HINTS & PINCHES

King Garlic & Queen Onion,

Unabashed Monarchs of Kitchendom, Tabledom, and Healthdom.

HINTS & PINCHES

A Concise Compendium of Herbs,
Spices, and Aromatics with Illustrative Recipes
and Asides on Relishes, Chutneys,
and Other Such Concerns

EUGENE WALTER

Illustrated by the Author

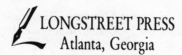

LONGSTREET PRESS
Atlanta, Georgia

For Betty Rossell McGowin,

A lady of charm and style in garden,
kitchen, and parlor.

Published by
LONGSTREET PRESS, INC.
2150 Newmarket Parkway
Suite 102
Marietta, Georgia 30067

Printed in the United States of America

1st printing 1991

Library of Congress Catalog Card Number 90-0638901

ISBN 0-929264-86-X

Grateful acknowledgment to the *Azalea City News and Review, Food Arts, Alabama Magazine,* and *Mobile Bay Monthly,* where some of this material, in somewhat different form, first appeared.

This book was printed by Arcata Graphics, Kingsport, Tennessee.
The text was set in Sabon by Typo-Repro Service, Inc., Atlanta, Georgia.
Illustrations by Eugene Ferdinand Walter.
Book design by Jill Dible.

Contents

Foreword

Dear Reader, I feel I should explain a few things about this book. It has evolved over more than half a century. It was brought on by my own interests and research, but ever pushed forward by the reactions and inquiries of readers who've read my pieces in the *Azalea City News and Review, Alabama Magazine, Mobile Bay Monthly, Gourmet, Harper's Bazaar,* the *Transatlantic Review, Food Arts,* and all such.

I made my first appearance as a culinary writer in the column of the famous Lucius Beebe, in the *New York Herald-Tribune,* when I was making my first visit to New York, on furlough from the Air Force cryptography school. I had written a friend enthusiastically of a then-famous restaurant called *Little Old Mansion* presided over by Miss Gladys Willcock and some superb black cooks, with murals by Ludwig Bemelmans on all three floors. The friend showed my letter to another friend who showed it to Beebe, who wrote me and asked to publish it. What could I say but "Yes"?

I was born and raised at the corner of Bayou and Conti streets in the old downtown section of Mobile, that Gulf of Mexico port under Spanish, French, English rule at various times, and site of the first Carnival celebration in what is now the United States. My grandfather of Bavarian origins ran his own three-story import-export produce company down on Water Street, with the river wharves on the east side and a railroad siding on the west. The bananas, plantains, guavas, and alligator pears (avocados to you) arrived from the Caribbean and went north in freight cars full of blocks of ice which returned from up there with apples and grapes, especially Jonathans and Concords.

Both he and my grandmother (a petite lady of French-Swiss background with clanking amethyst beads) were very serious about good food and good wine, and positively hectic in their insistence on fresh fruit and vegetables. Naturally they had a garden in the courtyard, as did most downtowners then. Nobody then would dream of buying salad greens or tomatoes or fresh herbs from a shop. A tiny garden it was, very neat indeed, with precise and manicured rows, flowers along the sides, and one plum tree onto which my grandfather had grafted several other kinds of plums. In the back corner of the yard, under the huge pecan tree, was, naturally, a huge compost heap.

If, in summer, corn-on-the-cob was part of luncheon, my grandmother would put the water on to boil and when she saw the first bubble she'd signal through the window to my grandfather out in the garden, and he'd pluck the ears from the plant, shuck them and hand them through the window. As I said, *fresh*. I earned my weekly allowance working in the garden and in the kitchen—weeding, raking leaves, picking crabmeat, peeling. There began my lifelong interest in good food and . . . if you are serious about good food, sooner or later you are concerned with gardening.

In Alaska and the Andreanof Islands during World War II, I enjoyed studying the wild plants and learning of the Indians' diet from a battered Department of Agriculture pamphlet I'd found in Anchorage; but three years in New York and then three years in Paris were frustrating. No garden. My first forays into the culinary worlds of Haiti, Japan, and Russia were in New York, and oh! the marvels of Paris, but in both cases in rooms with only straggling mint and basil in window pots. I covered every square inch of France, of course, and talked to ancient creatures in fields and woods gathering herbs and mushrooms, made an expedition into truffle country, interviewed famous chefs, sniffed out bakeries in back alleys, all that.

Then came several decades in Italy! All discovery! When I went to France I knew a long list of dishes and ingredients, streets and restaurants, poets and composers, like the beads of a French rosary, but the Gulf Coast in my early years had little or no Italian elements. Noodles were always of the Austrian variety, spaghetti was a Manhattan-Sicilian hybrid, with meatballs. Magnani, Moravia, Fellini, and pasta came later.

So I lived longer in Rome than anyplace else. I had a rooftop terrace half a block long where I grew herbs, salad greens, tomatoes, even pears, and more than fifty varieties of iris. And discovered the delights and subtleties of Italian food, thrilled to find the same insistence on freshness I'd learned as a child. Again, I covered every square inch of the country as well as Sicily, eating goat flavored with rosemary cooked outside in the mountains, discovering authentic pizza (thin, crisp, some two hundred different toppings; the thick doughy circle is purely American), chatting with the cultivators and gatherers everywhere. Same during six months of wandering in Greece and the Islands. Baby lamb flavored with dittany of Crete is something else again. In Egypt and Tunisia I learned the truth about how to use cardamom. And so it went . . . and goes.

The questions and comments of readers have guided me in making this book. The Dear Reader may note the absence of this or that herb or aromatic, but will certainly discover others. One of the mysteries of the table is how some things become universal, others hide for centuries. Columbus's crew smacked their lips over pineapple on the tiny Caribbean isle where it originated; by the mid-1600s the pineapple was already in cultivation in India, China, and the Philippines. But the guava, the papaya, the cherimoya, and actinidia are only now coming into the greater world. Pomegranate and persimmon are not exactly household words, even now. So many factors involved, such as getting such delicacies to table while *fresh*. One of the best greens is Good King Henry, as delicious as baby spinach or beet greens, but Good King Henry wilts within an hour of picking. There you are! Garden!

An aside to cooks: no one has ever questioned or expressed uncertainties to me about the use of "pinch," "dash," etc., as measurements. In the long run I feel "pinch" is much more precise than the "$1/8$ of a teaspoon" employed in more prissy-proper recipes. The great Southern cooks, well aware of differences of altitude, climate, temperament, astrological signs, mood, degree of appetite, type of stove, kinds of kitchen equipment, and most of all, the eaters for whom they cook, would never specify precisely such a measurement. They know what is meant by splash, dribble, dollop, lump, squirt, and hint, the difference between a dusting and a topping, between a dash and a pinch. Above all they know that recipes are to be *interpreted,* and so read a recipe rather as Wanda Landowska might read a page of Scarlatti for the first time, or Van Cliburn peruse a newly discovered Moussorgsky prelude. Above all, the serious cook knows who is coming to table, whether a ladies' luncheon of reducers, a gang of greedy-guts teenage boys, the steak-and-potato set in need of introduction to, say, a grits-cheese-and-garlic soufflé, thin Aunt Mayhem in from gardening, ravenous and tucking in, or fat Uncle Picky, soaked in rum, and taking only little forkfuls.

The best advice to cooks is, I feel, *seek fresh, avoid chemicals, keep a light hand, rise to the occasion, try what you don't know, have fun* . . . and good eating, you-all!

— **Eugene Walter**
Mobile, Alabama

ACHIOTE, ANNATTO
(*Bixa orellana*)

It is always strange to consider how close we are to those two thousand-odd islands of the Caribbean Sea and yet how far. Right up until World War I, many of the foodstuffs from down there landed in our southern ports. As a child I often breakfasted on fried red plantains; the delightful guava paste, with that vein of jelly in the middle, was often served as a dessert, with a little pat of Philadelphia cream cheese alongside. And so on and so on. Somehow, with the years the Southern United States of America has become more Anglicized, less Latinized.

a bunch of Reds, hunh?

Annatto seeds
(*Bixia orellana*)

Consider the annatto seeds and the oil derived from them. They come from a small evergreen tree called *urucu* by the Indians of Central and South America. The spiny pods are full of seeds surrounded by bright red

arils. The arils are scraped out to provide a virtually tasteless dye which has been used for more than a century to color butter and margarine (Cheshire cheese in England and many American cheddars).

The seeds are ground to provide a spice beloved in the Caribbean and Central and South America. Many dishes visitors eat, of an attractive red-orange color, are not made with tomato sauce, as one immediately assumes. No, it is the annatto or achiote seeds which give the color and a delightful odd, mild flavor. A favorite dish is roasted, quartered chicken which has been left twenty-four hours in a marinade based on onions, mild pepper, and annatto seeds ground in olive oil.

How can one describe the flavor? I've just chewed one or two annatto seeds and I think I could say the flavor is a combination of strong tea, dill pickle, and peppergrass.

You have probably eaten annatto without knowing it, in Mexican or Haitian food. You have gazed countless times on Mexican wool or cotton where a strong golden-yellow dye occurs. Annatto again.

But even if you eschew this seed in cookery or coloring, it still has a strange, wonderful, cranky place in history.

For . . . there are no Red Indians, no "redskins." In many parts of tropical America, the native Indians use oil of annatto to protect them from the powerful sun, smearing all their exposed skin when they work in fishing boats or in the fields.

This is what the first explorers saw: whole families dyed red with annatto. They reported tribes of Red Indians or "redskins" upon their return to Europe. And the fact that these Indians are not naturally immune to the sun's rays is part of the argument that they originated elsewhere, most historians preferring to believe that they are an Asiatic people who made their way across the Kurile Islands, the Adreanofs, the Alaskan archipelago, then down to our west coast and tropical America. There are no Red Indians, only people of beige, tan, bronzy pigmentation drenched in annatto oil!

The seeds are hard to find, but if you grind up a teaspoonful with a minced clove of garlic and a bunch of shallots, then marinate chicken pieces before roasting or barbecuing them, you have a treat in store. But they give a very appetizing color to any stew or gumbo, or a sauce to serve over boiled rice or boiled fish or whatever, besides a delightful mild spiciness.

If you find you like annatto you'll do well to have a pepper mill full of them, but you can smash them in a mortar and pestle or even powder them under a flat-bottomed jar or tumbler on a cutting board. Most Latin-American households — especially Peruvian — always have jars of annatto oil (they prefer the seeds' other name of *Achiote*) and/or annatto paste always on hand, for salads, cooking dozens of chicken dishes, and for Red Rice, so good with chicken.

Annatto Oil

1 cup corn oil, or light olive oil, or
clarified, strained pork fat
generous half cup of annatto seeds
a good dash of cayenne pepper
pinch of dried dill
handful of celery seeds
2 small bay leaves

Put everything into a small pan, heat slowly for five minutes or so until the color is a rich reddish yellow. Cool, strain, keep in covered jar in fridge. Will keep for months.

Red Rice

unsalted butter
1¹/₂ cups rice
3 cups warm water
2 small bay leaves
grated lemon peel
pinch of salt
¹/₂ cup finely chopped cherry tomatoes
2-3 tablespoons annatto oil

Put a good lump of unsalted butter in pot, turn 1¹/₂ cups rice until grains are transparent, add exactly 3 cups warm water, 2 small bay leaves, grated lemon peel to taste, pinch of salt. Boil on medium, stirring once or twice until water is absorbed and first grains go "click" as they stick to bottom of pot. Turn off heat, put dishcloth over pot. When ready to serve remove bay leaves. Add ¹/₂ cup finely chopped cherry tomatoes and 2 or 3 tablespoons annatto oil, mix well. Serve with chicken or broiled or fried fish.

AJOWAN
Omam, Bishop's Weed
(*Carum ajowan*)

Ajowan is closely related to caraway and cumin, but has a rather powerful taste of thyme, since it contains great amounts of thymol in its chemical constitution. An extract of this is chemically related to carbolic, making the ajowan a powerful germicide, and indeed, in India a beverage derived from the seed is prescribed for "traveler's tummy" and for cholera. Ajowan is powerful against flatulence too, and since the Indians eat enormous quantities of peas and beans, they use ajowan generously. In Hindu restaurants, you might think certain

cloves, pinch of salt, two pinches of sugar, strain and butter after one minute and send to table as a vegetable, there'll be "aaahs."

Even those big tan-colored farm onions we call Big Bang Repeaters in the South (the burp, the inner rumble, the sudden explosion) can be dealt with: cut them in half and remove some of the middle. Dust them with powdered cloves and mace, drench well with butter, honey, and syrup from preserved ginger and bake them. Not only very good but you'll note a difference in social life.

Most of the Alliums are very easy to grow. Don't buy chive seeds! Get a clump from a friend, takes much less time. Next time you prepare to serve leeks, cut off the roots with an inch of lower stem and simply plant them; in no time you'll have another bunch of leeks. If you can get Vidalia or Walla-Walla sweet onions fresh, they can, indeed, be eaten as you would an apple. A nibble of parsley afterwards goes a long way toward removing all traces on the breath.

ALLSPICE
Jamaica Pepper, Myrtle Pepper
(Pimenta dioica, P. officinalis)

Mother Nature went whole hog when giving the Americas their one true aromatic spice. To most people, allspice tastes like a mixture of cloves, cinnamon, and nutmeg, with cloves predominating. The tree which produces this spice is of the myrtle family and has leaves not unlike the bay laurel. The berries are a rich purple when ripe, but they are picked green and dried in the sun until they turn brown and look like oversized peppercorns. Since allspice is always being confused with mixtures such as the classic

Chinese five spices, it would be infinitely preferable to call it by its old names of Jamaica pepper or myrtle pepper, as it appears in many old cookery books and still today in certain English culinary writings.

In eighteenth-century America, this delightful spice saved the kitchen lives of many colonial housewives who couldn't obtain or couldn't afford the precious oriental spices and aromatics, for allspice blends well with New World foods: tomatoes, yam, pumpkins and squash. The famous lament of the New England housewife:

> We have pumpkins at morning
> And pumpkins at noon;
> If 'twere not for pumpkins,
> We should soon be undoone.

. . . makes one contemplate the problems of the limited fare available then. But the pumpkin can be differently presented at each meal, differently flavored with bacon, molasses, made into a pudding with cornmeal and allspice.

Allspice should be bought whole, not powdered. It quickly loses its warm and comforting fragrance. I keep an oversized peppermill with whole berries. Allspice goes into limitless numbers of curry, stew, spiced meat and vegetable dishes, is essential in marinades, in pickles, in cakes and pies. Once a cook is familiar with its uses, this becomes an everyday spice, not an exotic. The Scandinavians adore it in their Christmas goodies and in all their marinated raw herring dishes. Simple milk custards or puddings become Something Else Again if given a neat flavoring of allspice. Hot toddies, too. For the first symptoms of a bad cold, a mint tea laced with honey, orange, lemon, allspice works wonders. Here's a wonderful old Gulf Coast recipe:

Veal Roll

1 boned veal shoulder
1¹/₂ cups soft breadcrumbs
1¹/₂ teaspoons seedless raisins
skin of 1 orange, grated
1 tablespoon chopped shallot or mild onion
2 teaspoons mixed parsley
powdered bay laurel
mustard powder
1 teaspoon ground allspice
salt and freshly ground black pepper
orange juice
plenty of unsalted butter

Mix well breadcrumbs, raisins, orange skin, herbs, some pea-sized lumps of butter, and shallot or onion. Season with salt and pepper. Roll the meat up with this stuffing

inside; tie with string. Rub outer surfaces with plenty of butter and the allspice. Place in baking dish with more butter and juice of orange. Bake in 350-375 degree oven about 25 minutes to the pound and 25 minutes for the pot, basting frequently. If pan liquids reduce too much, add a little white wine or some stock. Remove meat and keep warm. Boil up pan juices, add more wine or stock if need be, and if too thin, thicken with a bit of cornstarch. Serve sauce in gravy boat.

Here's a bit of early Americana:

Pumpkin Pancakes

3 cups mashed pumpkin
1¹/₂ cups flour
¹/₂ teaspoon allspice
1 beaten egg

Beat all ingredients together very well. Drop by spoonfuls onto hot greased griddle or into hot deep fat. Dry, sprinkle with powdered sugar and serve at once.

They are delicious like that, but if you want to be Southern and pile Pelion on Ossa, use this alongside:

Rose-Geranium Jelly

about 1 heaping pint of rose-geranium leaves
5 cups sugar
juice of 2 small lemons
1 teaspoon whole allspice corns
4 ounces powdered pectin
4 cups water
a little Bing cherry juice for coloring

Wash geranium leaves, steep them in sugar, allspice and lemon juice for an hour. Place in saucepan with water and bring to a boil. Add pectin, then boil again, stirring for about a minute. Add coloring. Place rose-geranium leaves in small clean jars, pour in jelly, seal.

Unexpected Visitors' Dessert

Mix equal portions of brown sugar, unsalted butter and chopped apple. Add small splash rum, liberal flavoring of allspice. Spread this mixture on bread slice with a slice of apple on each one. Bake at 375 degrees till they sizzle. Perfect with strong black coffee.

ALOE

ALOE
Health Plant
(*Aloe barbadensis,* formerly *Aloe vera*)

This plant is the best argument there could be for using things fresh.

The earliest record we have of aloe is in an Egyptian account of medicines dating from 1500 B.C., where the implication is that it had long been in use. Cleopatra used the juice of aloe as a beauty cream, and Alexander the Great's soldiers took it to battle with them because of its extraordinary healing power. No kitchen windowsill should be without a plant of this, since a bit of the juice from its fleshy leaves cools a burn or cut and speeds healing. Since earliest times it has been used on bald spots, face wrinkles, as well as to effect amazing cures in arthritis, constipation, diarrhea, hemorrhoids and even insomnia! It is one of the very few ancient and traditional cure-alls that modern science has ratified. In fact, in recent years Dr. Wendell D. Winters, at the University of Texas Health Center, has conducted exhaustive research and pronounced that the ancient hearsays were correct, and that aloe (member of the lily, not the cactus family) is rightfully called Health Plant since antiquity. But he also discovered that the mysterious curative powers, which have not been exactly identified, vanish in bottled extracts or creams, wiped out by the chemicals used as preservatives. So FRESH, please, for basil, parsley, onion, garlic . . . and aloe.

ANCHOVY
Herring family
(*Clopidae*)

The anchovy is a small fish with a dark grey-blue back and a white belly, frequenting the Mediterranean and the Atlantic coast of France and Spain. The fresh fish, from three to eight inches long, has a white flesh, good flavor and is often fried or grilled. It gives no indication of the reddish flesh and odd pungent, mushroomy-Worcestershire old-cigar-box scent and flavor it acquires after a few months pickling in salt with attendant fermentation. But this has been understood and appreciated for thousands of years in the Mediterranean world, and both the fish and the juices are essential in hundreds of sauces and gravies.

The anchovy pastes and ready-made sauces, however, are abominations for the most part, being oversalted and colored with Armenian bole, a kind of red earth.

Try this: place some anchovy fillets to soak in milk a few hours, then drain. Cut green tomatoes in half, spread with unsalted butter, sprinkle with chopped capers, dill, basil, and inner leaves of celery. Place the fish fillets on them and cook in hot oven about 20 minutes. With toast and dry white wine this is a delightful first course.

Most great chefs make a fuss about preparing Steack Tartare (in French "steak" appears as *steak, steack,* and even *steacq*) and most of them include some finely chopped and pounded anchovies as a "secret ingredient" . . . listen to how Rainer Kraus prepares it at the Hotel Bodensee in Switzerland:

Anchovy

Steack Tartare

1¹/₂ pounds best lean steak
glop of Dijon or Creole mustard
ghost of grated garlic
finely chopped onion
chopped capers
yellows of 1 or 2 eggs
drop of best oil
freshly ground black pepper and
dash of paprika
dash of Lea & Perrins
2 or 3 best-quality anchovies, chopped fine

Mix well. Eat this along with hot buttered toast.

In the south of France the delicious *tapenade* is a spread made of anchovies, black olives, capers, thyme, bay, dash of wine vinegar, dash of brandy, all pounded together and served with fresh hot bread. In old Mobile there was a mushroom ketchup incorporating anchovies which went with any grilled white-fleshed meat and even beef and mutton. Any beef stew is heightened greatly with one or two desalted chopped anchovies added. The Scandinavians serve a quite delightful hors d'oeuvre where anchovy strips are arranged on a salad made of diced tart apples, beetroots and celery cut in small dice and flavored with oil, vinegar, salt, pepper, and dill, surrounded by halved hard-boiled eggs and parsley. A mixture of desalted anchovies, blanched, and pounded garlic, worked into unsalted butter and forced through a sieve, serves as basis for great grilled mushrooms. Chop the stems with a little parsley and some toast crumbs, mix with the butter mixture and stuff the big mushroom caps. Sprinkle with freshly ground black pepper and grill.

We all know the delight of anchovies on pizza, but even better is:

Tartine de Mobile

Lightly butter slices of whole wheat bread, place in 350-degree oven till butter melts. Spread a thin layer of Creole mustard, then a thick layer of crunchy peanut butter, then a slice of green or just-showing-pink tomato, sprinkle with chopped capers, top with anchovy fillets that have been soaked in milk. Put in oven about 15 minutes. Serve with mild pickled okra.

Tinned fillets in oil, of course, in all the above; never fresh, and NEVER paste.

ANGELICA
St. Michael's Plant
(Angelica archangelica)

This hardy annual, or biennial, or triennial, as the case may be, is a giant member of the parsley family. In almost every European language it is associated with angels and is considered a cure against the evil eye, as well as cure for numerous diseases. There are repeated legends of an archangel bringing it as a cure for the plague. It might be that the angelic association comes from the fact that it usually blooms around St. Michael's Day, May 8th in old calendars.

We know it in the form of the little green stem bits used in fruitcakes, but candied stems are only one use. Plant, root, and seeds are all delightfully aromatic. A resinous gum from the roots substitutes for musk benzoin in perfumery; the delicious flavor of muscatel grapes in some Rhine wines comes from a sneaky use of angelica. Seeds and root are in *Chartreuse,* it joins caraway in making *kümmel;* the seeds are one of the principal ingredients of gin. The tender ribs of the leaves can be eaten raw or braised like celery. The dried leaves make a tea rather like China tea.

It likes a little shade and a rich humus. When it finds a spot it likes, the plant reaches eight feet without trying, with huge leaves and round umbels of fragrant yellowish green flowers, a delightful accent plant in any garden. It is a biennial and dies after producing seeds; if the flowering stems are cut down before they mature, the plant grows on. It usually takes three or four years to reach vast proportions. Young stems are best for candying, collected in the second year of growth.

Snow Pudding with Angelica

1 cup orange juice
1 tablespoon Knox gelatin,
softened in ¹/₄ cup water
¹/₂ cup minced angelica
stems (fresh or candied)
¹/₂ cup sugar
2 tablespoons lemon juice
¹/₄ teaspoon salt
3 egg whites

Scald orange juice; don't boil. Add all save egg whites, stir over low heat until smooth. Let cool and thicken. Beat whites until stiff. Beat into the mixture a little at a time. Pour into mold lightly oiled with sweet oil and chill several hours. Serve with a custard sauce.

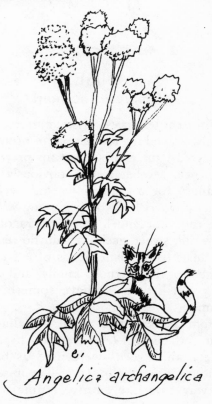

Angelica archangelica

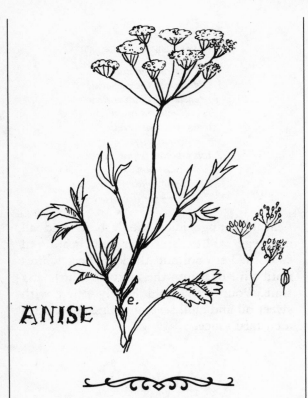

ANISE
(Pimpinella anisum)

From earliest pre-Christian times, anise has always had the reputation for protecting one against the evil eye and for preventing flatulence. Mother Nature obviously has a fondness for a certain warm, sweetish, mildly pepperish flavor, beginning with licorice root. But fennel, chervil, tarragon, caraway, dill, sweet cicely, certain flowers, the star anise (or badiane, seeds of a Japanese member of the magnolia family) and even a crazy mushroom all have something in common.

From earliest times until well into the eighteenth century (and even now in remote places), anise seeds were used as bait in mousetraps. Mice flip. Dogs like anise seed the way cats like catnip. Humans have always chewed anise seed the morning after heavy drinking or after garlic and onion feasts. American cooks seem not to have learned the European regard for mingling dashes of anise, cinnamon, and bay leaf to flavor fish, pork, ducks, game, and sausages. The leaves are delightful in a mixed salad.

Anise has always been sought for making a cure for colic, for infantile catarrh, for various candies and liqueurs which aid digestion. The seed in the center of our familiar penny candy, the jawbreaker, or gobstopper, is often an anise seed. All over the Mediterranean world there are apéritifs called *pastis* (brand names such as Pernod, Ricard, Berger are household words) which go into many dishes, for instance, Oysters Rockefeller.

In the late eighteenth century a widow in Bordeaux, Marie Brizard, began to bottle commercially one of the greatest digestive drinks, her famous anisette. Her *recette* calls for the following to be macerated and marinated: 60 grams of anise seed, 30 of corianders, 2 of cinnamon, 1 of nutmeg, 2 liters of *eau-de-vie,* and 1 kilogram of sugar. The secret ingredient was only recently revealed: some grated lemon peel. All the anise cookies and teas are tonic and healthy. But the seeds add a wonderful *je ne sais quoi* to poultry, applesauce, soups, beet salad, bread, and cookies. This is very good:

Mrs. D'Olive's Spicy Beef

4 pounds brisket of beef
4 tablespoons oil
1/2 cup soy sauce
1 teaspoon crushed anise seeds
1/2 cup sugar
1 tablespoon salt
1 cup sherry
pinch mustard powder

Heat the oil in a deep iron pot. When very hot, brown the cut-up meat all over. In a bowl mix all the other ingredients except sherry and enough water to cover the meat. Pour this mixture slowly over meat, cover the pot, put heat on medium, let come to boil, then put on low heat and simmer, basting from time to time. When the meat has cooked for 1½ hours, add sherry. Bring again to boil, turn heat to low, simmer another ½ hour. Very good with spoonbread or grits soufflé.

ARTICHOKE
(Cynara scolymus)

The artichoke is the flower bud of a prickly-leaved plant originating in either North Africa or Sicily. Cleopatra brought it to Rome, Catherine de Medici probably introduced it into France. When the Gulf Coast was Latin and when California was Spanish, the artichoke was common food, but the United States, generally, discovered it only after World War II. In the Mediterranean world, vast quantities of artichoke are consumed. Until recently it was believed to be a powerful aphrodisiac, right along with oysters and watercress and eggs, and it was considered scandalous if young girls or unmarried ladies seemed to enjoy it. Catherine de Medici consumed vast quantities; this undoubtedly explains her reputation. The artichoke has a special odd acidulous taste which is wrong with any wine that exists. I like to serve a thimbleful of ice-cold gin or vodka or *eau-de-vie* with an artichoke, or the palest of beers. A great way to prepare them is this:

Artichoke Boil

6 artichokes
6 tablespoons lemon juice
6 tablespoons best olive oil
2 garlic cloves
1 teaspoon salt
6 or 7 crushed peppercorns
dash of Tabasco

Cut off stems and a fraction of base. Cut off about three-fourths of an inch of the prickly top. With your sharp scissors cut off the point of each leaf. Drop artichokes into bowl of warm water with a pinch of sugar, a pinch of salt, and a splash of white wine vinegar. Place them base down in a big deep pan (steel or enamel, not aluminum or iron). Pour oil and vinegar over top of each. Add boiling water to cover, toss in other ingredients. Cover, boil, turn down to simmer, cook about 35 minutes or until leaves pick off easily. Let cool 2 hours, drain, serve as is or with dip of your choice.

Globe Artichoke

ASAFOETIDA
Devil's Dung, Stinking Gum
(Ferula narthex)

This is really something for the adventurous cook. This is a highly interesting flavor when used in minute quantities. It flavors many of the Eastern dishes most attractive to visitors and is part of the delicious distinction of many Hindu vegetable dishes. The ancient Romans knew it and used such quantities that their source, the *silphium* plant from Cyrenaica, was already extinct by Pliny's time and known to us only by an image on a coin, which suggests it is another member of the giant fennel family.

Ferula asafoetida is known as Devil's Dung and Stinking Gum, and in bulk has a perfectly hideous stink, like garlic gone bad. It is an evil-smelling perennial, with yellow flowers, growing about six to twelve feet high. The milky juice dries into a solid resin-like mass, but for us today it is preferable to buy a little bottle of extract from the druggist. Used by the dropful it gives an exquisite flavor to, for instance, any pan-broiled white fish. Dried salted cod soaked in many changes of cold water and made into codfish cakes flavored with a hint of dill and a drop of asafoetida are Something Else Again. A number of chutneys and pickles of North India, with delicate appetizing flavors, contain this paradoxical flavor.

BAMBOO SHOOTS
(Bambusa vulgaris,
Phyllostachys pubescens)

Bamboo shoots are a basic staple of diet in China, Japan, Korea. They occur in so

Bamboo Shoots

many oriental dishes that it is certain that, whether you realize it or not, you have probably eaten them at some moment of your life, if you've enjoyed Eastern cookery.

There is a bewildering variety of bamboos. Some are wild, some are cultivated. The shoots to be eaten are gathered at anything from six inches to one foot, and are usually simply boiled, then employed in hundreds of mixed dishes. They are salted and pickled as well, and all Chinese specialty food shops have them in cans. They occur in many salads, too. The young bamboo leaves are often used, along with seaweed, to wrap delicate fish such as bream when they are to be simmered in a flavored broth or slowly cooked over charcoal. A charming Chinese poem of the ninth century, by Po-Shui, describes the traditional spring delicacy (the Chinese feel about the first bamboo shoots of spring as we do about the first fresh asparagus) and the manner of preparation.

"I boil up the shoots with their weight in rice./The purple sections break like an old silk brocade; The white skins split, color of new pearls./Every day I recklessly consume them, too many, And enjoy the Spring, and am reassured about everything."

Chicken stuffed with bamboo shoots and mushrooms flavored with onion and mustard seeds, is a favorite. Or look at this:

Stir-Fried Snow Peas with Bamboo Shoots & Mushrooms

6 dried Chinese mushrooms
(soaked 30 minutes in warm water
with a little lemon juice)
1½ cups canned bamboo shoots
(sliced 1/8 inch thick)
1 pound fresh snow peas
1½ teaspoons salt
½ teaspoon sugar
2 tablespoons peanut oil
or sunflower oil

Discard the rougher mushroom stems, cut caps into fours, strain the mushroom water through a fine sieve and reserve 2 tablespoons. Put your wok or skillet over high heat for 30 seconds. Pour in oil, swirl about and heat another 30 seconds, but turn down heat if oil smokes. Stir-fry mushrooms and bamboo shoots about 2 minutes, then add snow peas, salt, sugar, mushroom water. Cook over high heat, stirring, about 2 minutes, or until water evaporates. Put on hot dish, serve at once.

You might just go to the nearest clump of bamboo in spring and do as I did down on Palmetto Street in Mobile. Cut six-inch-high fresh shoots, drop into boiling water for five minutes, then cool, clean, slice. In heavy skillet put unsalted butter and little cubes of ham fat and ham scraps from the last baked ham. When they are beginning to crisp, add a little dry white wine, a handful of raisins, and a good glop of Creole or Dijon mustard, plus a pinch of brown sugar and a pinch of cayenne pepper, salt to taste. Put in sliced bamboo shoots and mix well, cover and cook covered over low heat until just right. Serve with plain boiled rice, or with wild rice.

Or make a melange of vegetables: carrots, celery, bamboo shoots flavored with capers and chopped crisp bacon. Canned bamboo shoots are delightful in an easy vegetable soup: prepare a broth from chicken or turkey bones or bouillon cubes, into it drop chopped onion, garlic and sliced bamboo roots, a little grated lemon and a tiny glop of prepared horseradish. Cook over low heat 10 minutes, then bring to a boil and serve at once.

If you want to have the best introduction to bamboo shoots, pick fresh ones, clean them, boil them, put lots of butter on them while hot, salt to taste, and a good dash of freshly ground black pepper and devour them while hot.

NOTA BENE: The plant known as *Bamboo Briar (Aralia nudicaulis)* is employed in medicines the same as *Sarsaparilla*; it has a rhizome with a warm sweetish fragrance and scent. It is not employed in cookery.

BASIL
Kiss me, Nicholas
(Ocymum basilicum)

Most great cooks are unanimous in calling Common or Sweet Basil the greatest of all the culinary herbs. A member of the

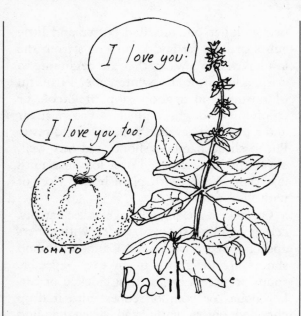

TOMATO

Basil

family of *Labiatae*, which includes the bewildering clan of mints, the plant has a very pleasing, very strong perfume and flavor.

It is by tradition a "masculine" herb, under the domination of Aries. All societies, ancient and modern, have recognized and celebrated the strength of the plant. But no two agree in dealing with the basil emblematically or symbolically. For the ancient Hindus (the basil originates in India), the plant had association with death and was planted on graves. Even today a good Hindu is laid out with a basil leaf in his hand. In the Latin countries the basil stands for love, and in many dialects is called "Kiss me, Nicholas." In ancient Greece, the basil represented hate, and to hand a man a sprig was to say without words: "Beware, someone is plotting against you."

When the British in India were looking for something sacred for Indians to swear by for courtroom oaths, since the Hindus have no equivalent to the Bible, they chose the basil plant, since it is held sacred.

The Common, or Sweet, Basil is a sturdy annual, reaching about two feet, with creamy white flowers. There is a larger, curly or wavy-leaved variety achieved through selection and cultivation, which is widely used from Rome to the south, including Sicily. A smoother, slightly smaller-leaved variety is most popular around Genoa for the famous sauce *pesto*. In *pistou*, the French form familiar in Provence, either form of basil is used. The origin of the name is unknown. Perhaps from Greek *Basileus*, meaning "king," another allusion to the strength and masculinity of the plant; perhaps derived from *basilisk*, the mythical serpent-like monster which could kill with a single glance.

A crazy legend associated with the plant since antiquity would have it that scorpions can be bred by crushing basil leaves and leaving them under a rock. There is also the confusing fact that basil leaves, macerated, are excellent for drawing out poison from the bites of insects or snakes.

Basil likes rich soil, full sun, and must be watered in the heat of the day. It is one of the few herbs which wants leaves and roots both wet. In warm climates you can cut it back and bring it indoors to have basil all winter, in a sunny window. It is fascinating to watch the seeds when you plant them. The moment water touches them, a blue gelatinous film forms on the seeds. Fermented basil seeds are the base for a drink in Malaya.

Basil can be used in many dishes, in meat loaves, sausages, pâtés, in the famous *pesto* (unforgettably delicious with spaghetti in the famous Genovese dish), with any eggplant dish, green peppers, with any fish, especially mullet, with any shellfish, in omelets, as an herb butter with steaks. But the great affinity for tomatoes is the chief fame of basil. Basil plants like to grow around tomato plants; they aid and abet each other. The greatest and most refreshing summer salad on earth is ripe tomatoes and shredded basil (shred, don't cut) dressed with lemon juice, the best pure olive oil, a touch of garlic, salt and freshly ground black pepper. One of the best sauces for spaghetti is that very same salad, let set awhile to "hatch" and added to hot buttered pasta.

One of the glories of Mediterranean cooking is what in Italy is *pesto Genovese* (literally, "Genoan pestle") and in Provence is *pistou*. This last is added to any kind of vegetable soup or stew, the Italian form is a sauce for spaghetti or any pasta. Here it is: *Pestle Sauce*:

The Famous Pesto from Genoa

4 tablespoons fresh basil
2 tablespoons ground pine nuts
or walnuts (I've used pecans)
3 crushed garlic cloves
3 tablespoons Parmesan cheese
5 tablespoons olive oil
2 tablespoons melted butter

Pound basil, nuts and garlic in a mortar, then add cheese and pound until a thick purée is formed. Slowly add oil and butter, then mix all together until smooth. This can be prepared and kept in the fridge. Add a few drops hot water and stir over heat before mixing into bowl of hot spaghetti.

Here's a wonderful South Italian sauce for pasta:

Spaghetti Sauce with Basil

2 or 3 zucchini
1 green pepper
1 crushed garlic clove
4 tablespoons pure olive oil

2 big fat ripe tomatoes
salt
freshly ground black pepper
1 or 2 anchovies
(soaked in milk, then pounded)
a few capers
6 or 8 black olives
a handful of shredded basil leaves
about 8 ounces spaghetti

Sauté zucchini, green pepper, garlic in oil. Add tomatoes, salt, pepper, cook slowly about 10 minutes over low heat. Add anchovies, capers, olives, basil, cook 5 minutes more. Pour over pasta, serve piping hot.

Stuffed Eggplant

A wonderful stuffed eggplant calls for cutting eggplants in two, parboiling just until fork will easily pierce skin. Scoop out flesh, leaving 1/2 inch attached to skins. Butter these shells, line with crumbs. Mix drained flesh, crumbs, butter, chopped capers and garlic, grated lemon peel, grated Parmesan and lots of torn basil leaves. Stuff shells, put on dab of butter, bake in moderate oven until kitchen, house, whole neighborhood smells good. (About 30 minutes.)

Golden Pasta

Boil up your pasta in plenty of water with a few drops of olive oil, pinch of salt, and 2 tablespoons of turmeric (curcuma). Prepare sauce: lots of big-leaf basil, torn, not cut, at least 2 cups very ripe red tomatoes, dash of celery salt, a few chopped capers, freshly ground black pepper, all mixed together with virgin olive oil. When pasta is just right, not soft, but *al dente* (bitable), drain well and mix the sauce into it. Serve at once.

Sweet Basil Sauce for Fruit

1 cup plain low-fat yoghurt
¼ cup honey or sorghum
juice and grated peel of lemon
handful of big-leaf basil, torn
dash of allspice and cinnamon

Bring honey, lemon, basil, spices to boil, turn off at once, mix well, let sit quarter of an hour, then whisk yoghurt into mix. Serve over berries, peaches, melon balls, or pound cake.

This is nothing if not sensational, very S'uthun, although European in inspiration. From Greenville, Alabama.

Grits Benedict

This is for breakfast or brunch or after theatre. Everything must be hot, plates, etc.

First make up some *Pesto Genovese* (see above). Boil a good quantity of best stone-ground grits. When done, stir in butter, a little salt, freshly ground black pepper. Put in baking pan 1½ inches deep. Let sit overnight in fridge to "jell." When ready to eat, dip 3-inch squares of grits into milk, then crumbs, and brown in butter. Place poached eggs on these squares. Or first a thin slice of Smithfield ham, then eggs. Pour hot pesto sauce over all and serve.

BAY
Sweet Bay, Laurier d'Apollon, True Laurel
(*Laurus nobilis*)

Bay laurel leaves are those used to make up the crowns for poets or victorious ath-

letes in antiquity. Hence the bay is sometimes called Apollo's Laurel or Poet's Laurel. In parts of Greece, it is called Daphne, referring to the nymph who was transformed into this tree when she fled Apollo's advances.

Laurus nobilis is a smallish tree, usually clipped to remain so, but in warmer climates it can reach sixty feet. The fresh leaves are slightly bitter; they are often dried for use in the kitchen. They are an essential flavor in all Mediterranean cookery, used in marmalades, in pickles, in the traditional *bouquet garni*. The bay leaf gives up its flavor slowly; that's why it is so often employed in slow-cooking stews and soups. It is an essential touch in almost all southern gumbos and should always be included in the flavorings for boiling shrimp.

Housewives of an earlier time always tucked a bay leaf or so into their jars or cannisters of rice, beans, prunes. This keeps weevils away, but also gives a pleasant aromatic presence to the foodstuffs. Leaves are strewn on shelves where flour and meal are kept; this discourages many pests. Rice puddings and milk-and-egg custards become

Something Else when bay leaves are boiled up with them, then removed. Certain pickles, quince, and pumpkin in particular are vastly improved by being cooked with bay. Bay berries are pressed and the resulting oil distilled. The thick greenish result goes into many mixed liqueurs and some of the vermouths. Bay is traditional with dried figs, placed under a pâté, inside a big fish when baked. The Italians use it in many marinades and stews, but are adamant that it should not be used with tomatoes. Dried bay leaves lose their perfume rather quickly; always buy small quantities unless you're cooking Apollo Veal, which is thick veal steaks bound with a branch of bay leaves and fried with butter. Here is a classic dish where bay leaves are all-important:

Daube à l'Avignonnaise
(Avignon Lamb Pot Roast)

4 pounds lean lamb, cut into nice chunks
4 ounces bacon cut into nuggets
4 minced garlic cloves
4 tablespoons minced parsley
4 sliced big onions
3 sliced carrots
5 tablespoons best olive oil
salt to taste
freshly ground black pepper
3 bay leaves
good pinch thyme
same of marjoram
about 1 teaspoon grated orange peel
½ bottle dry red wine
1 ounce brandy

Into each chunk of lamb insert a piece of bacon rolled in the parsley and garlic. Choose a dish which will just fit the meat nicely. Put it in along with half of the onions, carrots, bay leaves, seasonings. Cover with red wine and brandy. Let mari-

nate 4 or 5 hours, turning meat now and again. Remove and dry when ready to begin cooking. Put rest of bacon, olive oil in heavy pot and brown remaining onions, then brown meat. Pour in the marinade, taste for salt, add orange peel, let marinade simmer until reduced by one third. Then add enough boiling water to just cover meat. Simmer over very low fire 4 or 5 hours. Some cooks add stoned black olives and a few capers when they put it in the water. Daubes are made the day before they're needed, then fat removed and dish reheated. Always tastes better the second day.

BEER

Anthropologists never tire of pointing out that many primitive tribes have been so ignorant of the facts of life that they never dreamed that fathers were responsible for conception in mothers, *but* that there has *never* been discovered a tribe or community that did not know how to make a fermented, inebriating beverage from grain, usually beer, usually flavored with herbs.

The Babylonians, in their hanging gardens, sipped beer on those long summer evenings. In ancient Egypt men and women of all classes drank beer for nourishment as well as refreshment. The wine-drinking Greeks tended to look down on the beer-drinkers—so what's new?—but Xenophon writes, around 400 B.C., that beer can be most agreeable "to those accustomed to it." Medieval writers never let one forget that ales and beers are food as well as wine: "In ale is all included. . . ." And one has constantly to remind the bluenoses that there was more beer on board the *Mayflower* than water. In fact, the Pilgrim fathers, lacking

Melt butter, stir in crumbs, blend well. Press this mixture on bottom and sides of well-buttered springform pan. Spread the pineapple evenly in bottom of crust. Beat cream cheese until soft. Add cheddar, slowly blend in sugar, vanilla. Beat in eggs and yolks one at a time. Beat till all's smooth. Fold in cream, then beer. Pour mixture into pan. Bake at 300 degrees for 1½ hours. Remove, cool. Chill well. Top with whipped sour cream.

Beef in Beer

6 ¼-inch slices of round beef
3 carrots
3 leeks
3 dill pickles
3½ cups beer
1 cup unsalted butter
1½ cups beef stock
1 tablespoon cornstarch
1 cup sour cream

cows, might not have survived without their knowledge of beer making.

Beer is mostly water, but also contains protein, and an appreciable amount of B-complex vitamins, and enough mineral salts to be a highly useful salt replacement agent in hot weather. The resin of hops, the usual flavoring agent since the Middle Ages, is an aid to digestion. We all know cheese fondues with beer as a principal ingredient, but some of the grand old dishes made with beer seem to have been misplaced in the last half century. Take my grandmother's cheese cake, for *sin*stance:

Miss Annie's Cheese Cake

¼ cup unsalted butter
1½ cups smashed graham crackers
½ cup pineapple preserves
2 pounds cream cheese
½ cup grated cheddar
1½ cups sugar
1 teaspoon vanilla extract
4 whole eggs
2 egg yolks
¼ cup heavy cream
¼ cup beer

Cut each beef slice into two pieces about 3 inches by 6 inches. Cut carrots, leeks, pickles into quarters lengthwise, then 3-inch pieces. Place one hunk carrot, leek, pickle on each piece meat. Roll meat like a jelly roll, fasten with wooden toothpicks, place in bowl, cover with 2 cups beer. After 2 hours, drain. Melt butter in skillet, brown meat rolls on all sides. Place in casserole, cover with beef stock and remaining beer. Add salt, freshly ground black pepper, dash mace, splash of Worcestershire, simmer about 1½ hours until beef is tender. Remove rolls, place in hot dish. Add mixture to sour cream, then gradually all this to hot stock in casserole. Cook until sauce thickens; do not let boil. Pour over meat, glazing evenly.

Jumbo Shrimp in Beer Sauce

3 pounds big shrimp,
peeled and cleaned
1 large red onion,
coarsely chopped
1 mashed garlic clove
3 tablespoons olive oil
1 teaspoon salt
dash cayenne
2 cups beer
1/3 teaspoon dried dill
2 torn-up bay leaves
1 clove
2 tablespoons minute tapioca
1/4 cup chopped parsley

Add onion, garlic to hot oil, sauté until transparent. Add shrimp, spices, beer, lemon juice. Stir constantly, bring to boil, then simmer until shrimp are pink and firm, about 5 minutes. Drain off liquid and pour it over the tapioca, stirring constantly. Simmer until good saucy consistency. Return shrimp, reheat. Garnish with parsley and serve.

In the Netherlands and Great Britain, beers and ales are often used in marinades for tough beef, older fowl, all that. If you want something good, try soaking a good rump steak (in the fridge for four days, turning now and again in a marinade consisting of a bottle of dark beer with a half cup olive oil, garlic, bay, thyme, a little French mustard, and some powdered mace), then roasting as usual. Baste with marinade. This is Something Else Again. Or the same for an old hen.

Beer is used in cookery all over the world, but curiously enough American cooks have held back. The use of wine in cookery, which has been discovered by countless American cooks since World War II, has left beer in a kind of kitchen limbo.

Here's a dish from the old *Schimpf*'s restaurant in downtown Mobile, from the turn of the century:

Beerburger

1 pound lean ground beef
scant teaspoon salt
1 big or 2 small garlic toes, minced
2 tablespoons ketchup
8 hamburger rolls (or English muffins)
3/4 cup rolled oats
2 1/2 tablespoons minced mild onions
good dash Worcestershire Sauce
hint of Tabasco
pinch of dried or fresh thyme

Cut rolls or muffins in half. Mix everything else together, spread on rolls, put under broiler for 8 to 10 minutes. Pickled brussels sprouts are good alongside. Serve only with beer, never wine.

Foley Corn Fritters

2 eggs, separated
3/4 cup Pilsener-type beer
1 tablespoon corn oil
1 teaspoon salt
good pinch sugar
1 1/3 cups flour
2 cups fresh corn
1 1/2 tablespoons grated onion
1 teaspoon minced fresh parsley
pinch dried dill
freshly ground black pepper to taste
oil for frying

Separate eggs, put whites aside. Heat beer almost to boiling and set aside to cool, then blend in oil, egg yolks, salt, sugar. Then blend in flour. Cover and chill 2 or 3 hours. Beat egg whites until just stiff, fold into batter. Add corn, onion, then rest of ingredients. Heat oil in big skillet, drop by spoonfuls into hot fat, fry until golden brown.

Asparagus with Beer Sauce

2 pounds fresh asparagus
2 tablespoons unsalted butter
2 tablespoons flour
1¼ cups pale Hindu- or Oriental-type beer
1 teaspoon brown mustard
1 egg yolk
minced chives

Cook asparagus in salted boiling water until just tender. In saucepan melt butter, add flour. Stir until lightly browned. Add beer, cook a few seconds, stirring. Beat egg yolk with mustard, then add a little of the beer sauce. Mix. Then add to beer mixture and heat for a few seconds. Pour a little of the sauce over asparagus and serve, the rest of sauce in gravy dish or sauceboat. Sprinkle with lots of chopped chives. Some like to add a little prepared horseradish or grated lemon peel to sauce.

Eggs Beery-Detto

1 can condensed tomato soup
1 cup dark beer (Munich type) or dark English ale
2 thinly sliced onions
1 pound grated medium-sharp Cheddar cheese
3 whole eggs
pinch salt
good glop of freshly ground black pepper
1 teaspoon dry mustard
dash of Worcestershire
good pinch of celery seeds

Combine soup and beer. In this boil onions till soft. Add cheese, stir till it melts. Beat eggs with other ingredients, add a little of cheese mix to eggs, then put everything together over low heat for a second. Serve over hot toast or hot English muffins. Serves six. Watercress perfect alongside.

Beets

BEETS
Red Root
(Beta vulgaris)

The beet has been cultivated since pre-Christian times, used in countless ways other than as an edible root and leaf. We know that the old Romans used it to color wine that had lost color in the vat. Nobody knows how long it has been used to color fabrics, dye eggs, to make fake blood for theatrical representations. It probably originated in the Mediterranean world and was cultivated for its delicious leaves, although an edict of Charlemagne's specifies the root as a vegetable he wants grown.

German scientists and chemists discovered the high sugar content of a white variant of the beetroot and by methodical breeding perfected the sugar beet we know now. It was Napoleon who caught on to the possibilities and established a sugar beet refinery on the outskirts of Paris.

The bosomy dark red beet which everybody knows today was only developed just under a century ago, but the oval or smallish roots, some like a red carrot, some white, some a kind of golden-yellow or orange, are the beets which have always existed, and since in hot climates they are a winter crop, were very important for the Deep South in Reconstruction and Depression times. The big hard *mangel-wurtzel*, a brownish yellow or orange-tan root, has been used to feed cattle for centuries; humans when starving.

The beet has an astonishing quantity of vitamins, especially of potassium, the leaves more than the root.

Beet Greens

Most beet greens I've encountered are woefully overcooked. There is nothing (but nothing!) as good as steamed fresh young beet leaves with unsalted butter, salt and freshly ground black pepper. Quite as good as the first wild asparagus in Italy, the first young sorrel leaves in France. Tear them up, don't cut them, steam them, don't boil them! I serve them in individual ramekins with a little tray passed about full of toppings: crumbled crisp bacon, pine nuts, strips of Smithfield ham, toasted almonds. Most people don't know what the greens are. Many have simply never tasted beet

greens! Such exclamations of joy and mystified enquiries!

"It's a form of Turkish cabbage . . ." I say without a smile. Or, "You mean you don't know Provençal kale?" Only later do I explain. Sometimes one must tell the plain truth when first asked, embroider every subsequent version. Sometimes myth or invention should come first, truth emerge with a shy smile at the end.

Dear Gardener, even if all other crops fail for you, beets will still come in. Infallible. In September, for most of south and central USA, scatter seed thickly in well-prepared bed. When they're six inches high pull up three-fourths in making space for the others to mature. Eat those greens within an hour. Believe me.

Shy-Smile Beet Greens

Pick over your beet greens. Take out older, more wrinkled or yellow leaves. Cut off from roots. Wash in many waters. Tear up, don't cut. Put in steamer basket, don't pack too tightly. Sprinkle a few celery seeds, a light twinkle of freshly ground black pepper. Steam until just tender, turning once or twice. Mix with dollops of unsalted butter and hurry to table while hot. Pass a basket of lightly toasted English muffins cut into fingers and a selection of accents as related above.

Beets have a triple personality: leaves, stems, roots.

Beet Roots

When preparing roots for the pot, cut the stems about three-fourths of an inch above root. Don't touch the wiry bottom root. Don't peel. Wash well, put into cold water with a pinch of sugar and a pinch of salt, let simmer until fork goes in easily. Then wash in cold water, peel (skins slip off) and cut off root and lid. To serve, slice, dice, or cut into fingers, as you prefer, then heat in skillet in unsalted butter, or put back into steamer to heat. Serve mixed with heavy cream or yoghurt, with freshly grated nutmeg, or dried dill, or fennel seeds or caraway seeds or candied orange peel or candied ginger or paper-thin orange slices and paper-thin sweet purple onions.

Beet Stems

Stems? Check how tender they are. If suitable cut into 2-inch lengths and drop into boiling water with a bay leaf, cloves, allspice, mace, orange peel, whatever you fancy, boil till tender and serve as a vegetable alongside ham or roast pork or wild game. Or boil vinegar with any of those possibilities and pour over stems in sterilized jars.

In summertime I often serve as a first course a platter of devilled eggs (made with Mr. Underwood's devilled ham, a splash of cream, a splash of prepared horseradish, a drop of Tabasco) arranged on purple perilla leaves inside a ring of pickled beet stems and pickled baby brussels sprouts. Ooooohs and aaaaahs!

But if you want a different view into the nature and character of the underestimated beet, try this:

Southern Belle Ice Cream

(Whence the name? Oh, honey-chile,
that rose-pink color.)

³/4 pound beets, well-washed, ready to cook
1¹/2 cups sweetened condensed milk
(if you can find the traditional Southern brand called
Magnolia Milk, grab it; for desserts it's the best)

¹/2 cup warm water
2 cups heavy cream
3 eggs
¹/2 cup light honey
¹/2 cup finely chopped crystallized (candied) ginger
(refuse the dried-out crap)

Heat oven to 375 degrees. Have two big sheets of foil, put beets on one, sprinkle with water, wrap tightly, cook 20 to 25 minutes till tender. Peel and chop small. Bring milk, cream, water slowly to a boil, remove from stove. Add beets, let sit an hour. Strain. (Put beets in compost heap or save for salad.) Beat eggs till light, add honey, beat till thick. Add milk mixture. Put in heavy pot and cook until mix coats spoon. Put in icebox right away to let sit in cold for one day. Then freeze, adding ginger at the last. If you use ice cube trays to make ice cream, take the stuff out and beat it well when ice crystals form. Let freeze well. This serves four enthusiastic adults, four greedy-guts children, or twelve polite eaters.

P.S. Beet leaves, raw, are delightful in a mixed salad. Or mixed with crumbled bacon and ripe tomato slices. Or as a vehicle for crumbled Gorgonzola and chopped walnuts. Vinaigrette dressing, naturally, made at home.

Last thought: some like to add a splash of rose water. (Careful! *culinary* rose water, not *cosmetic*, to that ice cream.)

BERGAMOT
Bee Balm, Orange Tea
(*Monarda didyma*)

The bergamots are a group of wild American plants of the mint family (as their squared stems indicate), first recorded by a Spanish physician, Dr. Nicholas Monardez, for whom the plants are named. He described the medicinal properties of the herb, much used by the Indians, and provided the earliest account and illustration of tobacco, in his book *Joyful Newes out of the Newe Founde World*, published in London in 1577.

A tea made of the leaves is supposed to be relaxing, soporific, and sovereign against the first symptoms of a bad cold. The plant is variously known as fragrant balm, American balm, bee balm, red balm, Indian plume, Oswego tea, and horsemint. Bees go crazy over the red and purple flowers, are just as fond of the rarer lemon bergamot. The flower heads are delicious in salads, along with a few chopped younger leaves. Green caterpillars adore the plant, too, so look under every leaf when gathering. Eng-

Bergamot

lish hybridizers have created a whole scale of lilac, pink, violet, crimson bergamots, that are much appreciated in Europe as an ornamental garden flower.

NOTE: *Bergamot* is also the name of a bitter orange related to the *Bigarade* or *Seville*. These are the oranges too bitter to eat, used for marmalade. Oil of Bergamot is valuable in perfumery and is one of the elements in some of the most famous French scents.

BITTERS
Angostura, Peychaud, etc.

Since earliest times humankind has preferred bitter remedies for most ailments or upsets and our most up-to-date medical and chemical research tends time and time again to corroborate ancient herbal uses. Old medicines based on chamomile, chicory, fumitory, gentian, germander, hops, lichen, wild pansy, lesser centaury, quassia amara, cinchone, rhubarb and such are proven tonic and curative.

Medieval French recipe books contain endless variations for the making of *stimulating bitters* which serve to sharpen the appetite, settle the stomach, aid digestion, and prevent flatulence; the most-listed ingredients include some of the above as well as a peel of bitter orange, chestnut bark, the kernels of peach and apricot stones. Some of these all-purpose tonic bitters have survived to our day, chiefly because of their inclusion in famous drinks such as pink gin or champagne cocktails. But they have a place in the kitchen, too, even if half forgotten today. Nothing is better than very cold grapefruit with sugar and Angostura Bitters.

The late Mr. Hammond Gayfer swore by cold raw oysters flavored with lemon juice and Angostura. Early in the last century a Dr. J. G. B. Siegert concocted Angostura Bitters as a remedy for fever; it began to be consumed in great quantities, with cognac or whiskey, as a preventative.

Incidentally, there is not a bit of Angostura Bark in the mixture. The town on the Orinoco River where it was created was called Angostura (now Ciudad Bolivar). Angostura Bitters are still made in Trinidad from a secret formula said to include cinnamon, cloves, mace, nutmeg, orange and lemon peel, prunes crushed with their stones, quinine and rum, and have been distributed throughout the world since 1830.

A. A. Peychaud fled the island of San Domingo in 1793, along with other wealthy plantation owners, escaping with a few clothes, books, and a precious bitters formula: Many came to New Orleans (then Spanish) and here Peychaud set up an apothecary shop; the tots of cognac flavored with his own bitters which he served customers soon outranked his more conventional medicines. Peychaud's Aromatic Cocktail Bitters are still manufactured in the Delta City but even there you have to nose around in order to find them.

Pineapple sherbet liberally splashed with bitters is delightful. A wonderful old summer concoction is called *Juleb* and it's nothing on earth but a mint julep to which is added a little lemon and orange juice and a good splash of bitters. Thinly sliced boiled carrots glazed with butter, honey, and bitters are a surprise, and very good. Next time you boil a ham put lots of bay leaves in the water. Let the ham cool in its water (which you save to cook beans or turnip roots), then smear it well with a mixture of brown sugar,

mustard powder, port, and bitters, then heat in the oven. Mobile's own "sand" pears are delicious boiled, chilled, sliced, sugared, splashed with bitters. And both Angostura and Peychaud's bitters are a tried-and-true cure for hiccups. Sprinkle sugar and bitters on paper-thin lemon slices and eat slowly, chewing well.

BOUQUET GARNI
Marinades, etc.

One of the pitfalls for an adventurous modern cook are those phrases "season well" or "season highly" or "season to taste" which occur in Granny's recipes, or the old family cook's, or in cookbooks of earlier vintage. But all those old cooks knew perfectly well what was intended. It took two world wars and a depression, with subsequent interruption of the spice trade, to relegate that body of knowledge to the Department of Lost Arts. Yet Fannie Farmer, in her first cookbook edition of 1896, listed *bouquet garni* in her list of essential household staples, right along with baking powder, baking soda, beans, and bouillon cubes.

The classic *bouquet garni* in French cookery is defined by Escoffier as consisting of eight parts parsley to one part bay and one part thyme. In all of the Mediterranean a bit of orange or lemon peel is added as well. These flavorings are tied together or put into a little muslin bag, since they must, by all the traditions of classic cookery, be removed before the dish is served. But many different bouquets occur in all Latin and Eastern cookery: it is not unusual to find basil, celery, fennel, chervil, tarragon, burnet, rosemary, savory, cardamom, etc., according to the authority. English cookbooks often state "bundle of sweet herbs" or "faggot of herbs," depending on the cook's knowledge and taste, assuming always that the mixture is fastened together and will be removed before serving. Cracked peppercorns are ALWAYS added toward the end of cooking. The great cook pauses an instant, says a silent prayer, adds salt, tastes again, makes another silent prayer. Since many of the herbs impart a savory, almost salty taste, a light, even stingy hand with salt is imperative in good cookery.

"Parsley bouquet" means always some form of *bouquet garni* with parsley as principal element, but other selected flavorings as well. *Fines herbes* means finely chopped herbs, especially for omelets. Parsley is basic, chervil, shallots, basil, tarragon, on occasion mint, savory, thyme, lemon thyme: the artistry of the cook is at stake. The English "faggot" is sometimes the little bunch of sweet herbs in the sense of *bouquet garni*, but on occasion means literally the seasonings flung directly on the hot coals when cooking meat or fish. Stalks of fennel are widely used when cooking fish, even a bed of such when baking a big fish in the oven. But rosemary, garlic, hickory, or fruitwood is traditional in roasting turkey or beef; sage, thyme, and garlic for liver and spareribs.

A *ravigote* (from the French verb *ravigoter* meaning "to cheer" or "to strengthen") is a combination of finely chopped herbs: tarragon, chives, chervil, parsley, burnet, for adding to salads and sauce, or to mix with unsalted butter as an accompaniment for meat, fish or whatever.

A *mirepoix* is the mixture used to flavor stews, braised meat dishes, or heavy winter soups, and consists of 2 carrots, 2 stalks of celery, 2 onions (one with a clove stuck in it), pinch of thyme, clove of garlic, one quarter pound bacon or fatback, plus grated lemon peel the farther south you go. The Italian *battuto* is finely chopped carrot, parsley, celery, carrot, garlic, onion, and fatback, the basis of hundreds of Italian dishes. A *soffrito* is the same as the *battuto*, but with the herbs added and all sautéed lightly in preparation for almost ALL Italian soup, sauce, pasta dishes. (*Soffrito* means "underfried.")

Court bouillon, in both Creole and Cajun cookery, is a mixed dish in its own right, but the classic court bouillon in which to cook fish (and what a difference it makes!) is usually parsley, thyme, bay leaf, onion, garlic, peppercorns, pinch of salt, often some carrot, always a slice or two of lemon, and a cup of dry white wine. Again, there are many variations, and celery (especially the tender inner leaves, chopped) finds its way into the broth usually. The fish trimmings, one drop of vinegar and water complete the broth. Escoffier recommends that the broth be brought to a boil, simmered on lowest heat an hour, then strained. The peppercorns, of course, go in at the end. Many cooks add no salt whatsoever. After the fish is poached in this broth, it is often served with a sauce made of melted butter, some reduced broth, some white wine, a very little chopped dill. Or melted butter with chopped capers and lemon juice. The broth is saved for all kinds of soups and sauces.

Marinades to soak fish, flesh, or fowl before cooking are worth a later chapter to themselves, but this is the place to speak of seviche, where the mixture of flavorings actually "cooks" the fish without heat. Thin cut-on-the-bias slices of striped bass or some such fish are put into a marinade of lime, lemon, or orange juice, with sweet onions sliced paper thin, a dash of white wine, a dash of Worcestershire sauce, a little chopped dill, a dash of prepared horseradish, dash of cayenne and some thin rings of green pepper which have been blanched. This sits overnight in a cool place and is served with hot buttered toast. Salt on the side for them as needs or wants it. Very Good Indeed!

SALAD BURNET
(*Poterium sanguisorba*)

This was one of the essential salad herbs in Elizabethan England and is still widely used and much esteemed in France and Italy—one of the field herbs of varying crunchiness, bitterness, and flavor which go into the tonic spring salads. It used to grow wild all over the South, a garden escapee. Happily, it cannot be confused with any other wild plant, so one can pick it fearlessly. It has lovely matched leaves, a flower head of greenish knots feathered with long red-violet stamens.

Classically a part of such sauces as *ravigote* and *chivry*. Used like borage, too, to flavor lemon drinks and wine cups. Sometimes infused to make "burnet vinegar." Vaguely cucumbery in flavor, truly delicious in salads. It can be easily raised from seeds, and makes a useful tomato patch border. Grows in any soil. Try a mixed salad of lettuce (*not* iceberg), young celery leaves, burnet, dressed with tarragon vinegar, good oil, salt and pepper, and if you're capricious, two or three chopped capers.

BUTTER
Beurre, burro

The origins of butter go back to the earliest nomadic peoples, who churned the milk of the cows, goats, ewes, mares, she-asses, and even she-camels which followed along on their wanderings. The Aryans brought this art of churning to India, where butter came to be considered a sacred food. In Indian mythology, the Salmala is a river of butter which winds about the globe. The Hebrews used butter as a medicine, often as a vehicle for bitter remedies. The Scythians had butter; they taught the Greeks and, with that, to quote the *Larousse Gastronomique*, "butter entered into the realm of pure gastronomy. . . ." The Romans in their time, many southern Italians even today, as in southern France, especially Provence, have always preferred olive oil to butter in their cookery. An invisible frontier occurs just north of Rome: below the line is olive oil country, to the north butter country, best exemplified in the rich lush dishes of Bologna.

In all the great classic cuisines, butter means fresh butter and that means *unsalted*. Salt was added to keep butter from spoiling, and for some ungodly reason we have all been saddled with salted all our lives. Now that doctors are pointing to salt as a culprit in coronary ailments in our sedentary society, it would seem that everyone would turn to unsalted butter. And it does make a big difference in cookery. I made some delicate French almond cookies lately, using salted butter, since I couldn't find unsalted, and they really were not good. The taste of salted butter predominated. Land o' Lakes puts out a very good unsalted butter. If you fancy yourself a serious cook, you'll use only unsalted. One of the oldest and best French sauces is Black Butter. (In Rabelais a black eye is always described as "an eye with black butter.") For a grilled, baked, or boiled fish, there is simply nothing better than this sauce. Try it, you'll see.

Beurre Noir

You'll need 2 tablespoons of well-washed, picked, dried, chopped parsley, so do that first. When you are about to serve your fish (or veal chops or fillets), keep them warm and prepare the *beurre noir*. Cook 10 tablespoons of unsalted butter until it turns a dark brown. *Not* black. Immediately put it into a dish, and put a tablespoon of good wine vinegar into the pan and sling it around. Add the parsley and 1 tablespoon chopped capers. Add this to butter and mix well, and pour over fish. If you must wait to serve, return the mixture to pan and heat well. Some people like to add a bit of white pepper to this. In Marseille they often add a good dash of ground mace. When I have fresh dill in my herb patch, I often add finely chopped dill. This dish is no good made with salted butter, which somehow mixes the flavor of the capers.

You can add all manner of flavorings to unsalted butter to put between layers of a cake: vanilla, anise, tangerine peel and juice, crème de menthe, triple sec, etc. In France they make dozens of *beurres composés* (usually translated "compound butters") which are the basis of dozens of delicious canapes and hors d'oeuvres or served with fish or meat. Anchovy butter is one of such. Soak some fillets of anchovy in several changes of milk, dry them, then pound them in a mortar with about one scant cup of butter. Put through a fine sieve. This used to be a "must" with a steak or a lamb chop and is surprisingly good, giving that tang of flavor one sometimes wants from Worcestershire or mustard. Bercy butter is a classic French accompaniment for grilled fish or meat, either poured over, under, or served separately.

Beurre Bercy

Put one and a half tablespoons finely chopped shallots (the small reddish brown onions with delicate chive-like leaves) into one cup of dry white wine and boil down to one-half the quantity. When this is almost cold, add three-fourths cup of softened unsalted butter and one pound of beef bone marrow which has been diced and poached in salt water then drained, 1 tablespoon chopped parsley, and the juice of half a lemon. Season with salt to taste, and some freshly ground black pepper. Heat all well together and serve. Have some nice crusty bread or hot biscuits to dunk, dribble, and delight. Well-washed sardines and grated lemon peel, with some white pepper, added to unsalted butter, makes a very good sauce for fish, too. Tomato paste and paprika worked into unsalted butter is heaven with fried okra.

Green Butter

Green butter is unusual and good with shrimp: take a cup of mustard and finely chopped parsley, basil, dill, chives, inner celery leaves, and 2 or 3 blanched spinach leaves. A grand sauce for baked chicken consists of cooking finely chopped green or red (or both) bell peppers in butter with minced garlic then mashing and mixing into a

pound of unsalted butter, adding white pepper, a little grated lemon peel and a pinch of salt. Remember, *unsalted* butter, says the great chef . . . and the doctor.

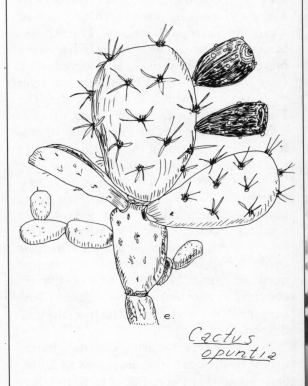

Cactus opuntia

CACTUS OPUNTIA
Prickly Pear, Cholla, Nopal, Bull Sucker

Alvar Núñez Cabeza de Vaca and three companions, the few survivors of an expedition formerly three hundred strong, stumbled into Culiacán, a city in northern Mexico, in 1536, with the wild story of how they'd been shipwrecked on an island off of

Texas six years earlier, enslaved by Indians until they escaped. They told, too, of Seven Cities of Gold to the north and of how they had survived because of *tuna*, the Indian name of the fruit of the prickly pear, *Cactus opuntia*. The prickly pear grows from Canada's prairies to the Strait of Magellan, throughout most of the hemisphere, and throughout the Caribbean. Curiously, the name of the plant comes from Greece, where a cactus-like plant was cultivated in the ancient village of Opuntian Locris. Introduced into the Mediterranean world in the 1500s and 1600s, one now sees hedges of this cactus forming fences around cow pastures just as in Texas or Mexico. In tropical and subtropical America, the flat leaves, known as *nopales* or *nopalitos*, thorns removed, are used in dozens of delicious local dishes. Roasted whole over coals, or peeled, cubed, cooked like green beans, strips served raw in salad (they taste rather like sweet bell peppers) stir-fried or deep-fried in a meal coating, included in countless stews or gumbo-like dishes, *Cactus opuntia* is an important green vegetable, and now begins to make its appearance in fancy food departments in many American markets and shops.

The *tuna*, known as Indian fig, has a soft texture and almost as many seeds as a pomegranate. It is sweet, and particularly refreshing on a hot day. Like the watermelon, it seems a natural antidote for heat exhaustion. In Chile they froth it up with sugar and water for a delightful drink. (Some add rum, gin, or vodka. Why not?) This fruit makes wonderful jellies, jams, syrups, or very heady liquors.

When boiled the leaves tend to a kind of okra-slickiness, upsetting to some diners. But here's a grand dish:

Cactus Creole

2 ounces diced cactus pads (leaves)
1 pound lean chopped beef
6 ounces tomato paste
1 cup water
1 diced jalapeño pepper
6¹/₂ ounces canned shrimp
salt and pepper to taste

Mix all together over medium heat about 20 minutes or until cactus turns a deep green. Serve hot over noodles, rice or potatoes . . . or in pita bread or in a folded tortilla.

Local variants of this easy dish include grated lemon peel, fresh cilantro, fish instead of shrimp, chopped onion, a hint of garlic.

There are now big cactus plantations in Italy and in Texas, and so *Cactus opuntia* is another American native who might yet catch up with the Caribbean pineapple in popularity.

CALENDULA
Pot Marigold
(*Calendula officinalis*)

The familiar orange flower with pale leaves native to South Europe and Asia is the pot marigold of old herbals and cookery books, not to be confused with the nasty-smelling pretty yellow and orange flowers we erroneously call "marigolds" and which might better be known by their botanical name of *tagetes*. Petals of calendula, both fresh and dried, have served as a poor man's substitute for saffron right back to earliest Roman times. It is much used in fish soups and stews for both color and flavor: a faint

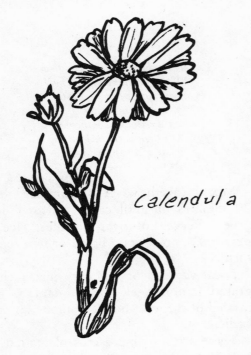

Calendula

leaves edgeways to the sun. Where it grows at earth level it has acquired spines; those in high rocks and old ruins have minor thorns. The best capers of all, now grown commercially in southern France, have no prickles at all.

The name comes from the Latin root word for goat, and some people claim that a pungent saltiness in capers reminds them of goats; I prefer the interpretation that the plant grows only where goats can reach it. In Cyprus the little fruit, like a tiny chubby *jalapeño*, is pickled, too. Pickled nasturtium buds and green seeds are often offered as substitutes and too bad; they're delightful in their own way and quite different.

Capers were once highly prized in sauces for mutton, in shrimp salads, with fish (especially the fattier ones), and in many meat stews and sauces, but since World War I seem to have been slightly forgotten, save in the Mediterranean world, which consumes quantities daily. Thin spaghetti tossed with unsalted butter, a splash of cream, and a handful of capers is a glory.

All the *beurre noir* (black butter) dishes are superb. You cook your fish fillets or veal fillets or even thin lean beef in butter, turning a few times; remove meat and keep warm. Add more unsalted butter, let it sizzle until brown; at once add a tablespoon of good white vinegar and a tablespoon of of chopped capers. Mix well and pour over fillets. Yum!

pleasant muskiness. The Dutch use quantities in meat soup. The petals, steeped in warm milk, give color to butter, cheese, and cakes. Try a handful of petals in your next beef stew. You'll be delighted. Or strew petals in your next green salad.

CAPERS
(Capparis rupestris)

This plant rather resembles the poet's myrtle of old-fashioned gardens: it has springing branches of tough oval leaves and white or pinkish pincushion flowers. If you've been to Rome, you've seen it sprouting from every ancient monument from the Colosseum to the Basilica of Masentius. It grows wild all around the Mediterranean basin, and has adapted in the most amazing ways. In the Sahara it has learned to turn its

Instead of the eternal dreary catsup sauce for shrimp cocktails, why not make a green mayonnaise with chopped chives, parsley (go easy on this), lemon peel, gherkins, and capers, along with inner baby leaves of celery and a glop of horseradish, and a splash of gin in place of lemon juice. Good on crabmeat or cold chicken breasts, too. Or spread on toast. Or rub it in your hair.

Capers, used in small quantities, do what Lea and Perrins or lemon peel or any of the "secret" ingredients do: point up a flavor, play *basso continuo* to a sauce or salad. When you've used them up, use the liquid in the jar to dress a salad of lettuce and radishes: you'll be surprised. With oil, salt and pepper, naturally. A few capers finely chopped in potato salad make the difference between so-what? and what's-that?

Try this marinade for a leg of lamb or a big hunk of beef (yes, I said beef): dry mustard, a little brown sugar, 1/2 cup of vinegar, 1 or 2 bay leaves torn up, teaspoon chopped capers, lots of chopped onion, a squirt of tomato paste from the tube, 5 or 6 garlic toes. Make holes in meat, stuff in garlic cloves. Spread, smear, mud-pie all the rest over the meat, turning several times and

Capers
(CAPPARIS RUPESTRIS)

letting sit about 12 hours, adding a little red wine to keep it moist. Roast in hot oven, not too long, baste with marinade (remove bay leaves), add cup or so of dry red wine to pan juices at end to make gravy, after you've lifted out the meat.

Appetizer: spread Melba toast with cream cheese, place a paper-thin slice of tomato, spread with chopped capers in cream, lots of lemon juice and freshly ground black pepper. Green tomato pies that are *not sweet* but full of sweet onion, capers and cream and black pepper and mace might start a new religious movement. I mean it!

CARAWAY
Kümmel, Alcaravea
(Carum carvi)

The name caraway comes from the old Persian *karavyja* and testifies to the ancient use of this plant. The Greeks and Romans knew it but seemed rather to slight it. In Oriental and Middle Eastern medicine and cookery it looms large, however. The Arab Ibn-el-Baltha and the Byzantine Aestius write at length of how it is valuable for digestion, against flatulence and all urinary problems. In the middle ages St. Hildegarde and the Salerno school emphasized caraway's all-round efficacy in aiding and strengthening all the internal organs. Shakespeare knew it; Justice Shallow invites Falstaff to his house for "a pippin and a dish of caraways."

This was a time-honored finishing touch for a meal: a roasted tart apple and some sugar-coated caraway seeds. An old gentleman writing in 1714 noted that he had eaten a roasted apple with caraway comfits every night for fifty years and had never suffered constipation, gout, stone, or any of the distempers of old age. Caraway was often included in formulas for love potions, while Dioscorides, the great Greek physician in the first century, prescribed it for adolescents with pale faces.

Caraway is a biennial, a member of the *Umbelliferae* family and is often confused with cumin, fennel, and anise, with all of whom it has qualities in common. Caraway is often referred to as "field cumin" or "cumin of the Vosges." In any cookery book dealing with curry, you can be certain there is a mistranslation if caraway is called for; cumin is intended. Caraway and cumin

e. Caraway

are often confused. The German-speaking countries put caraway into cabbage dishes, stews, breads, sweets, sprinkle the seeds over certain bland cheeses.

Caraway Bread
Caraway Dumplings

Caraway bread is wonderful for cheese or tomato sandwiches. You make your usual white flour and yeast bread, adding a tablespoon of caraway seeds at the last kneading plus 1 teaspoon of sugar for each pound of flour used. And caraway dumplings are great with goulash or a rich beef stew: Sift 6 ounces self-rising flour, 1 teaspoon salt, add 2 ounces shredded suet (white beef fat), grated rind of half a lemon, a heaped teaspoon caraway seeds, 2 tablespoons water. Mix well, gradually add a little water to make a rather stiff dough. Roll between your floured hands to make about 8 round dumplings, put then into your stew for the last half hour before the end of cooking. Chew caraway seeds after eating onion or garlic!

The plants like a semishaded location, are easy to grow, pretty with their feathery foliage and lacey white flowers. The black seeds have a distinct aromatic flavor, and are used to give interest to many rather bland foods such as carrots, turnips, parsnips. They are the seeds which flavor rye bread, spice cake, and are sprinkled into sauerkraut. The German name is *kümmel*; a very good digestive liqueur made of oil of caraway seeds is thus nominated.

The young leaves in spring are delightful chopped over baby carrots, for instance, in salads, with white cheese. The roots are like a very delicate parsnip. The seeds give a good spiciness to roast pork or ribs. The cheese of Münster is always accompanied by seeds, either caraway or cumin: the Germans prefer caraway, the French, cumin. In many German and Austrian provinces, a dish of caraway seeds is handed about after dinner with the sugar for the after-dinner coffee. Very good indeed. Here's a classic Spice Sponge:

Spice Sponge

3 eggs, separated
5 ounces sugar
4 ounces sifted flour
1/2 teaspoon baking powder
1 heaping teaspoon unsalted butter
1 tablespoon orange-blossom water
1 tablespoon cornstarch
grated rind of 1/2 lemon
1/2 tablespoon caraway seeds

Beat egg whites until stiff and dry; gradually add sugar and beat until it is dissolved. Gently beat in yolks. Sift flour, baking powder, and corn starch with pinch of salt three times, fold lightly into egg and sugar mixture. Heat butter, orange-blossom water, and about 2 tablespoons water at once, with caraway seeds which you have run over with a rolling pin to crack them. When all is mixed, pour into well-greased and floured tin, sprinkle some sugar on top, then bake about 20 minutes at 400 degrees.

Try making up your favorite roll recipe; before putting into oven sprinkle with cracked caraway seeds. After a rich meal of pork or beef, serve tart raw apples which have been sprinkled with lemon juice and caraway seeds then chilled, alongside any firm mild cheese such as Emmenthal, Munster, *Port de Salut*, even the milder American cheddar. Or wash some sauerkraut in several cold waters, then simmer with chopped onion and tart apple, with a generous cup of dry white wine, a few juniper berries and a good sprinkle of caraway seeds. Salt and freshly ground black pepper to taste. Serve with broiled pork chops, sausages, and boiled new potatoes in their skins. Carrots glazed with honey, butter, orange juice, and caraway seeds are nice too.

CARDAMOM
(Elettaria cardamomum)

Cardamom is said to have grown in the royal gardens of Babylon some seven centuries before Christ, although that must have taken some doing, since the wet hill forests of South India and Ceylon are its natural habitat, and there the plant springs up six to eighteen feet. The fronds are rather palm-like, although this is a member of the ginger family. The seeds are produced in a rather odd fashion; little wandering stalks come from the base of the plant and sprawl about on the ground.

Since the seeds ripen unevenly, repeated harvests are necessary. These seeds are in great demand all around the world and now there are extensive plantations in Central America.

But everybody likes these seeds. Sweden alone, for instance, takes one quarter of all the seeds produced on the Indian sub-continent. Russia, Germany, and Norway use mountains. The Arabian countries, especially Saudi Arabia, use staggering amounts.

The Arabs love coffee flavored with cardamom. Green cardamom pods are broken, pods and seeds dropped into a pot of hot water, with a touch of saffron or ground cloves, some sugar, and freshly roasted and ground coffee. This is boiled three or four

Cardamom

minutes, strained and served. The mixture is so aromatic that the coffee is barely noticeable; about two teaspoons of cardamom are needed for each medium small cup of coffee!

In much of Europe the seeds are required for pickles and for such delicacies as pickled herring and the German *sauerbraten*. The Scandinavians have hundreds of cakes, breads, rolls, cookies flavored with cardamom. Closer to the source, the seeds are essential for hundreds of mixtures of curry spices.

The seeds go into many punches and mulled wines. One of the most delicious custard desserts is made of hot milk in which cardamom seeds have been steeped. In many countries the seeds are chewed to sweeten the breath after partaking of garlic or onion. Cardamom has a natural affinity for apples. Pies or tarts or stewed apples flavored with ground cardamom are something special.

Because of the demand, the seeds of some related forty species of the ginger plant have been substituted or used to adulterate the real thing. This can be disastrous, for some taste unpleasantly of camphor or cough syrup, i.e. ghost of eucalyptus. Your best bet is to buy light-colored pods which have been dried in the sun, and pay whatever price is asked. Avoid big furry pods. I should like to quote Tom Stobart, the great herbal authority:

"When I was last in Bombay, an Indian friend of mine told me how, when dining out, he had discovered what he took to be a cockroach in his curry. He fished it out and called the waiter. The waiter called the manager, who, in turn, called the cook . . . the Indian cook respectfully pointed out that the cockroach was, in fact, a large hairy cardamom seed." He goes on to say that in another classic Italian story, it *is* a cockroach and the waiter eats it, smacks his lips, and says: "You do not like zis *wonderful* little fish?"

Here is Craig Claiborne's excellent curried shrimp dish, redolent of cardamoms:

Curried Shrimp

1¹/₂ pounds shrimp
2 teaspoons turmeric
¹/₄ cup vegetable oil
2 medium onions, sliced
1 medium green pepper, chopped
1 clove garlic, diced
1¹/₂ teaspoons salt
2 teaspoons diced fresh ginger or
¹/₂ teaspoon powdered ginger
1 teaspoon powdered cardamom
(or slightly more, if you like)

Wash shrimp and sprinkle them with turmeric. Place in a skillet, cover and steam without additional water until the shrimp turn pink, two or three minutes. Shell and devein the shrimp. Brown shrimp in the oil. Add the remaining ingredients and cook over low heat, stirring frequently, until most of the liquid in the skillet evaporates.

This is very fine:

Cardamom Apple Pie

Unbaked pastry for 2-crust, 9-inch pie
5 cups sliced tart apples
¹/₄ cup brown sugar
2 tablespoons unsalted butter
³/₄ teaspoon pure vanilla extract
dash of mace
1 heaping teaspoon ground cardamom seeds
(Grind them yourself, in a machine
or in your mortar and pestle.)

Place bottom layer of pastry. Arrange apples in layers, sprinkling each with brown sugar. Dot with butter, add cardamom, mace, and vanilla. Put on top pastry; seal and flute. Bake at 400 degrees for 10 minutes, then turn down to 350 and bake 30 or 35 minutes or until crust is lightly browned. Remove at once and cool to room temperature. No cream or ice cream with this, please, just strong coffee. Mmmmmmmm!

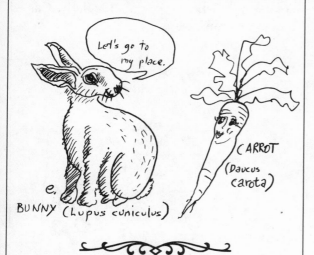

Let's go to my place.

CARROT (Daucus carota)

e. BUNNY (Lupus cuniculus)

CARROT
(Daucus carota)

The ancient Greeks and Romans used the wild carrot purely for medicinal purposes. A compress of pulped carrots was standard treatment for ulcerous sores. The plant, root, and leaf were the source of a yellow dye, and in the south of France are still used to heighten the color of pure unsalted butter, often pale. French, Italian, German cultivators in the fifteenth and sixteenth centuries developed the slightly poisonous root into the sweet vegetable we know now. There are varieties which are almost white, some red, some purple. Carrots have an elusive sweetish flavor which joins with celery

and onion in so many stews, marinades, ragouts, soups that many cookbooks simply state "add seasonings" since time was, assuming that any cook would know this trio is essential.

NEVER PEEL CARROTS! The flavor and the nutritive value are immediately beneath the skin. Soak in cold water, scrub lightly with a straw brush, flick off any obstinate specks of earth. That's what fingernails are for. The carrot is usually listed just after potato and parsnip in the list of valuable food roots. They are part of every kitchen garden and figure in a wider variety of dishes than most cooks think. The French make a *soufflé* or a *purée* of first spring carrots which is delightful. The English have always regarded the roots with esteem. A favorite adornment at the court of James I was great "plumes" of carrot foliage the ladies wore in their hair. Here is a North African salad which is unusual and great after any bland main dish:

North African Carrot Salad

1 pound fresh carrots
(scrubbed, cut in quarters, longwise)
3 or 4 cloves garlic
1/4 teaspoon pounded cumin seeds
pinch of coriander seeds
wine vinegar
salt
sugar
hot red pepper
parsley to garnish

Cook carrots with salt, sugar, garlic about 12 minutes. Drain, sprinkle amply with vinegar, a little more salt, cayenne pepper to your taste. Sprinkle coriander seeds on top, garnish with sprigs of parsley.

Carrots cooked with orange juice, grated orange peel, either honey or brown sugar, one clove pounded with a pinch of coriander seeds, simmered until liquid is reduced, then buttered, are delightful as a dish in their own right, but are also good wrapped in thin slices of ham and served with waffles.

Grated carrots and baby turnips, dressed with lemon juice, salt, sugar, black pepper, a drop of oil, are welcome with pork roast or spare ribs. A marmalade made with grapefruit peel and chopped carrots is very fine. Apple pie with grated carrot added and a dash of Peychaud bitters is very *ah!*-inspiring. So is this cake:

Carrot-Coconut Cake

1 cup sifted flour
1 teaspoon baking soda
1 teaspoon powdered cinnamon
pinch powdered mace
1 heaping teaspoon finely chopped orange peel
3-finger pinch of salt
1 cup sugar
3/4 cup corn oil
2 eggs
1 1/2 cups finely shredded carrots
3/4 cup flaked coconut

Grease a 2-inch-by-9-inch-by-12-inch baking pan. Sift flour, soda, spices, salt. Mix together sugar and corn oil. Add eggs, one at a time, beating well. Alternately add flour mix and carrots, a little at a time, mixing well. Stir in coconut. Pour into pan, bake in 350-degree oven 25 or 30 minutes or until cake springs back when touched. Cool 10 or 12 minutes. Remove from pan and let cool completely. Serve as is or with following frosting:

Cream Cheese Frosting

3 tablespoons cream cheese, softened
1 tablespoon light Karo syrup
1 1/4 cups confectioner's sugar
1/4 teaspoon vanilla extract
pinch ginger
pinch allspice

Mix cheese and syrup, stir in sugar, spices. Beat until smooth, add vanilla. This makes enough to lightly frost top of cake.

P.S. Recently published research bulletins would have it that lung cancer is rarest among men who eat carrots regularly. Carotene, vitamin A.

Cassia buds.

CASSIA BUDS
see also Cinnamon
(Cinnamomum cassia)

True cinnamon (as defined today) is a fairly recent discovery. Native to Ceylon, *Cinnamomum zelanicum* was known only to the natives until the Dutch spice traders discovered it in the 1600s. It is more delicate than the more common *Cinnamomum cassia*, which is what we usually know as cinnamon. Much "true" cinnamon is adulterated with the cassia form. In England alone, what is sold as "cinnamon" is just that. The common cassia form was recorded in China in 2500 B.C. and is one of the oldest known spices. It was known in Egypt in 1600 B.C. and gradually reached Europe.

They are both members of a genus of some forty evergreen trees, all native to Southeast Asia. They have recently been the subject of much study by Russian scientists, since they all contain aromatic properties. *Cassia camphora* yields camphor. Others give various essences for perfumes and the palliation of strong medicines.

Cassia buds, imported from China, are the dried unripe insignificant fruit of *Cinnamomum cassia*. They have a sweetish, yet spicy flavor of part cinnamon, part clove, part carnation. In the Far East they are the traditional emblem of good luck, and in Indonesia a drink flavored with cassia buds is always given to newlyweds. The buds are part of hundreds of old European recipes for pot pourri, are essential in flavoring Hungarian cherry soup, sweet pickles, chutneys, and many sweet confections. To make a completely delightful after-dinner cordial, steep a handful of crushed cassia buds with some brown sugar and a bit of grated lemon peel in a quart of very good French brandy, let sit a month, then strain through a muslin. Or if you wish to make people beg for the recipe, use cassia buds instead of cloves to stud a ham when baking. My! You should have a pepper mill just to contain them. Fresh peaches with lemon juice, honey, white port, and a good dusting of grated cassia buds are what the archangels discuss on New Year's Day.

CATMINT
(CATNIP)

CATMINT, CATNIP
(*Nepeta cataria*)

Catmint, or catnip, is a dear little shrubby perennial with a delightful perfume. It has lovely flowers, white with a mauve patch. If cut back after each flowering, it simply goes on forever. Seed is tiny; better shake the seedhead into a plastic sack, then strain through a fine tea strainer to remove stems, leaves and bugs.

Catmint has always been of medicinal value. A tea made from the leaves is mildly sedative, especially for children. In herbal therapy it is often prescribed for the overactive child, or the midnight tosser-and-turner, or indeed against nightmares. Usually taken very cold. Taken very hot it induces perspiration and is very good mixed with other herbs for a tea at the first sign of a bad cold.

Bees love it and flock to it, pollinating your garden and the neighbors'. Cats show highly individual reactions, as in everything, to the dried leaves sold in pet shops. But they love to roll on the plant; the one thing where all cats agree is the odor of the roots of this plant. If you're dividing a clump, they go quite mad and do the most odd and undignified dances and rolls. Some cats love to play with a catnip mouse; others remain on their cushions, glowering, "What is that nasty thing?"

CELERY
Celeriac, Celtuce, Celery Seeds
(*Apium graveolens*)

If you ask any serious cook what he/she would list as the ten most-used herbs or spices, you would be immensely surprised to find he/she would list even such as cinnamon or nutmeg, after bay leaf, pepper, thyme, garlic, onion, etc., and would not think to include celery, which is part of the culinary holy trinity of onion-celery-carrot in all classical cookery. So familiar one simply forgets it!

Archaeological research suggests that the very bitter small wild celery, known as smallage, which occurs all over the Mediterranean, as well as the British Isles, probably introduced by Roman legionnaires, was much prized as a bitter tonic, even though poisonous in large quantities. The Romans used it widely as flavoring and as medicine. Italian and southern French gardeners began, in the sixteenth and seventeenth centuries, to develop the wilder form into the sweeter, tenderer, more succulent celery we know today, hitting up on the idea of planting it in trenches, then drawing earth up about the developing stalks to make them grow long and to "blanch" them. This form was introduced into the rest of Europe and the British Isles in the eighteenth century, thence into America.

Selection and hybridization have produced both summer and winter varieties, as well as a form developed for its huge root, the *celeriac*, prized especially in France, where the huge bulbous root is boiled, then chopped or shredded and served cold with a vinaigrette or lemon sauce or a cream and dill sauce as a totally satisfactory hors d'oeuvre. In most of the Latin countries a small, more pungent form is cultivated as an aromatic to flavor soups, stews, salads, etc. It is simply the original *smallage*, cultivated but not tamed.

Many ancient writers, Livy the Younger among them, recommend a great draught of cold water and a few celery stalks as a cure for headache; I've tried it, it works.

One of the great oyster stews of yesteryear in Mobile restaurants consisted of chopped mild onion and celery sauteed in butter until soft but not mushy, then put, with the oysters and their juice, into simmering milk with salt, a bay leaf or two, a bit of cayenne pepper, a hint of nutmeg, then cooked until the edges of the oysters curled, at which a dash of dry white wine or dry sherry was dropped in, the stew removed from the fire and placed in a hot tureen with a sprinkle of very finely chopped parsley and served with homemade oyster crackers and brought to a table of diners panting with anticipation.

But celery is a grand cooked vegetable to serve with turkey, game, ham. Chopped in thumbnail-size bits, after removing the "strings" and putting the younger leaves aside, the celery is sauteed in butter to which is added a big glop of Creole or Dijon mustard, salt and pepper and one or two chopped capers if you wish. When celery is well coated with butter and starts to take color, pour in a little chicken or turkey stock, put on lid and simmer on very low fire until celery is soft but not mushy, then serve topped with either buttery, garlicky toast crumbs or chopped toasted pecans, and a good sprinkle of chopped inner celery leaves. (Variant stews consist of ham scraps, chopped and fried crisp, then added to a celery and milk stew, or celery and diced potato and milk stew.)

In all ancient herbals, celery is listed as promoting restfulness and sleep, as helpful in treating rheumatism, while any milk and celery combination — soup, stew, side dish — is excellent in calming fretful infants. The following is a perfect Italian dish from the Abruzzi mountains:

Celery & Chestnuts

2¹/2 cups diced destringed celery
1¹/2 cups cooked, peeled, chopped chestnuts
3 cups lightly salted water
4 tablespoons unsalted butter
¹/2 cup heavy cream
pinch sugar
salt
freshly ground black pepper
dash paprika

Cook celery in water until tender, about 15 minutes. Drain, save liquid. Blend butter and flour in top double boiler, stir in celery liquid and cream. Taste for seasoning, after adding salt, pepper, sugar. When mixture is smooth and thickened, add chestnuts, celery, sprinkle with paprika and there you are. Wait for the "Mmmmms!" Take center stage, smile a great self-congratulatory smile, shrug. *Fanfare.*

Celtuce is not a celery-lettuce hybrid, as some believe, but is a member of the lettuce family. The flavor is stronger than lettuce and the leaves become rather bitter as they mature. Most people enjoy the young leaves in salad, but a few of the stronger flavored, older leaves are quite good in salads made of any of the rather bland and uninteresting (save for texture) iceberg lettuces and such. But it's the stalk of celtuce that makes enthusiasts. When it's three or four feet high, one peels away the stringy bitter layer of the stem and finds a crisp, juicy, completely delicious crunchy center which is delightful in salads or served with capers and caper juice as a first course. A "Cream of" soup made with celtuce has many variations, one of the best having little strips of leftover baked ham. An oyster stew with mild onions and celtuce stems is very fine indeed.

Celery seeds have a flavor all their own and add life to dozens of sauces and gravies. When steaming asparagus or beet greens or lettuce hearts (to serve hot with butter as a first course), a generous sprinkle of celery seeds does something special that salt can't do. Always add celery seeds to potato salad or sprinkle on baked potatoes.

Medieval magicians put celery seeds in their shoes, believing this could make it possible for them to fly.

CHAMOMILE

CHAMOMILE
Manzanilla
(Anthemis nobilis)

Chamomile is one of the oldest cultivated garden herbs, and in much of Europe, one of the most widely used today. In France, Italy, Spain, it is very common for folk to take a digestive infusion of chamomile after a big meal, or to insure sound sleep, or, in the case of the very aged, an even stronger chamomile tea taken as a stimulus to appetite, drunk an hour before eating. For "hyped-up" children, it is one of the few calmants; it is the only known remedy against nightmares. The ancient Egyptians reverenced the many virtues of the herb, especially its power to cure ague, and so dedicated it to their gods.

The name, incidentally, is chamomile, not, as so often and so incorrectly written, "camomile." The fresh daisy-like plant has a highly pleasant aromatic scent something like apples, something like fresh hay. Imported from England, it grows wild over much of the southeast United States. The form preferred for herbal remedies, however, is a double-flowered cultivation form. The tea, taken by cupfuls, sweetened with honey, is made of about one ounce of the dried flowers to about one pint of boiling water. This is an old-fashioned but highly efficacious remedy for nervous and hysterical complaints in women, all manner of digestive problems in children, against colic, flatulence, indigestion, heartburn in everybody. Many Europeans, going off on summer vacation, take along packets of chamomile tea as a specific against summer diarrhea.

The Greeks called it *kamai melon* or "ground apple," referring to the scent. The Spanish know it as *Manzanilla*, or "little apple." The sherry called Manzanilla has, in past times, been flavored with the herb. This can be confusing: there is a town called Manzanilla. Not all sherries produced there are flavored with chamomile; there are also chamomile-flavored sherries produced elsewhere. In Tudor times, this plant, with its tightly woven, springy nature, was used for lawns. It tends to strangle any weeds which pop up; seems to love being walked upon. An old rhyme says,

> *Like a chamomile bed,*
> *The more it is trodden*
> *The more it is trodden*
> *The more it will spread . . .*

More than that, this herb has long been known as the "Plant's Physician."

Any plant which is droopy or pawky seems to perk up, thrive and flourish if a plant or so of chamomile is dug in next to it. Some European gardeners make a point of planting a ring of the herb about young fruit trees when they are set out. But since long before Christ, the blondes of this world have known that a rinse of strong chamomile tea, habitually used after washing the hair, will give "dishwater" hair new golden lights. Grey hair recovers some blonde coloring, and barbers have always used it on blonde beards and mustaches, which often grow out a slightly different tone than the head hair, especially in the case of first beards.

What else can one say of this totally delightful and useful herb? Only that insects will have none of it, leave it alone. And that it will grow on any soil at all. The better chamomile for medicinal purposes grows on poor land. Seeds are available from most of the bigger seed companies.

CHEESE

"How," General de Gaulle once asked in perplexity, "can one govern a country which has over 2000 varieties of cheese?" And how, in the space available here, can one deal with so vast a subject? Only a proper encyclopedia of cheeses and their uses, running to some six volumes, I should think, would be adequate, and not then exhaustive. But let's plunge and make a few bold statements!

At one end of the spectrum are the innumerable white farm cheeses, where the texture is all, the taste only a kind of pleasant lactic acidity; at the other the various "blue" or "dirty sock" cheeses such as Roquefort, Gorgonzola, and rising to the infamous

sweetish-rotten presence of Limburger and others. A Polish farm stinker, delicious with apples, is known as "Frighten Your Mother-In-Law." The aromas may be off-putting, but the flavors are almost always highly satisfying, slightly salty, an aid to digestion.

In cookery, cheeses have a way of blending in unobtrusively and sparking up the other flavors. The great French chefs use the Swiss Gruyère and Emmenthaler (as well as dozens of country cousins in Haute Savoie and Burgundy), and the Italian parmigiano or similar cheeses with high artistry. Parmigiano (parmesan) has a way of pointing up countless pasta sauces, but added to a meat loaf in judicious quantity, it gives another taste dimension.

In Italy fresh vegetables, steamed or quickly boiled—but not over-so—doused with oil (in the South) or unsalted butter (in the North), and sprinkled generously with freshly grated Parmesan, are one of the

wonders of everyday meals. And I should add to the High Church category of cheeses our old American rat-trap cheese, any one of a number of yellow-orange sharp farm cheeses from New York State, Wisconsin, even Washington and Iowa. The American combination of a highly spiced hot apple pie and a few slivers of sharp rat-trap cheese is completely delightful, part of our classic canon of national dishes. In classic seafood in a creamy sauce, a bit of grated Parmesan and a drop or so of dry sherry are traditional, but try, for instance, shrimp in a creamy sauce with a little prepared horseradish with a teaspoon of grated American rat-trap cheese and a pinch of cayenne. Something else. Here's something very good, using both Swiss and Italian cheese:

Tartlets Maria

(Mrs. Sylvia Humphrey's version)

CRUST:
2 cups flour
1 tablespoon grated parmesan
1/2 teaspoon salt
good dose of freshly ground black pepper
rind of 1/2 lemon, grated
1 cup softened unsalted butter
1 egg, beaten

Mix flour, cheese, salt, pepper, rind. Turn out on floured board, make a well, and put in egg and butter and mix lightly until amalgamated. Form into ball, wrap in waxed paper, place in icebox one half hour. When cool, divide into eight pieces and roll out each one to make a small tart. Use big muffin tins. Prick crust on bottom, cover with wax paper, then fill with rice or dry beans. Cook 15 minutes at 425 degrees.

FILLING:
1 pound cleaned, sliced mushrooms
2 tablespoons Marsala wine
butter
1/4 pound grated Gruyère cheese
2 egg yolks
bread crumbs

Sauté mushrooms in butter, dampening now and then with the wine, until cooked. Put aside to cool. Melt 2 tablespoons butter in saucepan, stir in flour. Add milk gradually, stirring with wooden spoon constantly, until mixture begins to thicken. Add salt and pepper. Stir in half the Gruyère and mix until blended. Remove from fire, beat in egg yolks, add ham, chicken and mushrooms. Sprinkle bread crumbs in bottom of tart shells. Put in the meat mixture. Sprinkle with remaining cheese, brown in your 425-degree oven, serve hot.

This is an old Mobile version of a favorite:

Potatoes au Gratin

Use small old potatoes. Scrub well, do not peel. Slice thin; if too big, halve or quarter slices. Butter casserole. Put in layer of potato slices, then layer of paper-thin sweet onion slices, then lots of grated rat-trap cheese, dabs of butter and freshly ground black pepper, a little salt. Repeat until dish is full. Put cheese on top, lots of pea-sized dabs of butter. Pour milk into dish until it shows. Bake about an hour at 350 to 375 degrees. Try with fork; when potatoes are easy to pierce but not mushy, remove and serve.

A nice end for a hot-weather dinner is to give each diner a plate with a whole lettuce heart (the small central portion of any garden lettuce with a knot of stem left on, NOT iceberg lettuce) which has been washed, shaken dry, sprinkled with lemon juice and chilled, no salt, no nothing. Serve on plate with a portion of this mixture, well-chilled: 2 parts Philadelphia cream cheese to 1 part any strong "blue" type cheese, mixed well and a sprinkle of celery seed added. Crackers on side.

Goat cheese, or *chèvre*, is delicious as a first course on a plate with Greek olives or eggplant caviar or toasted pecan halves. Always chives or shallots alongside. Always a drop of virgin olive oil poured over the goat cheese, of course, and a nice sprinkle of celery seeds or freshly ground black pepper. Fresh sage.

This is another delightful first course, good served with sweet mild black olives and cherry tomatoes, or bread-and-butter pickles.

Fried Cheese

10 ounces sharp cheddar
cut into ³/₄ inch cubes
¹/₄ cup cornstarch
1 big egg, lightly beaten
1 cup fine fresh bread crumbs
dash mild paprika
dash powdered ginger
oil for frying

Dredge cheese cubes in cornstarch, shaking off excess, then dip thoroughly in beaten egg, then into bread crumbs, being sure to coat well. Let stand on wax paper 20 minutes. Heat two inches of oil to 350 degrees, fry cheese cubes in batches, turning them for 1¹/₂ to 2 minutes, until they are golden. With slotted spoon remove and drain on paper towels.

CHERVIL
Cerfeuil
(Anthriscus cerefolium)

This is one of the prettiest and most subtly flavored of the culinary herbs. Mysteriously, it enhances other flavors. It came from southern and western Asia, but was grown in Italy in classical times. Pliny lists it, and recommends vinegar in which chervil seeds have been soaked as the best cure for hiccups.

It is an annual herb, grows quickly, goes to seed quickly; one must start new seeds about every three weeks if growing chervil in pots. Better to try and get plantlets from some specialist nursery. Once established, the plant seeds itself, doesn't mind our southern winters, goes on imperturbably. The seeds don't keep well in our climate, thus sometimes there's an initial frustration in getting a nice clump started. It grows

CHERVIL

about fifteen inches high, with charming fern-like leaves which turn pinkish purple as they die off, while the tiny white flowers, typical of the *Umbelliferae* family, are borne in umbels. The generic name, *Anthriscus*, was bestowed by Pliny, while the specific name, *cerefolium* means "waxen-leaved."

The flavor is sometimes described as a rarefied caraway, sometimes like a ghostly tarragon, but the faint, soothing, warming perfume is all its own, and blends well with meat or fish, eggs or salads. It makes a heavenly vinegar, and of course is basic in French cookery. In northern Italy it figures in some fine old dishes as *cerfoglio*, is known but little-used in England, and only grown in America by connoisseurs of the French kitchen. What a shame! It blends in the bouquet of herbs in an *omelette aux fines herbes* and if you want an interesting experiment, try such an omelet with and without chervil. You'll see its reason for being at once.

CHERVIL

The famous French soup is made of it; it is often chopped into little bits (the French word *pluches* is amusing: "pin-feathers") to toss into soups just before serving, to put on boiled potatoes, into unsalted butter to put on fish, to sprinkle on boiled crab or lobster. It is never really cooked; it's tossed in, sprinkled on, mashed into. Like parsley, you must pick the outer leaves, so that the inner ones keep on growing.

The French verb *ravigoter* means "to revive, to cheer, to help to perk up," and that's just what this herb does. This is the classic sauce, Creole version, wonderful with cold meat, fish, leftovers, avocados:

Sauce Ravigote

4 tablespoons best olive oil
2 hard-boiled egg yolks, mashed, fluffed
2 tablespoons French mustard
2 tablespoons white vine vinegar

You should also add freshly ground black pepper, pinch of sugar, salt to your taste, chopped chervil, parsley, chives and also, if you like, tarragon, burnet, and capers. (Burnet has a cucumber flavor; you could substitute one, yes, one, slice of cucumber, seeded, minced.)

Stir oil into egg yolks, as for a mayonnaise, add remaining ingredients, mix well. If too thick, one drop lemon juice, if too thin, more oil and chervil. Let stand in cool place; stir well before serving.

There are several versions; check M. F. K. Fisher's cookbooks for the hot ones. An old Mobile recipe requires a few drops of onion juice and one drop of Tabasco.

Chervil, incidentally, doesn't like dry places and loves half-shade. Chervil resembles another herb, sweet ciceley, and by association ciceley has come to be referred to, in English herbals, as great chervil, sweet chervil, and cow chervil. What you want, in this case, is just plain ole chervil. Always plant the seeds two or three days before the full moon. Last, but not least, if you want to impress the know-it-all quiche-makers, add 3 tablespoons finely chopped chervil, then smile like a cheshire cat, and don't tell 'em what it is!

CHINESE FIVE SPICES
Cinq Parfums
(Heung neu fun, Hung-liu, Ngung heung)

This mixture is classic in oriental cookery, and is not to be confused with any mixture such as pickling spices, or marinades, or any mélange whatsoever. And let us not forget that *allspice* might remind people of several spices at once, but is the berry of a member of the laurel family. Chinese five spices is a finely ground blend, in equal portions, of cloves, fennel seed, cassia (a kind of cinnamon), star anise seeds, and anise pepper. (Anise pepper is almost unknown in the West. A relative of the Rue, *Xanthoxyplum pipesitum* is a small, spiny, lacy tree whose red berries are dried to make the piquant aromatic Anise Pepper.)

Any Chinese or Vietnamese shop stocks Chinese five spices, and the mixture is worth trying. Perhaps on some occasion, dining in an oriental restaurant, you have licked your chops over "lacquered pork," a tender pork roast beautifully glazed with soy, honey, fruit, sometimes wine—the recipes are many—and the tantalizing flavors of the five spices. If you want to enchant your guests try marinating your pork ribs in

CHINESE FIVE SPICES

dry red wine laced with a little Creole mustard, some lemon peel, chopped onion, salt, and a good dash of Chinese five spices. Cook as usual, on grill or in oven.

This spice blend goes well in any kind of pâté, and I once made a grand beef dish of strips of beef (as for a stroganoff) simmered in wine with the five spices. Another delight: good country sausage served with stir-fried shredded baby cabbages flavored with the blend. I have an idea that some game birds and venison would benefit from a judicious use of the five spices, but haven't tried it yet. Hard pears, such as our old local Sand Pear, are a wonderful side dish for pork chops when simmered in dry red wine flavored with a bit of orange marmalade and a few pinches of Chinese five spices. Plain boiled turnip roots become rare exotics when dressed with lots of unsalted butter and this spice mixture.

Chives

CHIVES
(Allium schoenoprasum)

The chive is a tiny onion. They multiply so rapidly, they never stay alone, but make dozens of crowded bulblets. That's why we always hear "chives" in the plural. From prehistory it has been enjoyed, and grew wild over most of the northern hemisphere: Siberia, Corsica, Greece, Italy, southern Sweden, North America. Chives were part of Chinese cuisine already in 3000 B.C., valued as an antidote to poisons and a remedy for bleeding. They were also popular in Greek and Roman dishes. They're good for you! What with being mildly antibiotic and full of vitamins A and C, concentrations of iron, calcium, magnesium, phosphorus, potassium, thiamine, niacin. Always used

against high blood pressure, and to strengthen the kidneys.

(Romanian gypsies use them to tell fortunes. What more do you want?)

Chive Butter

Beat 2 tablespoons fresh, chopped chives into a pound of room temperature unsalted butter. Use on hot breads, potatoes, grits.

Chive Salt

Add chopped chives to non-oxidized salt, let sit a week or so, remove leaves, serve on almost anything.

Their hollow, grass-like leaves have a delicate oniony flavor which "points up" everything from omelets to soups to salads. They make a delightful edging to a vegetable or even flowerbed, with their mauve-pink flowers rather like thrift. Alas, the flowers should be discouraged, since the chives grow tough when the flower stem appears. Chives should be cut off, right to the ground, when you need them; snipping tops of leaves is wasteful, since the rest of the leaf dies. Chives have a definitely antiseptic quality, for they contain the volatile oil of sulphur typical of the *allium* family.

New potatoes, well buttered and rolled in finely chopped chives, are wonderful. Green tomatoes sliced thickly and sautéed in butter, then sprinkled with chopped chives, capers and basil are very fine. Pumpernickel spread with Philadelphia cream cheese and sprinkled with chopped chives and salt and pepper is also very fine. An omelet of chives and chervil ditto. Beet soup sprinkled with chives, ah, yes. Consommé . . . cold tomato soup . . . Vichyssoise without saying . . . stuffed eggs done with horseradish, black pepper, cream and chives; try that. Also crab salad made with lemon juice, horseradish, grated onion, capers, cream and a good sprinkle of chopped chives and parsley!

If your chives *do* flower, make a salad of lettuce hearts and chive leaves *and* flowers. Try paper-thin slices of little yellow squash, marinated in vinegar with bay leaves, then served with oil, salt, pepper, chopped chives. Then there's stuffed crab done with crabmeat, cream, chopped chives, a crushed shredded-wheat cushion, splash of heavy cream, cayenne, topped with Parmesan and a lump of butter. Dear chives! Universal application!

CHOCOLATE
(*Theobroma cacao*)

The name comes from the Aztec *chocolatl*; Prescott reports that the Emperor Montezuma *required 50 jars a day*. It was the principal beverage for the Aztecs, but also appeared in many stews and meat dishes. Chocolate is made from the seeds or "beans" of a tree native to the tropical lowlands of Central and South America; so long cultivated that probably nowhere does there exist a wild tree living today. These trees reach from twenty-five to forty feet, with shiny dark-green leathery leaves often a foot long. The flowers and pod-like fruits hang directly from branches and trunks. The fruits change color from green to orangey-green to purple-red when ripe. The inner pulp is pink and pads the mauve-pink seeds clustered around a central core.

Chocolate was unknown in Europe until Columbus, on his fourth voyage, noticed it on an Indian trading boat in the Bay of Honduras; Cortés took it to Spain in 1520.

The Spanish tried to keep the drink a secret, but it spread through Europe as a snobby luxury beverage. The first chocolate house, opened in England in 1657, was strictly high priced and high society; not until 1825 was chocolate available to the poor, after repeal of high customs duties.

The process which turns the ripe seeds into what we know as chocolate is long and complicated. The seeds are first fermented, then dried in the sun. They go to the factory where they are sorted, then roasted, then broken up, and the brittle shells winnowed out. A clever and indefatigable Dutchman, van Houten, discovered a way to press out the excess fat (cocoa butter) and make a more drinkable brew, as well as blocks of eating chocolate, also how to treat the drinking chocolate with an alkali and make what we know as cocoa. Cocoa should not be confused with the coconut or with the coca (*Erythroxylon coca*) leaves chewed by South American natives, which contain cocaine.

Chocolate is too well known as a flavoring for sweets, desserts of all kinds, to go into here, but it is less familiar as an ingredient for stews and sauces. In Mexico, powdered chocolate is an essential part of many of the powders known as *chili* in the United States, *chilli* in the rest of the world. In Spain and Italy, chocolate blends with onion, garlic, tomato, oil and spices for some of the most savory meat dishes, even with fish and octopus. This sounds odd, but the result is most delicious. One of the sweetest liqueurs is *crème de cacao*, made of infused cocoa beans, vanilla, cloves, and mace. The best way to serve this is chilled, with chilled heavy cream poured carefully on top, and a glop of the best cognac poured on top of the cream. The different weights of the liquids keep them separate.

Madame de Pompadour used chocolate in many of the aphrodisiac preparations with which she tried to get a rise out of Louis. One of these was fresh morel mushrooms in a heavy cream sauce flavored with sweet sauterne, bitter chocolate, and cayenne pepper. Solid block chocolate has always been considered as second only to honey to give quick energy; European students often eat it before an examination as a stimulus.

Every cookbook is full of chocolate recipes; every household has Aunt Boobalyn's chocolate this or that or Uncle Cranky's favorite whatever. There are cookbooks dedicated only to chocolate, every food column in newspapers and magazines eventually goes all over chocolate. Here are two old Deep South favorites:

Chocolate Mousse

12 ounces bittersweet chocolate
1 cup milk
1/4 cup dark rum
4 eggs, separated
1/4 cup sugar
1 cup heavy cream

Combine chocolate and milk and warm over moderate heat. Stir until chocolate is melted and mix is smooth and creamy, about 3 minutes. Remove from stove, beat and whisk in the egg yolks and rum until well blended. In separate bowl beat egg whites until just stiff. Gradually beat in sugar. Whip cream until soft peaks form. Now whisk the chocolate mixture into whites until well blended. Fold in the whipped cream. Put into 6 or 8 dessert bowls. Cover well with plastic wrap for at least 2 hours but no more than 6. Chill if you like.

Hot Fudge Pudding

1/4 cup shelled pecan halves
1 cup flour
1/3 cup sugar
1/4 cup unsweetened cocoa powder
2 teaspoons baking powder
scant 1/2 teaspoon salt
1/2 cup skim milk
1 big egg, lightly beaten
2 tablespoons vegetable oil
1 teaspoon vanilla extract
3/4 cup brown sugar
11/3 cups strong hot coffee

Put pecans in 375-degree oven on baking sheet for 10 or 15 minutes, cool, chop coarsely. In big bowl stir together flour, cocoa, baking powder, salt. In measuring cup combine milk, egg, oil, vanilla. Make a hole in center of dry ingredients and gradually pour in milk mix, stirring well until all is combined. Stir in pecans. Spoon into lightly oiled 8-by-8-inch baking dish. Spread evenly. Dissolve brown sugar in coffee, spoon over batter. Bake for 25 minutes, or until toothpick comes out clean. Let stand 12 minutes, serve hot or lukewarm. Twelve polite eaters, eight greedy-guts. If you wish to pile Pelion on Ossa you can sprinkle over each portion, before taking to table, the coarse sugar crystals from the bottom of the crystallized (candied) ginger jar or box.

These two recipes, just plain luscious, are clear indications of how chocolate has always been respected and honored in the lazy-making climate of the South, in contrast with the published opinion of Harriet Beecher Stowe. *She* claimed chocolate is a good example of the voluptuary immorality of the French and Spanish and should be banned from American tables. Not the first time the South has disagreed with *her*.

CHUTNEYS, RELISHES
All That

If one asks of a good cook, "What is a chutney?" the answers are as varied, startling, and hooty as if one had asked, "What is a Christian?" What, exactly, is a chutney? Well might one ask! Opening the *Oxford English Dictionary* I learned that chutney, chutny, chutnee are all correct forms of the word, derived from the Hindu *chatni*, which the *OED* defines as "any strong hot relish or condiment compounded of ripe fruits, acids, or sour herbs, and flavoured with chillies, spices, etc."

The *Larousse Gastronomique*, that treasure-trove of French culinary lore, is often quite dotty on things non-French and informs us that a chutney is "a kind of purée made with seeded Malaga raisins, which are pounded in a mortar with garlic, shallots, pimentos, apple, mustard, brown sugar, and

vinegar." Very well. I know that *most* chutnies in India are purée rather than coarse ground or chunky, but then *Larousse* appends a recipe which has nothing to do with the above, but is a tasty mix of ginger, mangoes, garlic and lemon peel.

Waverley Root, in his delightful *Encyclopedia of Food* gets around defining chutney by not mentioning it at all! The fact is, that Chinese, Persian, Arabian, French, British, and Deep Southern cookery all abound with sweet-sour relishes or acid-hot or sweet-hot or hot-sour pickles and accompanying garnishes which might be called chutney, but which are called many other things, such as relish, pickle, piccalilli, compote, conserve, confit, preserve, or even marmalade (as in onion marmalade made with ginger and red pepper to go with roast meats).

There is a basic dietary wisdom in all of these: the acidity of these side dishes, consumed by rich and poor alike, is helpful in

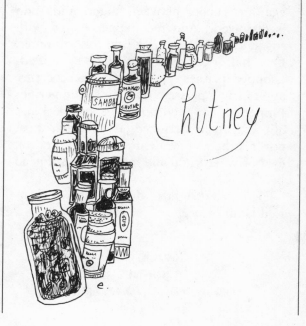

the proper functioning of the body's chemistry. The acidity helps to work in oils and starches and relieves the labors of stomach and liver. In old Persian cookery, they are called *torshi*, these chutney-like dishes. Here's a famous one:

———

Torshi Holu
(Persian Peach Pickles)

1 tablespoon powdered ginger
4 cups white wine vinegar
2 tablespoons coriander seeds
1 whole bulb garlic
1 pound fresh peaches
¼ pound dried tamarind (if available)
½ teaspoon red pepper
¼ cup sugar cubes
1 teaspoon salt
1 teaspoon black pepper

———

Soak ginger in vinegar. Toast coriander seeds slightly. Peel and separate garlic cloves. Combine peaches with ginger, coriander, garlic and remaining vinegar. (Tamarind, if available, should be soaked in vinegar and rubbed between fingers until pulp is dissolved.) Add red pepper mixed with sugar, salt, black pepper. Boil for 5 minutes. One half pound of any may be added: chopped prunes, plums, apricots, cherries, apples, figs, persimmons, limes, tangerines (unpeeled, chopped up, seeds and peel and all). Put up in sterilized jars. Vinegar must cover other ingredients. Seal, but check every few days and add more vinegar if need be.

Here is a delightful dish, to go with curried lamb or beef:

———

Mint Chutney
(Hindu)

One small onion or half a big one
1 green hot pepper
pecan-sized piece fresh ginger root
pinch cumin seeds
pinch salt
small toe garlic
cupful scalded mint leaves
squeeze lemon or lime juice
½ pint plain yoghurt

———

Pound all ingredients save yoghurt together in a mortar until you have a fine paste. Add yoghurt and either whiz in blender or whip well until a nicely flecked green mixture is the result. Chill before serving.

In some parts of India, chutneys are known as *sambals*. This one is delicious with boiled shrimp:

———

Cucumber Sambal
(Hindu)

Peel and shred a cucumber, mix it with a generous half cup of minced chives or thinly sliced onion, minced green hot pepper, a little parsley. This must be pounded together (or whizzed) with a little oil, vinegar, powdered ginger, salt and freshly ground black pepper.

Chatni is its Hindu name; we transliterate it as chutney, chutny, chutnee. What is called chutney in India is not the sweet bottled kind we know as chutney. In the East the relish called chutney is usually a paste made fresh for the occasion, with mangoes the base of many of them, but any piquant mixture of raw ingredients will serve: fresh ginger, fresh hot green pepper, onion, garlic, mint, coriander leaves, sour fruits, coconut, anything stimulating or refreshing to the palate, anything (remembering the predominance of beans and peas in Hindu cookery) useful against flatulence, and anything

CHUTNEY

(remembering the predominance of flies and questionable water supplies) mildly antiseptic.

The *cooked* bottled chutneys we know are usually of Indian inspiration and often manufactured there, but they would consider them sweet pickles. Many fresh chutneys, which are more like a purée than a preserve, are called *sambals*. Every country where the culinary arts are taken seriously produces endless variations of sweet-sour side dishes which stimulate appetite and aid digestion.

Many of our southern favorites have a longer lineage than we know: green tomato pickles were known as green tomato chutney way back when. In Italy, for instance, there is a wonderful, delicious relish called *Mostarda di Cremona*. All fresh chutneys are improvised: the cook takes what she finds and invents on the spot.

The principal manufactured chutneys available in jars or bottles are Bengal Club, Colonel Skinner's, Major Grey's, Hot Mango, Sweet Mango, and Tirhoot. They include mangoes, ginger, and various combinations of spices. The Tirhoot chutney leans heavily on oranges and lemons and is especially good with hot curried chicken.

An important ingredient in Hindu cookery is *dhania,* one of the most commonly used herbs on the planet. We know it as coriander. Under the name *cilantro* it is a basic ingredient in Mexican and Central American kitchens, usually the green plant. If the coriander seeds you buy at your grocer's are fresh, they'll easily sprout and you can sample these greens for yourself. Not only are they delicious they are highly nutritious, we are told by such authorities as Mr. Tom Stobart. Look at this:

Green Coriander Chutney

Chop and blend with about a half cup water a big handful of coriander leaves, a small onion, a teaspoon of salt, 5 fresh green hot peppers, the juice of half a lemon, a pinch of grated lemon peel. Now you need coconut, roughly 2 cups or even a little more. If using dried, grind it first to powder in your blender, then add to other ingredients till a nice smooth paste results. Use more coriander greens if you like, or more onion, or pepper, or more coconut. Hindu cooking is the exact opposite of *Good Housekeeping Institute,* it's what's in the market, *carpe diem,* and dare all!

With baked ham or pork chops this is surprising:

Quince Sambal

Peel and quarter some not-quite-ripe quinces, and for 2 or 3 quinces, take one sliced onion, a hot green pepper, a little salt and a little orange juice and pound (or whizz) all together and serve.

The following is a treat with plain boiled or broiled fish and a rice flavored with bay leaves, onion and 1 tablespoon (to about 2 cups rice) powdered turmeric (curcuma). A

good salad would be curly lettuce and fresh peaches dressed with garlic, salt, powdered ginger, lemon or lime, and good olive oil.

Shrimp Chutney

You'll need about a pint of boiled shrimp. Boil them in water with only a bay leaf, some lemon and orange rinds, a little salt. Let them cool in their water, then peel and clean. Mince them with a sharp knife and either pound in a mortar or whizz in your machine with 1 or 2 chopped green hot peppers, some finely minced chives or shallots, a dusting of powdered ginger, 2 tablespoons best oil to make a smooth paste, enough lemon or lime juice to acidulate the dish pleasantly. Crabmeat can be used in place of shrimp. Good with the plain boiled fish, as noted, but delightful on thin freshly toasted wholewheat Melba toast as a little first course.

We've been contemplating the family of accompanying dishes, myriad combinations of sweet-sour-acid-hot-pungent which are an aid to digestion. Well, one of the most delightful and the least known outside its native purlieu is *Mostarda di Cremona* (Cremona Mustard). There are two basic forms and many variations. In the great Italian restaurants there is always a *bollito misto* (mixed boil) which many visitors scorn. "Boiled meat? Really . . . We didn't come to Italy to eat boiled meat."

But a cart is wheeled in, a kind of portable hot table, with a great hunk of beef brisket, rump, or bottom round which has been boiled with carrots, onions, potatoes, green pepper, celery, canned Italian tomatoes (the flavor is different from the fresh), *and* veal, a chicken or so, a calf's head, and a *cotechino* sausage boiled separately. Various sauces and relishes are served, varying according to region and restaurant, but with the *bollito* there is always *Mostarda di Cremona*.

The most common variety is a great jar of whole fruit—seckel pears, small oranges, apples, kumquats, cherries, apricots, peaches, with slices of quince, pineapple, sometimes whole grapes or currants—pickled in sweet syrup heavily flavored with sharp mustard and powdered ginger. This combination occurs also in a finely chopped version. Rarely, one finds the fruits sliced and pickled thus. The tart fruit flavor underlined by mustard is delightful. As perfect a pairing with the boiled mixed platter as our Southern brandied peaches with ham or pork.

Southern Brandied Peaches

4 pounds firm ripe peaches
1 pint brandy
2 pounds white sugar

bay leaves
mace
cinnamon
1 clove stuck into each peach
dash powdered ginger
a few mustard seeds
a few celery seeds

Put peaches into enough water to cover with sugar and spices. Bring to boil, turn down to simmer, cook until fork just goes into peaches. Remove peaches, boil liquid uncovered until reduced by half. Turn off fire. Replace peaches in syrup, pour in brandy. Put in sterilized jars, close-packed, use what's left of brandied liquid over vanilla ice cream.

Here's an old Virginia recipe for piccalilli:

Piccalilli

Use, as you please, cauliflower, onions, gherkins, French beans, green pepper, green nasturtium seeds or capers. Cider vinegar, mustard, ginger, turmeric, curry powder, mace and cayenne.

Break and/or cut vegetables, cook about 3 minutes in a boiling brine strong enough to float an egg. Drain well, spread on platters, let them remain in sun until perfectly dry. Cook up your cider vinegar with about ½ ounce each of curry and turmeric to each quart of vinegar. Add spices. Bring just to boil. Mix mustard powder smoothly with a little cold water and add to liquid, but don't let boil. Place prepared vegetables in jars, cover completely with hot liquid. When completely cold, quite cold, cover closely and store.

Here's a chutney from the old hotel at Mentone, Alabama.

Mentone Apple Chutney

12 tart apples
12 ripe tomatoes, firm
6 medium white onions
3 red peppers
3 green peppers
1 pound seedless raisins
1 orange cut fine (peel, seeds, the works)
1 cup finely chopped celery
1 teaspoon grated lemon peel
2 cups sugar
pinch of salt
mace, cinnamon, powdered ginger,
cayenne pepper as you like

Chop vegetables, then apples, unpeeled. Combine all, cook until thick with 2 quarts best cider vinegar. Pour into jars and seal at once.

CINNAMON
(Cinnamomum zeylanicum)
Cassia (Cinnamomum laurii)
Cassia (Canella alba)

Now, for the Department of Total Confusion. There are two kinds of cinnamon.

The flavor we all know as "cinnamon" is common in milder and nippier degrees to a host of trees and shrubs producing either strongly perfumed bark or berries or both. There are four hundred members of the cassia family, forty of the cinnamon. The cassia (Chinese cinnamon, *cannelle de Chine*) is one of the oldest of all spices, recorded in China in 2500 B.C. (It is one of the elements of the Chinese Five Spices, a mixture widely used in Oriental cookery.) In Egypt it goes back to 1600 B.C. The milder "true" cinnamon was discovered in Ceylon by Dutch spice traders. The tree, which grows to twenty or thirty feet in height, grows best in almost pure sand, requiring only one percent of vegetable matter. The Dutch, fearing the bark would have less flavor if cultivated, only allowed plantations to be established in 1776. Now it is grown in many localities.

Among the many varieties of plants producing the "cinnamon" flavor, only the laurel *Cinnamomum zeylanicum* is medicinal, being astringent, carminative, antiseptic. It stops vomiting, relieves flatulence, and combined with chalk or other astringents has been widely used for diarrhea and internal hemorrhages. In many countries, only the bark of this tree, whole or powdered, may be sold under the name cinnamon. Which is why in England and the Commonwealth you will find also powdered cassia on sale in shops, especially as an ingredient for curries. But for sweets and mulled wine and fig preserves and apple pies and such, it is the

CASSIA

real thing which is required. Much more delicate. But ATTENTION! If you see something marked "cassia" at your druggist's or in the health food shop, remember that is a common appellation for senna pods, a powerful laxative.

In the United States, what we buy as powdered cinnamon is usually the cassia. This comes from China, Vietnam and Indonesia. It is darker and stronger than cinnamon, which is lighter, more delicate in flavor and comes from Ceylon. In England it is illegal to sell cassia as cinnamon. The Mexicans prefer the milder cinnamon and use a great deal of it. In the United States, we rarely see real cinnamon, save as stick cinnamon, the curled papery type. This has had the bark scraped off. Cassia is sold in hunks, too, but with the bark intact. If you like cinnamon in sweet dishes, buy real cinnamon bark and keep it in a jar of granulated sugar; use that sugar for your desserts. Real cinnamon bark is papery and pale beige. Cassia bark is usually thicker, or twisted, of an orangey-brown with characteristic spots, or scars, or markings. I confess I like strong powdered cassia, pungent and bitey, to make a classic cinnamon toast, but when I make bananas flamed in cognac I use only the "real" cinnamon, along with mace and a hint of nutmeg.

On a rainy afternoon, or for children home after examinations, or for the blues, the lows, the foozies, mollycobbles, undiagnosed sadnesses, hangovers, stresses, strains, beginnings of a cold, after an unexpectedly high bill, bad news in a letter, tantrums by pet dogs or cats . . . after any and all of such, there is nothing, but nothing, more cheering than strong unsweetened tea and cinnamon toast. Take some slices of whole wheat bread, put them in a 350-degree oven a minute or so to dry them a bit, then spread them lavishly with *unsalted* butter mixed with sugar and ordinary store-bought powdered cinnamon and put back into oven until they begin to bubble slightly. Serve at once. Lots of paper napkins.

In the Arab countries, cinnamon is important in meat cookery, especially for lamb and mutton, where it takes away the muttony taste unpleasant to some.

Beef Stew

Try marinating cubes of beef in red wine with chopped onions, some grated lemon peel, a glop of Creole or Dijon mustard, and a good dash of cinnamon and freshly ground black pepper. After about 4 or 5 hours of marinating, put into a thick covered casserole dish and let cook about an hour or a bit more in a moderate oven. Serve from the pot, with lots of hot biscuits or hot bread to slurp up the sauce. Or make an apple sauce ice cream loaded with cinnamon and splash a dash of Triple Sec over it before serving.

Cinnamon (let's call them both that) is one of the rare sweet spices. It seems to stimulate the taste buds. It also contains an essential oil strong in phenols, which discourage the bacteria that make food go bad. Cinnamon is probably the first spice used by humankind; it occurs in every record in old civilizations as something precious, powerful, helpful. The Chinese emperor Shen Nung (2700 B.C.) wrote in a treatise that no doctor would write a prescription without including *kwei* (cassia) or *tien-chu-kwei* ("cassia of the Indies,") for the spicy flavor, but also for the comforting therapeutic values, borne out by the latest scientific find-

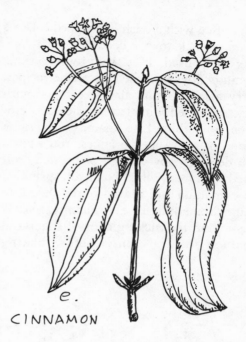

CINNAMON

ings that have identified the elements in the essential oil of cinnamon that are stimulating to the gastrointestinal and respiratory systems, besides being antiseptic and a strong killer of harmful bacteria.

Cinnamon enters into the preparation of holy incenses and holy ointments in all the religions of the ancient world. As the sacred unguent used for ritual anointment, cinnamon occurs frequently in the Bible (as *kaneh* or *quesiah* — the Greek is *kinnamon*, the Latin *cannula*, Italian, *cannella*, French, *cannelle*) as in Exodus 30:23, in Psalm 44, as the symbol of wisdom, used to perfume the tunic of a royal bridegroom; in the Song of Songs when the bride is compared to a garden of fragrant plants, cinnamon predominating. From the remotest past, the spice is praised as efficient in helping to cure colds, fevers, chills, "winter colics," diarrhea, and *gloom*!

A dash of cinnamon is the secret ingredient in many of the chocolate desserts.

Black coffee with a dash is delightful. Use a cinnamon stick to stir cocoa or chocolate. Sticks can be used, dried, kept for next time. Cinnamon goes into the best pickle recipes, but try a fresh fruit salad sweetened with honey, sprinkled with lemon juice and cinnamon. Something Else Again. Or the same combo on fresh sliced oranges. You want a quick dessert? Any cooked or canned fruit topped with (real) whipped cream sprinkled with cinnamon and shaved bitter chocolate becomes Something Else. Cinnamon toast is a classic, but try tucking dabs of sugar and cinnamon inside biscuits before baking them.

This is very good, too:

Sweet and Sour Beans

Wash one pound of navy beans (white beans) and soak overnight. Do not throw out water. Next day simmer in 2 pints of that water for thirty minutes, then add 1½ ounces brown sugar, ¼ cup cider vinegar, 1 tablespoon cane syrup, 2 teaspoons salt, a good piece of cinnamon stick, a few cubes of fatback, some freshly ground black pepper, a little grated lemon peel. Simmer another 30 minutes until beans are tender and just right.

CITRUS

Everybody knows orange, lemon, lime, grapefruit, tangerine, much of the Gulf Coast loves the sweet-skinned acid-fleshed kumquat and the tangerine-type Satsuma orange which has loose skin and sweet flesh, but many of the literally hundreds of varieties and hybrids making up the citrus world are unknown, although easily grown in the warmer parts of our country. Some of the citrus family can be easily grown in window pots if they get at least four hours of light daily, and terra cotta, not plastic, pots. Calamondin oranges (*Citrifortunella x mitis*) are among the easiest, if you take the trouble to read up on their habits. They're small and tart and make a marmalade which puts Seville oranges to total shame.

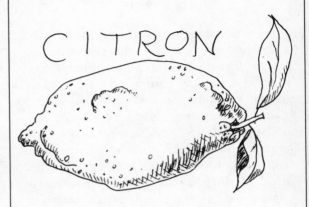

The citron (*Citrus medica*) is a big bumpy thing looking rather like a quince, and is candied, used in curries, endless relishes. In Bayonne, France, a local delight is the *pâté de cédrat*, pickled with spice and wild mustard seeds. The botanical name of this fruit has changed—its origins still disputed (Persia? Media?), its history vague. Is it the "Median apple" referred to by ancient writers? Some Bible scholars since the beginning have argued that this is really the forbidden fruit Eve offered, and refer to little indentations on the fruit as "Adam's bites."

To add to the hubbub, there is a hard-rinded melon called "citron" which is candied for use in cakes and puddings.

This member of the citrus family is said to have been cultivated in the Hanging Gardens of Babylon, and appears to be the only variety known to the ancient Latin world. Under varying names (*citrium, citreum, citrum, citrus*) it is referred to in many contexts. It is a big knobbly, warty yellow or greenish yellow lemon-like fruit, sometimes weighing as much as five pounds, growing on a thorny tree fifteen to twenty feet high.

The wood of the tree was used for fine, expensive furniture, the leaves used for perfume and to flavor vinegar. The extremely acid juice was used in medicines, and to strengthen vinegars. The peel is the part most employed; it yields a volatile oil which adds immeasureably to countless perfumes, *eaux de cologne,* rubbing oils, hair tonics, etc. The peel is, of course, best known in its candied (artificially colored) form. Cultivated nowadays in both the Mediterranean and West Indian countries, one half of the world's supply of candied citron peel is consumed in the United States, and it would be amusing to know what percentage goes to the southern states, since it is one of the traditional ingredients of our Christmas fruit cakes.

In old Mobile and New Orleans recipes it sometimes occurs under its French name *cédrat.* Candied citron peel is delightful in its own right. A chilled honeydew melon dressed with lime juice, slivers of candied citron and candied ginger, is one of the most delightful summer desserts imaginable, and any plain tea-cake becomes a treat with bits of citron and grated lemon peel added.

One of the wonders of the citrus family is its adaptability. Cuttings from the same parent plant, raised in Florida and California, display different characteristics. The California orange will be brighter in color, slightly more acid; the Florida twin will produce paler, often greenish fruits, much sweeter. In other cases, sizes will vary, noticeable alterations of flavor.

Grapefruit (*Citrus paradisi*) was a thick-skinned unattractive citrus in the Malay peninsula centuries ago. It went to China, changed under cultivation, then moved on to India, finally the Mediterranean, from there to the West Indies early on. In the West Indies the grapefruit really took off, changing its character completely. A Frenchman, Count Odette Phillippe, brought the fruit to the Tampa Bay area in 1823 and set up what became the world's largest area producing grapefruits. More than fifty million crates of grapefruit come from Florida every year.

Just as many events which affect the world (Gutenberg, Mozart, Edison) occur quietly, perhaps the biggest news in citrus history is the recent discovery of a single example of the grapefruit's ancestor, thought extinct, growing on the West Indies Isle of St. Lucia. Grapefruit, known now in ten varieties, is the only citrus thought to have originated in the New World, is the hybrid of two Southeast Asian fruits, the pummelo and the sweet orange. Discovery of this ancestor makes possible breeding for resistance to pests and diseases, even new varieties.

Blood oranges have a lush sweet flavor, part orange, part raspberry. They are a commercial crop in the Mediterranean but their color seems unpredictable in the New World.

Pummelos (*Citrus grandis*) are the biggest of the citrus family, ancestor of the grapefruit, and the fact that some markets sell pummelos as "Chinese grapefruit" makes for confusion. The flesh is sweet, but what will eventually make pummelos much more sought after is the fact that the soft thick rind peels off as easily as, then, do the enclosing membranes and inner skin. You can arrive at thick lush slices of flesh without any chewy white bits.

Pummelos, still called "shaddocks" in some places, after a Captain Shaddock who reportedly brought the first seeds to the West Indies in the eighteenth century, can be traced back to 1187. The fruit is sacred to certain Buddhist cults, and exists in many local variations, ranging in color from pink to yellow to white.

Kumquats, who don't mind a little cold weather, and will cross with almost any other citrus, are parents to some completely surprising (and delicious) new hybrids:

Orangequat is bigger than the kumquat, is bright orange, has mildly sweet rind and tart flesh.

Limequats make lovely trees with abundant fruit, bright green to yellowish green to pale yellow fruit, and are a great substitute for limes.

Mandarins exist in many varieties, there's news of new ones every year. One variety, "honey," has exceptionally sweet fruit.

The juices of the various citrus fruits have always been employed worldwide to enhance or heighten the flavor of countless dishes.

CLOVEPINK
Gilly flower
(Dianthus caryophyllus)

Modern clovepinks have little scent, just like their big brothers the carnations, often being hybridized for size or color or what have you, raised in hothouses. But the old-

fashioned clovepink, a universally beloved flower lauded by Shakespeare, Spenser, Herrick, and many another, is delightfully perfumed and a great pleasure in any garden. In the last century there were literally hundreds of varieties: speckled, fringed, particolored. A garden society in the British Isles is combing old gardens to rescue many of the "lost" forms. Hummingbirds are dotty over the single-fringed varieties, and visit faithfully at precisely the same hour every day, you can set your watch. In European gardens, the hummingbird hawk moth, which imitates the hummingbird, does the same!

The Romans felt that petals of clovepink in their wine cups delayed inebriation. They are the "sops-in-wine" floated in the wine cups of engaged couples in seventeenth- and eighteenth-century England and Virginia and the Carolinas.

The petals, gathered in early morning, can be steeped in warm cream which is then used to make a cream custard or a sauce to pour over cooked pears or peaches. Or sugar the petals, steep them in cognac, strain, and use to flavor dry white wine as a dessert beverage with sherbets or fruit. Or pour hot sugar crystals over the petals, steep, strain, and use to make a sherbet of fresh fruit or ditto a pie. Completely delicious and unexpected. Clove-like and something else again. Ghost of tea roses. Early morning in the garden. Summer.

CLOVES
(Eugenia aromatica, Eugenia caryophyllata)

Clove is one of the best known of all spices, the dried flower bud of a handsome evergreen tree native to the Molucca Islands (Spice Islands) of which every part is aromatic, and the wood of a fragrant purplish grain, employed for precious coffers, reliquaries, etc. The volatile oil of cloves is a powerful antiseptic and analgesic.

In preplumbing days, many folk carried a spiceball or pomander, an apple or orange thickly studded with cloves, to hold to the nose when traipsing through the streets or even passing in a litter or carriage. Powdered cloves, like the dead dust sold as pepper, is as far from the flavor of a freshly crushed clove as Helsinki is from Las Vegas. A fascinating volume could be compiled on the history of this spice.

In the third century B.C. one of the Han emperors in China ordered that all courtesans should hold cloves under their tongues when they were in his presence, as a breath sweetener. Hence the Chinese name for it,

Ki-she-Kiang, variously translated as "bird tongue spice" or "chicken tongue spice" since presumably their strong presence under the tongue gave the nobles a birdy look. The Emperor Constantine sent the Bishop of Rome gold and silver vessels filled with cloves, considered the ultimate in princely gifts. Throughout ancient and medieval times, the spice was heavily taxed, a luxury item much used in medicines and aphrodisiacs. Both the Dutch and the Portuguese attempted to gain a monopoly, but it was broken when an intrepid Frenchman, Pierre Poivre (his name translates "Peter Pepper") stole ashore at Amboise and made off with some seedlings, which he introduced to *Isle de France* and *Bourbon.* A sole tree survived: from it descended all the plantations in Africa and America. The people of Amboise now keep all their cloves to add to their smoking tobacco. We get our supplies from Zanzibar, Madagascar, and the West Indies.

Cloves are powerful, should never be used in excess. They are a most fortunate combination with onion, reducing the strong flavor of the bulb and bringing out its sweetness, and should be included in every beef or pork dish, whether stew or roast, daube or ragoût. This is standard practice in the great dishes of France and Italy. One does not taste the clove, but when it is lacking, the absence is noticeable. Same for bay leaves. On a cold winter day, nothing is better than fresh salt pork, slowly simmered with bay, cloves, cracked peppercorns. The water is used to cook white (or navy) beans. Braised celery on the side with a light dry red wine.

Apples studded with two cloves and with the core hole stuffed with brown sugar and sherry, baked, are good with pork or as a simple dessert. You are not acquainted with onions until you try this with pork chops: parboil some fairly big onions for 20 minutes. Drain. Scoop out two-thirds of the flesh and chop it fine, salt to taste, mix with butter, honey, tomato paste. Stuff onions. Stick a clove in each onion. Place in a baking pan with a splash of white wine and a few drops of vinegar. Lightly lay a sheet of aluminum on top. Bake 30 minutes at 350 degrees, remove foil, baste, bake a little longer.

Coffee strongly dosed with cloves has lately been prescribed widely as a relief for asthmatics.

COGNAC

There are many brandies and brandy-type distilled liquors, but "brandy" and "cognac" are two words never to be confused.

In the ancient small town of Cognac in France, nothing has changed, literally, in distilling the spirit, since the fifteenth century. The oak casks in which the cognac ages for as long as eighty years are still made by hand. They are really works of art, carefully cut and fitted wood: no nails are used, cognac must never make contact with metal, only oak. But the potstills in which the cognac is distilled twice are the very ones brought to this region in the twelfth century by the invading Moors. The lengthy processes involved in preparing the spirit have never been altered or speeded up to satisfy modern impatience. The long-trained master blenders sniff and taste hundreds of individual cognacs, then carefully blend as many as 100 different varieties to achieve their end

product. Because everything in the village of Cognac goes slow, the villagers are called *cagouillards*, a *patois* word for "snail."

Brandies are used to flavor many dishes, but cognac is usually served straight or, at best, as a few drops in the morning coffee during very cold weather. Since forever, it has been medicinal and restorative: for faintness, after childbirth, for fits of melancholy or low spirits.

But . . . but . . . some very grand cooks claim that only real cognac can give the proper taste to these:

Cognac Cookies

1 stick unsalted butter
1/2 cup firmly packed dark brown sugar
1/3 cup molasses
1/2 teaspoon powdered cinnamon
1/2 teaspoon ground ginger
3/4 cup sifted flour
2 teaspoons Cognac
1 ounce chopped white chocolate
1 cup crushed pecans

Heat oven to 300 degrees. Grease big baking sheets. Mix butter, sugar, molasses, spices. Cook till butter is melted; stir well. Little by little, mix in flour, then cognac. Drop by teaspoonfuls onto sheets, about 3 inches apart. Bake about 12 minutes until golden. Cool 1 or 2 minutes. Then remove 1 cookie at a time and shape it into cylinder around handle of a wooden spoon (greased). Work fast; they harden. Put back into oven if they do. Cool on racks. Melt white chocolate in cup set over simmering water. Put pecan bits into a cup or small bowl. Brush ends of cookies in melted chocolate, then into nuts. Let sit on racks to cool. About 45 cookies.

Comfrey

COMFREY
Boneset
(Symphytum officinale)

According to the most ancient *and* the most modern herbal usage, two plants could halve all the ailments of the Western world: garlic and comfrey. Garlic is universally known as helpful for all circulatory and digestive problems, but the "miracle worker" comfrey seems less familiar. Its old names, "boneset" and "boneknit," indicate its time-honored use as a poultice for fractures. The leaves are pulped, mixed with wine, applied. In some of the great tuberculosis sanatoriums in Scandinavia, comfrey is an accepted medicine and is credited with amazing recoveries where tissue damage has been prolonged and severe.

Comfrey contains a substance called *allantoin,* which has been identified as a cell proliferant, a substance which speeds up the natural replacement of body cells, hence its use both internal and external. Put through the juicer and sipped as a juice (with a bit of celery and parsley for taste), comfrey goes to work in the bloodstream, its natural calcium and B_{12} vitamins penetrating the entire system. A poultice of the leaves has been proven nothing less than astounding in treating stubborn cases of acne or acne-scarred skin. Ditto burns and scar tissue. But this bountiful plant doesn't stop there.

The abundant leaves work as a quick and easy manure. Chop up some of the fading older leaves, dig them in around your plants. Their quick decomposition will free nitrogen and calcium into the topsoil. A few leaves chopped into the salad bowl add color and flavor, but since they are slightly hairy, like borage, not everybody will like them. So use smaller leaves. The same smaller leaves, dipped in a light batter and deep-fried, look like little green fish, and are an amusing conversational gambit for cocktail parties or first course to a dinner.

European farmers often use it to break up new heavy ground, for the roots go deep into the subsoil, dredging up minerals and nutrients missing in depleted topsoil. When the plant dies down, it is hoed to bits, and dug into the earth to make compost.

The plant is perennial, grows about three or four feet high, spreads out about three feet. The bright green leaves grow up to eighteen inches long, and grasshoppers and caterpillars, knowing what is good for them, will choose comfrey first in any kitchen garden. The plant hates droughts and must be watered in summer, otherwise it is unflappable. The pretty drooping bell-shaped flowers are a soft purplish color, sometimes mauve, bluish, or even yellow. The plants grow better and stronger if you nip off the flower buds.

COMPOTES

Once upon a time, when ladies had maids and cooks, if they felt it behooved them to do something in the kitchen, after they had ordered the meals and surveyed the provisions, it usually meant making special cookies or candies, Christmas fruitcakes (which involved practically the entire family; Papa helping by pouring brandy or bourbon over the finished product a few drops at a time for the two weeks aging process) or . . . or . . . working in the stillroom.

Houses downtown were often built with a pantry on the north side, often with a diamond-shaped window which opened on a pivotal shaft. These pantries or stillrooms

Compôtes

were usually cool. They were the "cool larders" where hams and roasts reposed, where pickles and preserves were lined in jewel-colored array. Ladies made toilet waters by cramming scented flowers into tumblers buttered with unsalted butter, often putting in new pickings twice a day. The tumblers were washed out with pure alcohol at last, the butter scooped and blotted away after steeping, and voila! a delicate faint flower perfume to dab on feverish temples and fragile wrists. But these same ladies prepared, as well, a whole warehouse of pickles, preserves, marmalades and . . . *compotes.*

The word "compote" means something vague today, generally a dessert of cooked pears or such. But the oldtime compotes were wonderful sweet-sour relishes to eat with roast meats and especially game. Roast venison usually was accompanied by an *épergne* or a flat relish dish, each having four, six, or more little dishes containing freshly prepared sweet mustard, freshly prepared hot mustard, mustard with horseradish, mustard with herbs . . . and several kinds of compote. The recipes here are from my grandmother, the Misses Ebeltoft, and Miss Ruth Huger.

Lemon Compote

Peel 1 lemon and 1 orange. Remove every bit of white pith, then mince the yellow part of the skin and all the flesh into dice. Bring to boil with just enough water to cover. Just to boiling point, not beyond. Add a glass of red wine, a tablespoon of brown sauce, a little salt, cayenne pepper, and the juice of one more lemon, one more orange. (Note: brown sauce would be, for all practical pur-

shire, half dry sherry. The brown sauce can also be read to mean 1 tablespoon Worcestershire sauce mixed together with ½ tablespoon cornstarch.)

Cranberry Compote

Wash berries well, dry on paper towels. Allow 1 pound of sugar to every 2 pounds of berries. Cook slowly until berries are soft but not mushy. Lift out berries, then boil up syrup until it is thick, then mix the berries into the syrup, add a splash of the very best French cognac, pour into jars and cover tightly until cool.

Sweet Tomato Compote

You need about 7 pounds of nicely sliced tomatoes. Let them stand 24 hours sprinkled with salt. Soak 24 hours in fresh water, then drain well. Take 4½ pounds sugar, 1 ounce cinnamon, 1 ounce cloves and enough vinegar to cover this mixture. Boil together and pour over tomatoes. Let stand 24 hours, bring to a boil once more, then pot it, tie it down and store in a cool dark larder.

Cherry Compote

Pick over fruit, remove stems, discard soft ones. Now boil up some best wine vinegar with a bay leaf, a few cloves, 8 or 10 peppercorns to each pint of vinegar used, let it cool, but not completely, pouring over packed fruit while still lukewarm. Cover and keep. Small plums, pitted, are delicious this way. Both cherries and plums are delicious with pork in any form.

Windfall Compote

Go out into the backyard and pick up any sand pears that have fallen. Wipe them, remove stems, cut out bruised or decayed parts. Fill a pot three-fourths full, and boil in enough water to cover; cook to a pulp. Drain off every drop of juice and weigh it. To each quart add 1 pound sugar, 6 or 7 cloves, about a teaspoon grated nutmeg, a little cinnamon and the juice and thinly pared rind of half a lemon. Some like a good dash of powdered ginger. Boil until thick and pot it. When cold it should be solid. (Nowadays you could make this with the mostly unripe pears offered in the supermarkets.)

CORIANDER
Cilantro
(Coriandrum sativum)

Coriander is one of the ancient ingredients, going back to earliest Egypt, but we know it by a Greek-derived name coming from *koris*, meaning "bedbug." Culinary writers have puzzled over this for centuries. I think it is easy to figure out. The fat seeds with their little whiskers do look like some tiny bug. And if you crush the green seeds before they're full-size, there is an odd greenish odor which is fairly unpleasant.

The green leaves of the plant and the seeds of the plant are two totally different flavors with widely differing uses.

Under the labels of Japanese or Chinese "parsley" the leaves figure in dozens of dishes, are eaten as a cooked green with a pleasant unfamiliar warm musky taste.

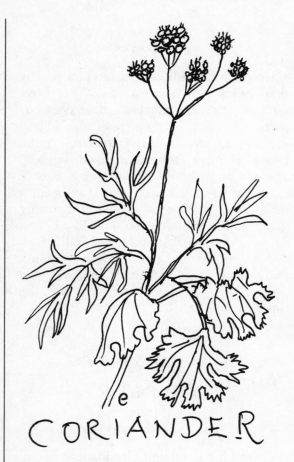

CORIANDER

Essential in authentic curries, the seeds, dried, have a wonderfully attractive fragrance and taste, reminding munchers of everything from burnt orange peel to sandalwood.

The dried powdered leaves, under the disguise of cilantro, form one of the most common seasonings in Mexican cookery, used in rice, bean, meat dishes. All the wonderful eastern Mediterranean mixtures of mostly onion, eggplant, garlic, onion, celery and zucchini, labelled *à la grecque,* depend on coriander seed and lemon peel for the distinctive and satisfying flavor. Coriander seed can sex up the dreariest rice pudding on earth. It is a secret ingredient in gin and

chartreuse and is often the seed in the middle of a jaw-breaker or gob-stopper.

—

Mexican Oysters

(This recipe counts 4 oysters apiece for 4 diners, as a hot hors d'oeuvre. Adjust quantities for more.)

16 oysters on the half-shell
4 slices lean bacon
4 tablespoons unsalted butter
3 tablespoons minced onion
3 tablespoons minced fresh cilantro (coriander)
pinch dill
couple good splurts of Tabasco
lemon juice as you feel
salt and pepper

—

Cook bacon in skillet over low heat until golden but still soft, put on paper towels to drain. In a bowl stir together butter, onion, coriander leaves, Tabasco, salt and pepper to taste. Arrange shells on flat baking dish, divide butter mixture among them, place oyster on each, sprinkle with lemon juice, put piece of bacon on top of each, bake in preheated 450-degree oven for 10 minutes.

COSTMARY, ALECOST
(*Chrysanthemum balsamita,* formerly *Tanacetum balsamita*)

Strange the caprices of fashion. And herbs and flowers go in and out of fashion, too. The aromatic, spicy herb, much beloved, much cultivated, used in dozens of dishes, in perfumes, in medicines, that we are contemplating here has dwindled from being an inhabitant of everything remotely resembling a herb garden to being a rarity. Yet it grows like a weed anywhere on earth, if given full sun and soil that is not too moist. Doesn't like shade. Spreads like mad; has to be thinned out every three years. "Cost" comes from *costum* or *costis* (variously interpreted to mean "oriental herb" or "spicy herb"); the "mary" comes from the plant's association with the Virgin Mary since earliest times. Its historic prevalence is borne out by the dozens of names by which it is known, such as *Our Lady's herb, mace, Mary's mace, Mary-mint, sage o' bedlam* (i.e. Bethlehem), *sweet sage, Ageratum achillea, goose tongue* (from the shape of the leaf). The American names (the Pilgrims brought the plant from Holland) *Bible-leaf* and *geranium mint* are derived from the custom of using the aromatic leaves as bookmarkers in the family Bible; and from a fancied resemblance to mint and scented geraniums in the plant's perfume.

The herb has a minty, sagey, pleasant, soothing aroma. I once created a sensation by flavoring pork sausage patties with grated onion, grated lemon peel, and chopped costmary.

For centuries the plant was used to give an elusive spiciness to beers and ales, hence its other name, alecost. The dried leaves were once mixed with dried lavender flowers to place amongst stored linens; I've tried this: the fragrance is completely delightful and lingers in towels and sheets. The "herb pillows" of the eighteenth and nineteenth centuries (little sacks of aromatic herbs thought to be a remedy for sleeplessness) always included lavender, clovepinks and costmary as principal ingredients. Costmary has been used, too, to make an ersatz "violet" perfume! The lemony quality of the young leaves make them very good to sprinkle in salad and on boiled or roasted fish, along with dill, while boiled new potatoes liberally doused with unsalted butter, dill, costmary, and black pepper are a

show-stopper. Vegetables which are slightly vapid in themselves, such as our dear little all-season yellow squash, can become important dishes when stuffed, for instance, with their own flesh mixed with bread crumbs, ham scraps, chopped costmary leaves, butter, and a dash of Cayenne, then baked. Costmary leaves are wonderful in mixed salads, in wine punches, in meat loaves, or try this:

Stuffed Breast of Veal

Get your butcher to cut a neat pocket in a 2-pound breast of veal. Sprinkle the meat with salt, freshly ground black pepper, a dash of Worcestershire diluted in white wine, and lemon juice.

COSTMARY

Stuffing

*³/₄ cup bread crumbs soaked in
a little milk and lemon juice
2 eggs, slightly beaten
1 slice bacon chopped fine
1 minced garlic clove
1 tablespoon minced parsley
1¹/₂ tablespoons minced costmary
2 tablespoons Madeira or cream sherry
salt and pepper*

Mix all together, stuff pocket in meat. Roll the meat, tie it, place in fairly tight oven dish so it won't have a chance to dry out. Put slices of bacon over it, a few dabs of butter, roast at 350 degrees until tender, roughly 1¹/₂ hours.

CRANBERRIES
Mossberries
(Vaccinium)

The botanical name for a genus of over 130 species of shrubs and small trees of the *Ericaceae* family (which includes the heathers) is *Vaccinium,* which in turn, is an old Latin name of disputed origin, used by Virgil and Pliny and probably a corruption of *Hyacinthus.*

Well, all right. But when the botanical authorities then add: ". . . distinct from *Chiogenes, Gaultheria,* and *Pernettya,*" my eyes begin to cross.

The most important subgenus in the *Vaccinium* group is the blueberry in its many forms, but what we are concerned with here are two worldwide favorites: *V. oxycoccos,* the small-fruited cranberry, and *V. macrocarpon,* the large-fruited cranberry. The first is native to Europe, the British Isles, northern Asia, and North America, and figures in cookery in those places since time immemorial. It is used interchangeably with lingonberries (the fruits of the rowan tree or mountain ash — red berries which look rather like cranberries) in many sauces, jellies and relishes to accompany game of any kind, where a sweetish-acid side dish is wanted. But cranberries are the basis for a whole world of desserts, too.

V. macrocarpon is an American variety with bigger berries; it has been successfully introduced into Europe, has been grown and even naturalized in the British Isles since 1760. Cranberries are an integral part of American Christmas tradition and are an important commercial crop in the northeastern United States.

The cultivation of these jewel-like little red berries is of interest. A patch of wild low-land is chosen, flooded for two or more years, then cleared and spread with three or four inches of clean white sand. Cranberry cuttings five to ten inches long are stuck five inches apart through the sand into the peat. These cranberry bogs are flooded from November through April, then drained so that the plants can flourish and bear.

The classic cranberry sauce to go with turkey or venison is simplicity itself: I quote the French gourmet Dr. Leclerc, who waxed eloquent over the dish:

"Cook the berries, which have been covered fairly liberally with water, until they are soft, for about 15 minutes, then add one and a third cups of sugar for each pound of fruit and cook again until the consistency of a thick syrup is achieved, which will form into a jelly when cool."

Less known are the completely delectable desserts employing these berries or their juice. The following is one of the triumphs of Scandinavian cookery, which is an unknown world unto itself, full of many delights.

Finnish Whipped Cranberry Pudding

3 cups cranberry juice
6 tablespoons sugar
1/2 cup uncooked cream of wheat

Boil your juice over moderate heat. Sprinkle in the sugar as it boils, then slowly add the cream of wheat, stirring constantly with your wooden spoon. Reduce heat, simmer about 6 to 8 minutes, with an occasional stir, until you have a thickish purée. Now, scrape your purée into a big solid mixing bowl and get your electrical mixer. (It takes several lifetimes to whip this by hand.) Beat at high speed 10 to 15 minutes, until mixture has tripled in volume. It must be very fluffy. Pour into individual dessert dishes. DO NOT REFRIGERATE. Keep no longer than two hours before serving. Ginger wafers are great alongside.

Cranberry Pie

You need enough pastry for a shell and lattice work.

2 cups cranberries
1 cup sugar
2 tablespoons flour
1/2 cup water

Mix ingredients, boil gently about 10 minutes. Put in pastry shell, arrange lattice strips on top, then a second rim to cover ends of lattice strips. Bake at about 450 degrees for roughly 25 minutes. Serve with heavy cream.

This is delightful with tea or with black coffee or dessert for a turkey dinner. White fruitcake dripping with white rum, chilled and thin-sliced. Never harmed anyone when served alongside.

Cranberry Sherbet

Mix 2 cups of buttermilk, 1/4 cup lemon juice, 1/2 cup sugar, 1 1/2 cups white Karo corn syrup, and freeze to mush with fridge at coldest. Meanwhile cook 1 cup of cranberries in very little water with 1 teaspoon sugar and some grated lemon peel. When cool, squash berries coarsely with masher or wooden spoon. Remove mush from freezer, beat smooth, add berries, beat again, return to fridge and freeze firm.

When you serve, each portion should have on top a fresh violet, or candied violet, or violet leaf, or candied rosebud, or tiny piece of candied ginger, or a mint leaf, or a lavender leaf, or a hundred-dollar bill wadded up in gold foil. MERRY KISSES AND HAPPY NEW YOU!

Cranberry Rollers

2 cups fresh or frozen cranberries
1 cup sugar
1 teaspoon grated orange peel
1/2 cup finely chopped almonds
2 cups flour
1 1/2 teaspoons ground cardamom seed
good pinch salt
1 stick unsalted butter, soft
1 large egg
1 teaspoon vanilla extract
pinch mace

Combine 1/4 cup sugar, the berries, the orange peel and cook over medium heat, stirring once or twice. When berries have popped open and juice is cooked away, about 15 minutes, stir in the chopped almonds. On wax paper, mix flour, cardamom, mace, and salt. Beat butter, 3/4 cup sugar, egg and vanilla till light and fluffy. Add flour and spices, mix well. Divide dough in half. Roll out each half into a 7-by-12-inch rectangle on waxed paper. Spread out cranberry mix evenly. Roll up like jelly roll, using the paper, not fingers, to lift and move dough. Wrap and chill half-hour in freezer, or 2 hours in fridge. Preheat oven to 400 degrees. Grease large baking sheets. One at a time, unwrap rolls and slice into 1/4 circles with a sharp knife. Place these about an inch apart on sheets. Bake 12 minutes or until edges brown. Remove from oven to racks, let cool completely.

Cranberry Bread

2 cups sifted flour
1 cup sugar
1 1/2 teaspoons baking powder
pinch salt
1/2 teaspoon baking soda
1/4 cup solid vegetable shortening
3/4 cup fresh orange juice
1 teaspoon grated orange rind
1 wee-beaten egg
1 cup coarsely chopped fresh cranberries

Sift flour, sugar, baking powder, soda, then cut in shortening until mixture resembles coarse meal. (Some baroque types like to put a pinch of mace, or a good pinch or so of powdered ginger in this, to "sex it up," as they say.) Beat juice, egg, peel lightly and add to previous mixture, tossing with fork until evenly distributed. Fold in berries. Put batter into loaf pan, bake until knife comes out clean, roughly 1 hour at 350 degrees. Cool pan 10 minutes, then turn out bread and let cool to room temperature.

CRESSES

Watercress *(Nasturtium officinale)*
Garden Cress *(Lepidium sativum)*
American or Land Cress *(Barbarea verna)*

The nomenclature and use of the plants called "cress" (until the end of the last century almost always referred to as "cresses," never in the singular) are mired in testy opinions and stubborn stands, as barbed as the endless discussions on the proper way to make a martini cocktail or, even more complex, a "true" mint julep. The name probably comes from some ancient word for "creep" or "creeper" and is similar in dozens of languages, referring to the watercress of spreading habit which thrives in or near running water. Or beside an intentionally-let-drip faucet in a semi-shaded corner of the garden.

Since earliest recorded history, the plant has been used as an antiscorbutic, as a stimulant to jaded or pallid appetites, to spice up salads and herbs of indifferent flavor.

We all know the watercress. Delightful as a garnish, too, instead of parsley. With steak, as in France. Splendid in a salad with thinly sliced tart apples flavored with a few pounded fennel seeds, a pinch of dill, a pinch of marjoram, dressed with oil and lemon. Delightful chopped into a good oniony chicken broth with some grated lemon peel, just before serving: stir half a minute, then hot to table. The second cress, often called garden cress, is the component of the familiar "mustard and cress" sandwiches so ubiquitous, so delightful, on English tea tables. The cress seeds are raised on damp cloth or even blotting paper, and at two weeks, when the first leaves have appeared, harvested to combine with mustard sprouts of identical cultivation and spread on unsalted butter generously applied to small fingers of bread. In tea table mythology, the equivalent of Lady Bracknell's favorite, the cucumber sandwich.

But the cress sprouts are altogether delectable chopped over cold boiled shrimp dressed with oil, vinegar, dill, lemon peel. Or in a hot consommé with a splash of dry sherry, or a cold consommé with a dollop of cottage cheese hidden in it.

When we get to American, or land cress, confusion is compounded and reigns supreme. Other names for it are Belle Isle cress, mustard greens, spring cress, treacle mustard, treacle wormseed, upland grass, winter cress, roquette, garden rocket, yellow rocket. It is NOT, however, OUR familiar mustard greens. But all the members of the *cruciferae* family (meaning "form of a cross," since they all have white or yellow florets looking like little St. Andrew crosses) have a bitey-peppery flavor, are all useful in salads, soups, stews to give pleasant piquancy and often replace salt.

This is the vast cabbage and mustard family of which cress is part, and "pepperwort" and "peppergrass" are names given to eight or ten members indiscriminately. The important thing is that this native of continental Europe has been naturalized in America since the eighteenth century and is easy to grow, if you have fairly rich soil and keep it well-watered until it is established. For winter and spring on the Gulf Coast, it is easy and unbeatable and you can find it in any of the older or larger seed companies' catalogues, usually under Land Cress. They all do better with chives and basil planted near to ward off various *cruciferae*-loving pests, but are very accommodating and undemanding other than for water while young. The cress family, in turn, scares off certain beetles. Here's an old English dish which is wonderful:

A Grand Sallet of Watercresses

Watercress, finely picked, washed, and laid in the middle of a clean dish. Sliced oranges and lemons finely carved, one against the other in partitions, or around the dish. Garnish with some celery, boiled or raw, capers, oil and vinegar, tiny pinch sugar, bolder pinch of salt.

CUCUMBER
Cowcumber
(Cucumis sativa)

Cucumber is almost universally relegated to mixed salads today, or to the pickle jar, but it has an ancient history of uses for boudoir, table, and pantry which are still relevant. In the east this trailing vine has been cultivated for some 3,000 years. The Greeks and Romans grew it. Pliny tells us that the Emperor Tiberius had cucumbers on his table daily, all year long, and his description indicates a small vegetable

e.

Cucumber

roughly the size of our gherkin, which is only a baby cucumber.

The fruit is always used green, whether at table or for the *toilette*. The eighteenth-century travel writer Hasselquist says of the cucumber, after speaking of its Biblical history: "They still form a great part of the food of the lower-class people in Egypt, serving them for meat, drink, and physick." Known early in England, it went out of use, was revived under Henry VIII, and widely cultivated after the middle of the 1600s.

The dietary value is negligible, being 96 percent water. But that other 4 percent is the *flavor* beloved of all. If you think cucumbers disagree with you, try peeling them, making runnels along their surface longwise with a fork, slicing them thin, then soaking them an hour or so in water with salt, sugar and a little lemon juice. Drain and use as

you would. This way, the feared BURP! is usually banished.

Pickles of cucumber, usually flavored with dill, are too well known, recipes too easy to find, for us to discuss them here, but let's consider some forgotten delights. The flavors of salmon and cucumber go together as propitiously as tomato and basil or liver and onion. But any mild Gulf fish is delicious broiled or baked, served with this sauce:

Cut cucumber longwise in quarters, remove seeds, toss into simmering salted water. Cook for 15 minutes. Blanch, drain well, cut into small cubes. Mix with freshly grated onion, or chopped chives or shallots, a few chopped capers, a little chopped parsley, a good pinch of dill, a pinch of cayenne, a few inner celery leaves chopped fine, and enough yoghurt and fresh cream to make a moist but not runny mixture. Salt to taste. This is a wonderful sauce with fish. Make plenty; it tends to vanish down those little lanes.

Or, if you wish a hot sauce to serve warm, prepare the cucumbers by parboiling as above, then chop into dice and add a green tomato peeled and seeded and likewise diced. Turn in the skillet in unsalted butter until all is faintly golden, then add lemon juice, a dash of dry white wine, salt, pepper, dill, a hint of thyme, enough cream to make creamy but not runny, and serve very small croutons of whole-wheat bread well-browned in butter with a peeled garlic clove which you remove after cooking. Delicious with plain broiled fish.

Cucumber boats filled with baby shrimp are good. Halve cucumbers, parboil as directed, remove all seeds. Fill with peeled, cooked, small shrimp, a little onion, celery and very little green pepper, all chopped small and sautéed lightly. Salt to taste, dash cayenne. Add cream and a good dusting of Parmesan cheese. But canned red salmon, mixed with cream and grated Parmesan, with grated onion and dill and lemon juice, makes a good stuffing for cucumber boats, too. Or bits of leftover white fish judiciously flavored. Cucumber has a wonderfully soothing effect for sunburn, and since pre-history, ladies have rubbed raw cucumber on their faces to keep skin soft and white. Southern belles of the last century swore by this lotion: "Ah swair-yuh bah it."

Cucumber Lotion

Peel 1 or 2 large cucumbers, cut into slices and place in closely covered double boiler; cook until soft. Put into fine linen bag and squeeze until all juice is extracted. Add to the extracted juice one-fourth part of good bourbon whiskey, one-third part of either elderflower water or rose water. Shake mixture well, put into small bottles for use. Or another:

Cucumber Lotion for Sunburn

Chop up a cucumber, then squeeze juice out with a lemon squeezer. Mix with a quantity of glycerine and rose water in equal parts.

Cucumber is used, surprisingly, in many floral soaps and colognes. In Paris, around 1902, when ladies wore mother-of-pearl houseflies glued inside their ears and butterflies embroidered on the "clocks" of their colored silken hose, cucumber perfume had a brief highly fashionable season. It is made by repeated extraction of the freshly sliced fruit with strong alcohol and subsequent distillation *in vacuo,* and naturally, is *very* expensive. Cucumber soaps and creams are still made and used today.

CUMIN
(Cuminum cyminum)

Cumin seed is listed in the Ebers Papyrus (1500 B.C.) as one of the medicinal plants grown in Egypt; the name derives from the Hebrew *kamon,* a word of Babylonian origin which became *kuminon* in Greek. The old Romans used vast quantities of it, both as medicine and as a flavoring agent in many meat dishes, and in breads. The seed is symbolic of the miser, of the stingy (because of its smallness); Marcus Aurelius was nicknamed "Cumin" for his cupidity.

Cumin seeds, powdered, have been an important element in a wide range of curry dishes since remotest antiquity. St. Hildegarde, that great doctor and gourmet, thought that mild cheeses should always be

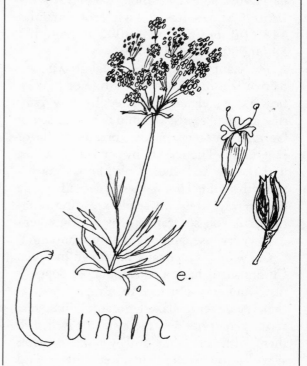

Cumin

eaten with a sprinkling of cumin seed and pepper. All great French restaurants serve a little side dish of the seed with Munster even today; they will bring the cumin on command with any cheese. In the Middle Ages it was the most popular of all seasonings. *Le Mesnagier de Paris,* an early cookery book (1393) speaks of what sounds like a delicious dish of chicken baked with cumin seed. For centuries, a favorite Easter confection was a light bread flavored with cumin, saffron and anise.

Cumin is an important commercial crop in Russia, Japan, France, Egypt, China, Mexico, and dozens of other countries, but oddly enough, is not much grown in the United States. This is indeed curious, for cumin is an essential part of *chili con carne* and of many Mexican dishes, and the importation of these seeds from Iran, Indonesia, India, Syria, and Turkey into the United States has grown from around 148,000 pounds in 1900, to roughly 5,900,000 pounds in 1990.

The plant is a feathery annual growing up to two feet high with tiny white or pinkish flowers, which are followed by tiny fruit that are the "seeds." Cumin is much used in German sausages, pickles, breads, to flavor sauerkraut. The Dutch love cumin in soups, with beans and cheese. A famous cordial bears the name *kümmel* but is actually made of caraway; the two seeds are often confused. If you see caraway as an ingredient for a curry, use cumin; it's a mistranslation. Caraway is practically unknown in India. Cumin seeds have a warm, almost peppery taste and if you'd like to sample them at their best, serve baked potatoes like this: scrub your potatoes, pierce them well, rub them with salt while still wet. Bake them, serve at once with unsalted butter and

cumin seeds. Try these for your next cocktail party:

Cumin Seed Wafers

3/4 cup softened butter
1 cup grated sharp cheddar
2 cups sifted flour
1 teaspoon minced mild onion
pinch mace
1 1/2 teaspoons cumin seed
pinch salt

Cream butter and cheese together thoroughly. Sift flour, salt and mace, and mix in onion and cumin, then blend into butter-cheese mixture. Form this dough into rolls about 1 1/2 inches in diameter. Wrap in foil or wax paper and chill a few hours or overnight. Heat oven to 400 degrees, grease lightly a baking sheet, then slice rolled dough thin and spread on sheet. Bake about 10 minutes or until lightly browned. Remove carefully with spatula and serve either hot or cold. Makes about three dozen.

Ranch Eggs

Mix one 8-ounce can of tomato sauce with 1 teaspoon chili powder and 1/4 teaspoon ground cumin seeds. Spread in lightly greased 9-inch pie plate. Place 6 eggs on top. Sprinkle with salt, pepper and paprika. Bake at 350 degrees for about 25 minutes. Serve with crisp tortillas; top with shredded cheese and sour cream.

Dutch Dip

(to serve with fresh vegetables)

Soften one 8-ounce packet of cream cheese, mix with 2 tablespoons cream, 1/3 cup minced cucumber, 1 teaspoon grated onion, 1/2 teaspoon salt, 1/4 teaspoon ground cumin seeds.

For a delightful salad, try kidney beans dressed with chopped parsley, chopped green onions, a good sprinkle of cumin seeds, lemon juice, olive oil, dash of dill, salt, pepper. Any bean soup is improved with a good sprinkle of cumin seeds, and next time you make cornbread or muffins, sprinkle the top generously with cumin seeds. Your guests will be delighted.

CURRY
Kari, Cari

Curry (*kari* and *cari* in East Indian dialects and some old cookbooks of the last century) is any one of hundreds of combinations of spices ground to a powder and cooked slowly in butter, vegetable oil or soured milk before being added to fish, meat, eggs or vegetables to be "curried."

"Kari" is from a South Indian word meaning "a sauce." Every province, every family, almost, has dozens of combinations, ranging from gentle, aromatic mixtures to real wig-flippers. The commercial curry powder we buy is usually a combination of fifteen or twenty herbs, seeds and spices. These were first put up for British civil servants returned to England and for use on British ships carrying these worthies. But in India the curry mixture is determined by the dish, the family's taste, and the availability of ingredients.

The basic ones which give the "curry" taste to what we in the West know as curry are the curry plant (*Chalcas koenigii* of a plant family including rue and the lemon tree), the turmeric (or curcuma, the powdered root of a member of the ginger family, often called as "poor man's saffron," since it smells of ginger and saffron, and is often substituted for the more expensive, harder-to-find genuine saffron; turmeric is used to give mustard its yellow color, too), and the hot chili peppers. Many curries include garlic *and* onions, some of the gentler ones are fragrant with basil, fennel seed, cumin seed, and nutmeg. Mint goes into many of the combinations intended for cooked vegetables, as do poppy seeds, sumac seeds, juniper berries and that warmly fragrant and attractive herb known as fenugreek. (The name means "Greek hay," it grows wild all over the Mediterranean world, but is very cooperative as a garden plant here; its botanical name is *Trigonella foenumgraecum*.)

A good way to move toward creating your own personal curry powder is to use small quantities of the store-bought product and add on one occasion or another your personal preferences. Try baby turnips, peeled, dropped into simmering water containing bay leaves and lemon peel, remove when a fork will just penetrate. In some unsalted butter, put a pinch or so of curry powder, a dash of cloves, a dash cayenne, a pinch of fennel seeds and turn all together in a skillet. When well heated, put in your baby turnips and a good splash of cream. Serve this as a vegetable or for your next curried beef stew with onion, celery and carrots, try adding pounded caraway and cumin seeds to store-bought powder, and more red pepper.

For curried cabbage: use 1 heaping teaspoon of bought powder, 1 ditto of turmeric, plus pounded fennel and anise seed, some grated lemon peel, and the tiniest pinch of powdered cinnamon. Boil torn (not cut) cabbage in water with salt and sugar just till fork will pierce thickest part of leaf. Remove from fire at once, drain well, add unsalted butter in which you've heated your curry ingredients, taste for salt, add some freshly ground black pepper. Very good.

Commercial curry powder is very useful as is, in perking up bland soups and stews. A pinch is enough. Some of the most delicious dishes in the Charleston repertory have a little "edge" which is nothing on earth but a judicious pinch of curry. Since we have all the foods right here on the Gulf Coast which are used in India's polycurried cookery, it behooves us to get a good Hindu cookbook and contemplate these delightful possibilities. Okra, eggplant, fish, shrimp, chicken, the works.

Creole Curry

1/2 cup coriander seeds
2 teaspoons hot paprika powder
2 teaspoons mustard seeds
1 teaspoon powdered ginger
1 teaspoon cumin seeds
1 1/2 teaspoons fenugreek seeds
1 teaspoon black peppercorns
3 1/2 tablespoons turmeric (curcuma)
pinch salt

Grind this mixture to powder in blender or spice mill or in mortar. Store in a tightly lidded jar or tin. This makes a good cupful and will keep in a cool place for about three months. During summer in hot climates, keep in bottom of refrigerator.

This is a good basic curry to play with. Add other spices you like, omit some of these; try different combinations until you find your favorite.

Gandhi Gumbo

1/2 stick butter
1 big onion, chopped
2 stalks celery, chopped
1 cucumber, peeled, seeded, chopped
3 cups cooked corn kernels
3 teaspoons curry powder
salt to taste
drop or so of Tabasco
2 1/2 cups chicken or beef broth
2 cups half-and-half or light cream
For garnish, chopped green onions
watercress, parsley,
or inner celery leaves

Melt butter in big heavy pot. Cook onion, cucumber, and celery over low heat until soft. Stir in curry and flavorings, cook over low heat 15 to 20 minutes, then stir in corn. Add broth, heat well, then put in cream, simmer till hot, serve at once in heated bowls with garnish sprinkled on top. Unsalted crackers alongside. This, too, is subject to many variations: tomatoes, okra, etc.

CURRY LEAF
(*Chalcas koenigii, Muraya koenigii*)

This bush is of the same plant family as rue and lemons, the *Rutaceae,* and lemons can be grafted onto its wood. If one closes one's eyes and tastes a leaf (I only know the

Curry Leaf

dishes of the region. Many Indian specialty shops have dried leaves, but the aroma is almost gone from them. The wood has a handsome red-gold grain and is used for knife handles, small carvings, etc.

CURRY PLANT
(Helichrysum angustifolium)

The botanical names come from Greek: *helios*, sun, and *chrysos*, golden. The completely delightful warm spicy smell of the plant reminds almost everyone of curry, hence the popular name. If you drop leaves of this shrubby plant into your soup or stew you won't get anything like a taste of curry, but you will get a nice mild spiciness unlike any other flavor.

The family of plants called *Helichrysum* has about 300 species spread over the warmer parts of the world. The American Indians used several varieties in medicinal preparations and especially in cures for snakebite. Dyes are prepared from the yellow flowers of many species. Almost all the plants of this family can be dried for winter bouquets. A few leaves can be added to almost any herbal tea to relieve symptoms of the common cold. The variety known as curry plant is usually grown for the sake of the cheerful golden flower heads and the wonderful hot spicy perfume which pervades the garden even in coldest winter.

The plant is usually about two feet high but can reach four feet. It likes a rather alkaline soil and full sun. Trim it back in spring or summer, a couple of times, not too early and not too late. Gather mature flower heads in early morning and hang upside down to dry, for your dried arrangements. A

dried, but am assured it is a ghost of the fresh) there is something like horsemint, something like a hint of rue, a taint of white pepper, a touch of thyme, a suspicion of clover. Think about that for a moment!

And, of course, neither of the above plants should be confused with any of the thousands of curry powders made up of bewildering combinations of spices and aromatics, different in every Indian locality, even in every household. Other than, as we have said, the use of this curry leaf in the south Indian, especially Madras, vegetable dishes.

This "curry leaf" is not to be confused with the "curry plant." This plant, which grows wild in the foothills of the Himalayas, is practically unknown in the West, although attempts have been made to grow it in California in recent years. In south India it is in almost every garden, for it is an essential ingredient in the vegetarian curry

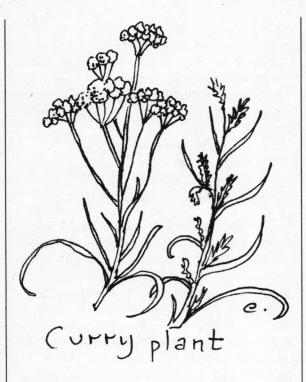

Curry plant

A ghastly custom has grown up in American restaurants which would have a tasteless iceberg lettuce salad coated with some kind of glop or axle grease plonked down before the hapless diner in advance of the meal. Since pre-Christian times, in older traditions, a bitter or piquant or acid or crisp salad course occurs after the meat course, to refresh the palate before the cheese, the desert, the fruit, the savory.

And the bitter dandelion leaves are greatly satisfying in a salad of mixed greens, dressed with the classic seasoning of salt rubbed with garlic, lemon juice or wine vinegar, pepper, and olive oil. In England a delicious wine is made from the flower heads. In the 1950s in the Soviet Union, rubber was produced from roots of certain varieties. In the South, during the War Between the States, coffee substitutes were

bunch hanging in your clothes closet or wardrobe is just as pleasant as lavender or whatever. And put a few chopped leaves in your next beef stew for a surprise. A somewhat rarer item, but essential in any complete herb garden.

DANDELION
(Taraxacum officinale)

In all the Mediterranean countries, as well as in England, the charming plant (considered a pest on lawns and tennis courts) known as dandelion (transliterated from the French *"dent-de-lion,"* "lion's teeth," referring to the deeply serrated leaves) is eagerly sought for a wonderful and bracing bitter and tonic salad herb.

Dandelion

created chiefly from toasted yam skins and toasted dandelion roots. In Italy, the cooked young leaves, tasting like some celestial combination of spinach and turnip, are a "must" in the way of spring tonics.

A salad of young early-summer dandelion leaves combined with chopped fillets of anchovy and chopped capers, accompanied by crusty bread and a bit of white farm or cottage cheese is very good indeed.

DAY LILIES
Orange and Lemon Lilies
(Hemerocallis, many varieties)

Everybody knows the day lily. Settlers brought them from England and Europe; they've escaped from gardens and one finds them wild throughout North America. They are among the most unflappable of flowers. They'll hold together a sandy or rocky bank and grow just as happily in moist soil near water. Few insects bother them; they have no notable diseases. In the South, two varieties, one yellow, one a rusty orange, were common and known as orange and lemon lilies. Modern hybridizers have created a whole new gamut of shades and tints ranging from rose to mahogany, a nearly pure white, a pale lime green, and have, as well, concentrated on the scented varieties. They'll grow in full sun almost anywhere, but in the Deep South prefer partial shade. The name is from the Greek: *hemera*, "a day," *kallos*, "beauty," so "beauty for a day." The flowers last only one day from dawn to dusk, but since every stem has six to ten buds, there is no sensation of these lilies being as short-lived as, for instance, the cereus. One variety, *H. citrina*, opens at four

in the afternoon along with four-o'clocks and stays open until dawn.

What are day lilies doing in this compendium, you ask? Because for centuries they have been a highly esteemed foodstuff in China, Japan, as well as among the nomadic peoples of west and central Asia. Modern nutritionists tell us that these lilies are highly nutritious, in fact.

Often Chinese recipes call for *gum fum*, known in Chinese specialty shops, in English, as "golden needles" or "tiger flowers." The latter name has led to a confused notion they come from tiger lilies. No, nothing but dried day lily petals. I remember a friend proudly showing me a little bag of "golden needles" she'd brought from New York in order to try a recipe in her Chinese cookery book. Outside her picture window, as she enthused, I could see banks of day lilies in full bloom. I didn't tell anything. Why disillusion?

You can prepare your own to use fresh: in the morning just as the blooms open, remove the six stamens and long central pistil, for the petals alone are used. Here's an oriental classic:

Day Lily Chicken

1 whole chicken breast
(skinned, boned, chopped thin)
1 small chopped onion,
another small onion sliced
1 tablespoon soy sauce
1 tablespoon cornstarch
1 teaspoon chopped fresh ginger
3 tablespoons oil
3 cups fresh day lily petals
¼ cup water

Mix together chicken, chopped onion, soy, cornstarch and ginger. In a skillet (or wok) heat 2 tablespoons oil until very hot

e.
Day Lily

(but not smoking). Add the chicken mixture and stir-fry 2 minutes. Remove and set aside. Wipe out pan or wok and in same vessel brown sliced onions in remaining oil. Add lily petals, water, the chicken mixture. Cook and stir 2 minutes or until sauce has thickened. This is for two people.

Shrimp which have been boiled 5 minutes and let cool in their water can be used instead of the chicken. The same recipe is delightful adapted to any white non-oily fish.

But the unopened buds of the day lily are wonderful used as the Italians use zucchini blossoms. Cut off stem end of blossom, removing stamens and pistil without opening bud. Put a bit of mozzarella and 2 pieces of anchovy fillet into each bud. Dip bud in a thin beer-and-flour batter and deep fry. Or put 1 teaspoon grated onion, a dash of marjoram, and lots of butter into a skillet

and sauté the buds without any ado. A very pretty vegetable dish in summer is zucchini in narrow strips, yellow baby squash in rounds, and day lily petals stir-fried in butter and a drop of oil with a little grated onion and a little grated green pepper. Go ahead, try a new taste.

NOTE: Better stick to old plain garden varieties — orange and lemon lilies — for cookery: the lovely modern hybrids on some occasions cause diarrhea.

ELDER
Black Elder, Common Elder, Pipe Tree, Bore Tree, Bour Tree, Hylder, Hylantree, Eldrum, Ellhorn, etc.
(Sambucus nigra)

The rose and the elder are the two plants which are the most surrounded by myth and legend, in every country where they grow. The name "elder" comes from the Anglo-Saxon *aeld,* "fire," since a pipe made of a hollowed stem of this plant was used in remotest times to blow up the embers. Pliny speaks of *Sambucus* and of musical instruments made of the wood. Small boys in the country, since time immemorial, have made popguns of these stems, and Culpepper writes in his great *Herbal:* "Needless to write any description of this, since every boy that plays with a popgun will not mistake another tree for the Elder."

Ancient lore would have it the tree on which Judas hanged himself. Sir John Mandeville, in the sixteenth century, describes elders near the Pool of Siloam in the Holy Land. Another tradition has it that the Cross was made of it. An old rhyme goes like this:

Bour tree, Bour tree: crooked rong,
Never straight and never strong,
Ever brush and never tree
Since our Lord was nailed on thee.

Many people are loathe to cut or burn the elder, and gypsies have an old custom which forbids them to burn elder in their campfires. In the Scandinavian countries the elder is always associated with magic. The Hylde-Moer (Elder-Mother), a kind of dryad, is said to dwell in the tree; if the wood is used for making furniture, she haunts the owners for generations. If a cradle is made, she will come and pinch the child's legs and never give it peace. In various countries and regions this dryad is the "Ellhorn Lady" or the "Ellan Lady." But the tree is planted near the house to ward off witches.

Lady Northcort, the folklorist, writes: "The Russians believe that the Eldertrees drive away evil spirits; the Bohemians go to the tree with a spell to take away fever. The Sicilians think sticks of the wood will kill serpents and drive away robbers, while the Serbs introduce a stick of elder into their wedding ceremonies to bring good luck."

It is generally thought to be a tree which is never struck by lightning, and a twig twisted into three or four knots, carried in the pocket, is a powerful charm against rheumatism. If an elder twig is stuck into the earth of a new grave and "takes" and blooms, it means the person inhumed there has a soul happy and at peace. Since the tree is associated with evil, it has long been held that if a child is switched with an elder wand, the child will cease to grow. In rural Denmark it is thought that if one stands under an elder on Midsummer Eve one will see the King of Fairyland ride by with all his entourage.

The whole tree has a narcotic smell; it has always been considered very risky to sleep under an elder. Another tradition would have it that an elder stake used in a fence enclosing gardens or forage grounds will last longer than an iron one. Most insects shun this plant; a decoction of the leaves sprinkled over delicate plants and flower buds is the earliest recorded insecticide.

For centuries a very fine port-like wine has been made from the berries; they are used to color and flavor many inferior wines. Distilled, it is the basis for the Italian digestive *Sambuco*. A delicious naturally sparkling wine is made from the flower heads, which are also very good indeed dipped into a light batter and deep-fried. Elderberry jelly and jam are too well known to describe here. All the products of the berries are helpful in colds, asthma, bronchial troubles.

With the discovery of the properties of viburnic acid, present in all parts of the plants, the elder returned to its old official place in pharmacy. There are many recipes for elderflower teas, vinegars, wines, elderberry chutneys, jellies, etc., as well as wine.

ELDER

ELECAMPANE
Elfwort, Elf Dock
Horseheal, Velvet Dock
(Inula helenium)

This is another aromatic herb which has simply been forgotten, although much employed by the ancients in both medicine and cookery. It is a very handsome plant. It grows straight and branches into many downy stems, with large, bright yellow flower heads, three to four inches across, from June to August, rather like double sunflowers. It once covered the damp meadowlands of England but has been so sought by pharmacists and confectioners over the centuries that it is now rather rare. Brought to America, it soon escaped from gardens and spread from Canada to North Carolina, westward to Missouri.

The roots have a very high incidence of the drug inulin, which is powerfully antiseptic, and highly effective for persistent coughs, catarrh, all pulmonary complaints. Up until World War II, country sweet shops in England always carried the candied roots, which have a distinctive aromatic flavor with something of violet or iris, something slightly camphory. The herbalist Gerard, explaining the origin of the botanical name, *helenium,* says it was called thus because Helen was gathering it when Paris stole her away. Another myth would have it that the plant sprang from Helen's tears. But mention of the herb occurs in almost all the ancient writers, who have universal praise for it.

All parts of the plant are aromatic; a poultice applied externally was common for centuries in treating sciatica or any neuralgia. It is easy to grow; many modern seed catalogs carry it, and for any herb garden it would make a delightful tall accent, besides supplying showy cut flowers. In Neuchatel, in Switzerland, elecampane is still one of the principal ingredients of the Swiss form of absinthe, while in France a delightful *apéritif* wine, of the school of the gentian and wormwood appetizers, is the *Vin d'Aunée* (the French name of the herb is *aunée*). The root mingled with whortleberries and ashes produces a fine blue dye. An ancient homemade cordial common to most of Europe is made by steeping elecampane roots with white currants and sugar in white port. It has a most delightful fragrance and pleasing taste. The German form, sometimes based on a sweet white muscatel, has the wondrous name of *Alantwurzelwasser.*

If planted in semi-shade and kept watered, elecampane will thrive on the Gulf Coast. It loves damp meadows and, given a chance, would probably run wild down here. Good thing, too, it discourages many insect pests.

ENDIVE
Chicory, Witloof
(Cichorium endivia,
Cichorium intybus)

The names "endive" and "chicory" have become so confused and intermixed, we'll probably never get two people to agree on which is which and why. With that, I take a deep breath and point out that there are two basic plants, from which dozens of varieties have been developed. The *Cichorium* family tends to have a bitter taste, which is why so many of them are blanched by being grown in cellars or dark sheds, covered with straw.

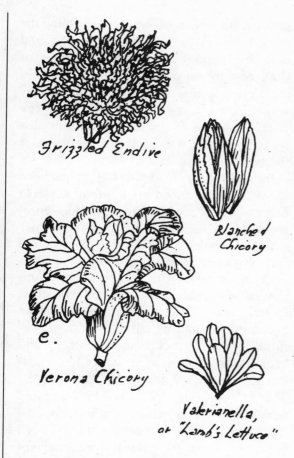

Frizzled Endive

Blanched Chicory

e.

Verona Chicory

Valerianella, or "Lamb's Lettuce"

One of the most delightful winter salads is a chicory called *Rossa di Verona,* which has red spots and streaks, often red stems, which become redder with cold. A few young leaves of this do wonders to give interest to a salad made of the hopeless iceberg lettuce. A great winter salad consists of frizzy endive, some young leaves of chicory, and dandelion leaves, all dressed with lemon, oil, salt, pepper, and lots of garlic.

Both endive and chicory bear delightful china-blue flowers like asters; it's worth it to let a few plants go to seed to see these cheerful blossoms on a grey winter day. The roots of chicory are, of course, dried, roasted, and ground to be blended with coffee. This not only for flavor, but because the chicory seems to make the coffee more digestible for many people.

Seeds of all the plants mentioned are available from the more serious seed and plant companies.

EUCALYPTUS
Fever Tree, Blue Gum Tree, Stringy Bark Tree, etc.
(genus of about 300 species)

Almost all of the species of eucalyptus are indigenous to Australia. The name comes from the Greek *ecalyptos,* meaning "well-covered" and refers to a little lid-like top of the cup-shaped bud. This top is thrown off as the bud blooms. These trees are amazingly quick growers and many species reach a great height. *Eucalyptus amygdalin* is the tallest tree known, reaching as high as 480 feet, higher even than the sequoias in California. The essential oils derived from the various members of the family vary widely, and many of them have become of

The curly or frizzled varieties of endive we usually call just that: endive, although "curled chicory" is not an uncommon appellation. We all know the delightful white, crisp pod-like heads of "Belgian endive," usually the variety "witloof" ("white leaf" in English), a standard winter salad on most of the Continent, especially France and Italy. Well, Belgian endive *is* chicory: the plants, blanched by being grown under peat, or sand, or loam, with little light. The curly endive and the rather lettuce-like chicory can take very cold weather. Endive is an annual or biennial and chicory is a perennial; that's the bit to remember.

great commercial importance in Australia, and begin to be so in California and North Africa.

They fall into three distinct categories: medicinal, commercial, and aromatic. The eucalyptus oil derived from the species *E. globus* is probably the most powerful natural antiseptic. The German Baron Ferdinand von Muller, who was director of the Melbourne Botanical Gardens from 1857 to 1873, introduced this plant family into all the world. He was first to suggest that the mere presence of such as *E. globus* might serve as disinfectant in fever districts; he has been triumphantly justified. Seeds planted in Algiers in 1857 thrived, and the botanical supervisor there, M. Trottoir, appropriately

Phascolarctos cinereus clinging to Eucalyptus.

enough (the lines of eucalyptus along the sidewalks of Algiers are well known) found that the fragrant antiseptic exhalations of the tree were far exceeded by the astonishing drying action of the roots in marshy soil. Five years after planting the eucalyptus, one of the most unhealthy districts in Algiers was converted into one of the healthiest and driest.

In Sicily, since World War II, it has been extensively planted to combat malaria because of its property of absorbing enormous quantities of water. Apart from their many beneficial qualities, the trees of the different species are quite beautiful with degrees of silvery or bluish foliage and flowers of white, pale yellow, and pale pink. In Italy and Greece, bunches of flowering branches are sold as cut flowers and perfume a parlor or sickroom delightfully and beneficially. They were introduced into California following a trip to Australia by Teddy Roosevelt. He was photographed with a koala bear which was quickly imitated by toy manufacturers as the "Teddy" bear. A surge of popular enthusiasm resulted in the creation of groves of certain species of eucalyptus to provide a habitat for koalas brought from Australia. They live exclusively in these trees.

Among the fragrant varieties, *E. citriodora* has a nice lemon scent much used in flavoring soft drinks and household cleaners; *E. odorata* is a 75 percent geraniol and much employed by soapmakers. *E. Sturtiana* has a fresh clean scent of ripe apples. Another, *E. piperita,* is used to synthesize menthol, while both *E. dives* and *E. radiata* yield slightly different peppermint flavors. Countless gargles, cough medicines, and cough drops contain some kind of oil of eucalyptus, as you will see if you read the list of ingredients in fine print. For a stuffy nose and clogged sinuses, a good handful of fresh leaves can be tossed into a pot of boiling water and the steam inhaled. Pleasant and effective. In all areas where flood control is a question of interest, the many members of the eucalyptus family are devoutly to be wished for, with their rapid growth and amazing greed for water.

FENNEL
(Foeniculum vulgare)
Florence Fennel, Fennel Seeds

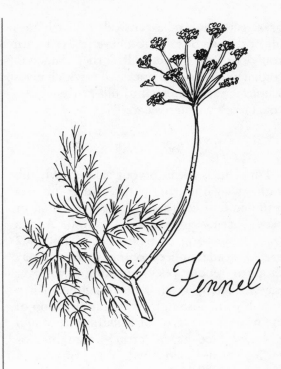

Fennel is related to both parsley and dill; it looks most like the latter. It has tall celery-like stalks, feathery green foliage, flat yellow heads of flowers. The Chinese, Indians, Egyptians all esteemed the plant since remotest antiquity, employing it in remedies for coughs, asthma, rheumatism. It still goes into the "gripe water" given to babies for digestive problems. A more compact form of the plant, *Foeniculum azoricum* is the famous "Florence fennel" eaten both cooked and raw in Italy, Greece, and Spain, and always one of the culinary surprises for Americans visiting those countries the first time.

Florence fennel forms a thick, rather bulbous lower stem, which is boiled as a vegetable, or sliced thin and sprinkled with lemon juice to eat as an appetizer. One of the most delightful hors d'oeuvres possible is a mixture of these fennel slices with fresh orange sections and sweet ripe olives (rather than the salted or pickled ones) dressed with lemon juice, pure olive oil, pinch of salt, pinch of freshly ground black pepper.

Fennel in all forms is so firmly linked to fish cookery since early times that a number of proverbs in every European language speak of the rich eating fish and fennel, and the poor eating the fennel by itself.

Common fennel is a perennial often grown as an annual, reaching up to six feet, with yellow flowers and bright green feathery leaves. Brought early to American soil, it grows wild in many places. If you would have it in your garden, place it in poor or sandy soil, away from your regular herb beds, in open space where it can develop. It needs to be well-watered in its first month, then you can more or less forget it. It produces enormous amounts of seed, which are used, according to which dish, both green and dried.

Don't plant anywhere near tomatoes or coriander. An English saying is, "plant fennel near the kennel," for it does indeed discourage fleas and ticks; they hate fennel. Stalks of fennel are used to make a bed to bake fish. It is used extensively in marinades for pork, fish or veal. You haven't lived until you've had red mullet grilled, then flamed in cognac on a bed of fennel stalks, which gives a unique take-me-back-to-old-Provence flavor. Here's a grand salad:

Verona Salad

Put a little salt into your salad bowl; rub with raw garlic, toss garlic aside. Put in a little lemon juice, a small glop of Dijon or New Orleans mustard. Mix well. Add a scant tablespoon of fennel seeds. Put in 2 peeled, seeded, sliced oranges, some finely chopped tender celery, including younger leaves. Freshly ground black pepper. Then thumb your nose in the general direction of the nearest purveyor of iceburg lettuce and add any nice green lettuce, romaine, or endive to the salad bowl. Torn, of course, not cut up. When you're ready to serve, toss in pure olive oil and mix well.

A few fennel seeds sprinkled on bread, cake or cookies add a nice ghost-of-anise flavor. The seeds are good to chew at weddings, funerals, committee meetings, or any place where the stomach might rumble with hunger. Aid to digestion, too.

Fennel seeds are something else again, and have many uses. If you don't know this flavor, it's eminently worth investigating. If you actively dislike liquorice you might not care for fennel seed, for it has a sweetish astringent quality. But with rich or oily fish such as salmon or mackerel, they play down the oiliness of the fish, and combined with lemon, make a most delicious flavor. They are widely used to sprinkle on pastries and confectionery, sweet pickles, go into countless fish dishes. Crush a few fennel seeds and add to your crab or shrimp salad. It makes that indefinable and teasing something in

the same way that absinthe sexes up Oysters Rockefeller. The Puritans liked to chew fennel seeds in church, called it "the meeting seed," thought it helped improve the sight. Incidentally, the young fresh leaves, chopped fine, add immeasurably to chowders or any fish dish, sprinkled over them before serving.

This next is unusual and delicious. Serve with plain buttered noodles. Follow with salad of raw fennel and oranges, or at least celery and oranges.

Italian Lamb Stew

2 pounds lean lamb shoulder
2 tablespoons olive oil
1 tin (2 ounces) anchovy fillets
3/4 teaspoon fennel seed
1/2 teaspoon minced lemon peel
1 minced garlic clove
2 tablespoons red wine vinegar
1/2 teaspoon freshly ground black pepper
2 teaspoons beef stock base, or concentrate
1 cup hot water
2 teaspoons arrowroot
1 tablespoon cold water

Trim excess fat from lamb, cut into 1½-inch cubes. Brown slowly in olive oil in iron skillet or Dutch oven. Wash anchovy fillets in warm water, chop fine. Crush fennel seed. Combine anchovies, fennel seed, lemon peel, garlic, vinegar. When meat is well browned, pour off fat, sprinkle with pepper, and stir in the mixture you've prepared. Dissolve the beef stock base in hot water, pour over meat. Cover and simmer slowly for about an hour or until meat is tender. Mix arrowroot with cold water and stir into stew. Cook, stirring constantly, until sauce is thickened. The anchovy and beef stock are both salty. DON'T salt the stew. Leave that to the individual diner's taste.

Flambéed Fish with Fennel Seed

2 pounds of fish fillets or a whole fish, split
1½ teaspoons chopped parsley
some freshly ground white pepper
juice of half a lemon
½ cup brandy
bit of onion or garlic, as you prefer

Arrange fish in oiled metal baking pan. Rub both sides with bit of frayed onion or garlic. Salt VERY lightly, sprinkle with part of lemon juice. Broil without turning until fish is done. Meanwhile, crush fennel seed and thyme, combine with parsley and pepper and remaining lemon juice and spread mixture evenly over fish. Heat brandy, pour over fish, set aflame, serve at once.

Seeds of Florence fennel are listed in many American seed catalogs; it is easy to grow. But keep it far away from the dill! They tend to cancel each other out, both plants developing an anonymous "fill" or "dennel" taste! The Chinese, incidentally, used dried fennel stalks of equal length as markers to cast when telling the *I Ching*.

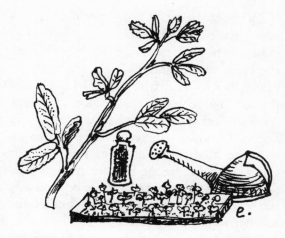

GREEK HAY

FENUGREEK
Greek Hay
(Trigonella foenumgraecum)

The proper botanical name means "three-leaved Greek hay," and the plant, a leguminous annual similar to lucerne, growing about two feet high, has been used since prehistory to flavor inferior hay. Horses and cattle love the plant, with its distinctive perfume, while the seeds still go into condition powders for livestock sold today.

The seeds have been used medicinally since earliest times. They yield a bitter fixed oil which can be extracted by ether, proteids, a volatile oil, two alkaloids (*Trigonelline* and *Chaoline*), as well as a yellow dye. The chemical composition resembles cod-liver oil, rich in phosphates, lecithin, nucleo-albumin, and considerable quantities of iron in an easily absorbed organic form. Fenugreek seeds, pounded when you're ready to use them, have always been part of many Caribbean and Gulf Coast dishes, and are the "secret ingredient" in most gumbos, for instance. So you can find fenugreek seeds in most shops that sell Creole and Cajun spices.

In much of North Africa, especially in Egypt, a thick paste called *Helba,* made by soaking fenugreek seeds in water, is still widely used as a medicine against fevers of many kinds. This is also an old remedy for diabetes. The flavor is very stimulating to the appetite. The paste is used externally for boils and carbuncles. And in warmer countries a kind of mucilage from the seeds is a cheap substitute for cod-liver oil in treating sickly children.

The great herbalist Culpeper considers a paste made of Fenugreek seeds, dates, and honey, to be the best and healthiest of sweets for both young and old. He thought the plant, with its little lupin-like yellow flowers, to be native to France, but later scholars feel it originated in western Asia, and it is known to have been cultivated all over the Mediterranean since most ancient times, both for forage and for human consumption. The young plants are cooked as a bitter and tonic green not too unlike the southern mustard greens.

Both leaves and seeds are essential in hundreds of Indian and Indo-Chinese curry dishes, and even those who think it totally unfamiliar, when biting a seed, will have a dim recollection of curry at once. The unadulterated flavor is distinctive, bitter, attractive, in the manner of lovage or celery. Curiously, although of the pea family, it has a classic reputation for preventing wind. But for us, unless we keep livestock, the reason to make acquaintance with fenugreek is for the sprouts, grown just like alfalfa or mung bean or whatever. Tom Stobart, the herb specialist, says, "If fenugreek seed is sown in boxes and grown to the two-leaf (cotyledon) stage like mustard and cress, it makes a five-star salad when dressed with oil and vinegar. The taste is refreshing, new and unusual."

Personally, my idea of a grand luncheon for very hot weather is very ripe tomatoes sliced thin, a nice glop of Philadelphia cream cheese, a little heap of fenugreek sprouts, sprinkled with lemon juice, a handful of Calamata olives, and some icy beer. If you study the seed catalogs you'll find fenugreek seed more available than you thought. Try this unfamiliar plant in your garden; you'll thank me.

Gumbo Filé

Sassafras

FILÉ
Sassafras, Gumbo filé
(Sassafras albidum)

The sassafras, according to fossils, has existed for some 100 million years. There are three known species, and *Sassafras albidum* is native to North America. The genus is a member of the *Lauraceae* family, which includes camphor, cinnamon, the true laurel and the spice bush. In the southern states, it can easily reach forty feet in height. The largest recorded specimen was in Owensboro, Kentucky, and was some one hundred feet high with a trunk five and a half feet in diameter. A distinctive feature of this plant is the wild variety of the foliage, especially in younger trees: some two-lobed leaves, some three-lobed, some simple ovals, some skinny. They make beautiful specimens on a lawn or in a garden if you tend them closely; they send out suckers and turn into a grove while you're not watching.

Every bit of the tree has a delicious perfume, reminding most of oranges and cinnamon. The root is the strongest but leaves, twigs, bark are all scented. The yellow-green flowers are borne in clusters in late April or early May, before the leaves, and in September the trees turn brilliant colors. In colonial America, the bark was used to dye wool, the wood used for beds and cradles (keeps fleas away), to build henhouses (since it is thought to repel chicken lice), and for building boats and furniture.

The roots make an aromatic tea, but the reason sassafras interests the Gulf Coast world and all the new fans of Creole cooking everywhere is that the leaves and pith are dried and powdered as a thickening for gumbos: this is the famous *gumbo filé*.

GARLIC
Theriac, Cure-All,
Poor Man's Treacle, Stinking Lily
(Allium sativum)

Even to touch upon the facts and lore of garlic would take a volume of some 2000 pages. It is part of every cuisine on this planet, has at some time or other been prescribed for every known ailment. The fact would seem to be that it is indeed a natural antibiotic, and more than that, a stimulus to appetite. Two universal and eternal claims made for garlic are that it is a natural aphrodisiac and a powerful antidote for vampires, plague, evil spirits. Every historian and commentator eventually has something to say about this bulb. Perhaps the great chef Louis Diat had the last word: "There are five elements," he said. "Earth, air, fire, water . . . and garlic." I like, too, the comment from the somewhat forgotten Thomas

Nashe (1567-1601), that delightful anti-Puritan Elizabethan who wrote countless witty and opinionated pamphlets, but also is author of an early English adventure novel *Jack Wilton*. Nashe put it simply: "Garlic makes a man winke, drinke, and stinke." And why not, Tommy, why not?

In the ancient world, garlic was known as *theriac,* or cure-all, and the old English name poor man's treacle was derived from that, but the Anglo-Saxon *Gär* (spear) *Leac* (leek) became the common appellation. Garlic is so entwined with human history on this planet, as medicine and as the most universal of all cooking flavors, that it is difficult to determine its point of origin, although nowadays most botanical historians feel that it originated in southwest Siberia, then spread to southern Europe where it became naturalized.

I think that the reason some folks have a passionate hatred for garlic is because they've been exposed to a dish made with garlic which isn't as fresh as it might be, or have been at close quarters with someone who has partaken of a dish with such elderly garlic. Garlic keeps well in a cool place, but inevitably it begins to germinate — which means ferment — and a powerful presence makes itself known.

If I were teaching beginner's classes in cookery, I'd dedicate the first three months to this maligned, adored, almost religiously worshipped cousin of the lily, and the diplomatic uses for it.

Most great chefs either rub their steaks with frayed garlic or put an unpeeled toe into the skillet and remove it when the butter or oil begins to bubble. I wouldn't dream of cooking a fowl of any kind without rubbing it first with half a lemon, then with frayed garlic, then a little salt, then lots of either butter or bacon fat or olive oil, as the case might be. For ducks I use orange instead of lemon. For geese I use sage instead of citrus. But garlic always! Nobody ever guesses garlic is part of the act, but seem to enjoy the crispy skin and pleasant appetizing aroma.

Theophrastus tells how the ancient Greeks placed garlic on piles of stones at crossroads for Hecate's supper. Even today people rub the door and windowsills of a new dwelling with garlic to keep away witches, ghosts, and ill fortune. The mysterious *moly* which Athena gave Odysseus to use as a charm against Circe preventing her from changing him into a pig, was nothing more than yellow garlic (*Allium moly*). In many parts of Europe, runners still hold a garlic clove in their mouths to keep competitors from outdistancing them. Hun-

GARLIC

garian jockeys fasten a clove to their horses' bits. All the ancients list garlic as remedy for endless diseases and complaints. Alexander Neckham, in the twelfth century, says it prevents heat exhaustion or sunstroke: in the Mediterranean world today field workers chew it during hot weather.

A number of modern medicines for heart ailments contain garlic. Antiseptic and stimulant, garlic as a cleanser of the blood is an ingrained article of faith for rural people since the dawn of time. It seems to bring out the flavor of other ingredients in cookery, especially meat, mushrooms and many vegetables.

There are many varieties, white, pink, mauve, of varying sizes, some as delicately flavored as flowers, others strong and overpowering. Some people claim to loathe garlic, but express delight in every single dish where it is the secret ingredient. Cloves of garlic tucked into a leg of lamb and left in a marinade seem to work at tenderizing the meat as well as flavoring it. Usually any unpleasant taste or odor comes from garlic that has been stored too long or has discolored spots.

A good cook buys small quantities, checks each clove for any "spots." Again, people who think they dislike the bulb praise green salad prepared in European fashion: put salt into the bowl, rub this with garlic, discard garlic, dissolve salt with lemon juice, add pure olive oil and freshly ground black pepper. Be sure your salad greens are dry after being washed. Don't mix the salad until you're ready to eat it. So simple, so good!

The folk in the Midi region of France like to rub dry bread crusts with garlic, soak them in oil, vinegar and salt, and use in a salad of curly endive. A beefsteak taken out of the refrigerator a few hours before required, spread with grated garlic (which is discarded) before sautéing the steak in unsalted butter with a little bacon fat, served with a sauce of pan juices boiled up with a little red wine, is another kind of steak altogether. Most casseroles, stews, roasts, and soups benefit from the addition of garlic in quantities greater or smaller, removed before serving or wolfed down, all as the case may be.

A wonderful relief for colds, a splendid pick-me-up, a great comfort in any emotional or climactic situation is this classic *soupe d'ail* (garlic soup) from the south of France:

Classic Garlic Soup

Put two quarts of water (or good broth if you want your soup richer) on to boil, lightly salted. While it comes to a boil, take a whole head of garlic and peel and purée it, and add to water, along with a *bouquet garni* of some parsley, very little thyme and 2 bay leaves (attached so they can be removed later). Cover tightly, let simmer 5 minutes. Put 2 tablespoons best pure olive oil, and 2 egg yolks into your soup tureen and beat them well. Now remove your *bouquet garni* and whisk the 2 egg whites quickly into the soup. Carefully pour the soup into the tureen, never stopping the whisking for an instant. Thin slices of hot toast have been placed in the soup bowls. Serve the hot soup over them at once, adding a little finely chopped parsley and freshly ground black pepper.

Sausages with Garlic and Cider

8 or 10 sausages
2 apples
4 shallots
3 or 4 cloves garlic
cup cider
2 tablespoons flour
sage and parsley
salt and freshly ground black pepper

Roll the sausages in flour and fry them lightly all round in a little clear fat. Put them in casserole with layers of sliced apple (cored but not peeled), finely chopped shallots (including the green parts), finely chopped garlic, and a bit of chopped sage and parsley. Season with salt and pepper, add the cider; cover and cook in medium oven about an hour. (Buttered, boiled pearl barley is good with this.)

Steak Rolls

Make a stuffing of 3 ounces soft breadcrumbs
2 slices of bacon cut into small bits
3 cloves finely chopped garlic
heaping teaspoon each of chopped onion, celery, parsley
1 tablespoon melted butter
dash mace
dash cayenne

Take 1½ pounds round steak, cut into strips, stuff with mixture, fasten with toothpicks. Roll lightly in flour, brown in fat. Place in baking dish, pour 1 cup of dry red wine over, simmer in medium oven for 2 hours, adding a little stock, or water, or more wine, as need be. Sprinkle with chopped parsley before serving. Good with buttered noodles.

Mushrooms on Toast

Clean mushrooms, slice, "acidulate" them by tossing into simmering water with juice of a lemon, then at once turn off heat. After 2 minutes run cold water over mushrooms and drain. In skillet heat unsalted butter, 2 finely chopped strips of bacon, 2 finely chopped cloves of garlic. Salt and lots of freshly ground black pepper. Add a little broth or water, cook covered about 15 minutes. Uncover, pour in 2 tablespoons dry sherry, cook 15 minutes longer on low heat, then add 1/2 cup cream, heat well, serve on toast.

Apart from the famous bulb, there are also garlic chives from China, delightful chopped into cabbage soup or with lemon and butter on broiled fish such as mullet or cod. There is also the elephant garlic, only recently introduced to us by the Nichols Garden Nursery, 1190 N. Pacific Highway, Albany, Oregon 97321. This huge bulb with beautiful flower head was brought to the United States by immigrants from Czechoslovakia or Yugoslavia, say the Nichols family, who discovered it in a backyard near Scio, Oregon, in 1941. They were bowled over by its size and its mildness and it figures always in their catalogue nowadays. Perhaps it is the best for this Mediterranean dish which is not for the chicken-hearted:

Baked Garlic

1 head elephant garlic
4 tablespoons virgin olive oil
salt to taste
freshly ground black pepper
thin triangles of toasted French or Italian bread

Cut off the top fourth of the garlic bulb, put in center of a big piece of foil, sprinkle on 2 or 3 teaspoons oil. Wrap foil completely around bulb and bake in middle of preheated 425-degree oven. Brush bread with remaining oil and toast on baking sheet, turning once, for 10 or 15 minutes. When garlic has cooked for 40 minutes, remove from foil, squeeze flesh out of skin, and spread on toast.

Greek Beans

1 pound fresh green beans
1 cup tomato juice
1/4 cup virgin olive oil
3 cloves fresh garlic, smashed
3 tomatoes cut in fourths
1 chopped onion
1/2 cup chopped parsley
1/2 teaspoon crushed oregano
1/2 teaspoon paprika
salt and freshly ground black pepper to taste

Cut beans into thirds, cook in tomato juice until tender. Meanwhile, sauté in oil the garlic, tomatoes, onion, parsley and oregano until they begin to soften but are still crisp. When beans are tender, mix everything, simmer about 5 minutes longer, then serve.

Zucchini Appetizer

4 cups zucchini, grated
1 3/4 cups biscuit mix
3/4 cup grated Parmesan cheese
1/2 cup virgin olive oil
4 beaten eggs
1 big onion, chopped fine
3 tablespoons chopped parsley or cilantro
1/2 teaspoon crushed oregano
salt to taste
3 minced fresh garlic toes

Mix everything well. Spread in greased baking dish 2-by-9-by-12 inch-and bake in preheated 350-degree oven for 25 to 30 minutes till nicely browned. Cut into bite-size pieces, serve hot or cold.

Gulf Coast Fish Chowder

2 pounds fresh or frozen fish fillets, cut into chunks
1 big onion, minced
2 tablespoons olive oil
2 cups chopped potatoes
1 small carrot
1 inner celery stalk, chopped
2 or 3 garlic toes, chopped fine
2 cups milk
2 tablespoons flour
2 bay leaves
salt to taste
freshly ground black pepper
good pinch dried dill
dash Tabasco
splash dry sherry

Sauté onion, carrot, celery in oil about 5 minutes. Remove from heat and add 3 cups water, potatoes, vegetables, garlic, seasonings. Bring just to boiling. Reduce heat, cover, simmer 15 minutes or until potatoes are almost tender. Combine milk and flour and slowly stir into soup. Add bay leaves and fish. Simmer on low about 15 minutes, don't boil. Take a fork and see if fish flakes. Remove bay leaves. Taste for seasoning. Add a good splash of dry sherry, cook a minute longer. Sprinkle with parsley and paprika when serving. Serves 6 to 8 polite guests, 4 greedy-guts.

In all the Mediterranean world there is some version or other of a garlic-and-sweet basil sauce known as *pistou* or *pesto,* which translates as *pestle,* referring to the principal ingredients being pounded together. The sauce goes with pasta, but also with plain boiled rice, with vegetables, with fish and crustaceans.

Pesto

3 cups fresh Genovese or big-leaved basil
5 or 6 garlic toes
3/4 cup grated Parmesan, Romano or Swiss cheese
1/2 cup olive oil
3-finger pinch sea salt

Wash and dry basil and tear up, don't cut. Peel and smash garlic. Put garlic, basil, salt in big mortar and pound hard until you have a paste. Some like a few chopped capers or a little grated lemon peel added, if sauce will be served with seafood. Add cheese, then oil, mixing until smooth. You can do this in traditional mortar with pestle, or in a blender (high speed, only a few seconds) or with elbow grease, using a jelly jar or tumbler to pound in a heavy mixing bowl. With blender you may have to repeat process another few seconds to get smoothness.

And here's a dish to convert the unconverted:

Baked Potatoes

Scrub 4 medium-size Idaho potatoes. Pierce them to the center with 2-pronged fork from several directions. This lets the whey escape in baking, makes them less fattening. While still wet, rub potatoes all over with salt in which you have left peeled halved garlic toes for at least 4 hours. Bake as usual. Serve with lots of unsalted butter and when the unconverted say, "What good potatoes!" say something like, "Yes, they're Mediterranean . . ." or "they're flavored with Bye-bye Dracula salt," or whatever seems right.

To diminish the presence or let's just say reek of garlic, several things are helpful: a handful of fresh parsley or cilantro consumed after the meal, or an apple or an orange.

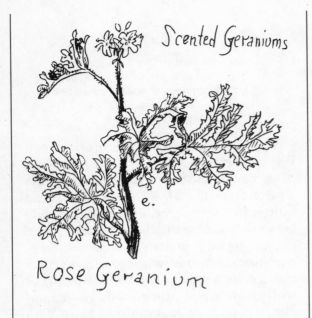

Scented Geraniums

Rose Geranium

SCENTED GERANIUMS

Recent studies of plant perfumes have shown that a plant gives off, in its perfume, molecules of the plant's substance. So sniffing a posy is not only pleasant but therapeutic as well. The nosegays, tussie-mussies, and pomanders which ladies and gentlemen of earlier times carried to shield them from the unbearable stench of open sewage were also powerfully antiseptic as well, especially two of their strongest components, cinnamon and marjoram.

The scented geraniums are praised in many old herbals as both protective and healing. The leaves, bruised, are often mentioned as the best kind of poultice for minor cuts, scratches, stings. Insects hate the scented geraniums, as they do garlic chives (Chinese or ribbon chives), lavender, parsley, pennyroyal, rue, santolina and tansy, so it is wise to plant combinations of these in proximity to roses, salad greens, or any of the more vulnerable plants. *Geraniums*, to those who insist on correct botanical usage, are the wild *Crane's Bill* and the single scarlet-flowered *Herb Robert*, and all the modern tribe descended or hybridized from them. Most of the scented varieties and the bi-colored and speckled and mottled show plants are properly *pelargoniums*. The most familiar scented varieties are:

ROSE GERANIUM (*Pelargonium graveolens*) A plant with beautifully cut leaves, a rather sprawling habit. A quick grower, highly and deliciously perfumed. Insignificant pinkish or mauvish flowers.

LEMON GERANIUM (*Pelargonium limonium*) Large deeply cut leaves, strongly perfumed, will grow into a bush five or six feet high unless cut back occasionally. Tiny pinkish mauve flowers in spring. There is another lemon-scented variety called *Pelargonium crispum variegata*, which is low and compact, with tiny curly green leaves of a paler chartreuse green on the tips of each stem.

PEPPERMINT GERANIUM (*Pelargonium tomentosum*) Soft and velvety, with ivy-shaped leaves and tiny white flowers. Rather pokey in growing, likes less sun than other geraniums. Surprising and delicious peppermint perfume, or maybe like peppermint with a dash of clovepink or tearose.

In the Old South, many attentive cooks liked to put a dash of rose water into their pies, their cakes and cookies, even into those delightful sherbets made of white Karo (corn) syrup and buttermilk and fruit. I mean culinary rose water, not the cosmetic rose water! Look out! That rose flavor adds immensely to apple, peach, pear, plum pies, puddings, etc. Curiously, rose water is almost impossible to find, although mirlitons, cardoons, annatto seeds turn up even in provincial shops, with the new interest in fine food.

Well, you can always use rose geranium leaves. (I presume no chemical insecticides or fertilizers have been near your geranium plants.) Line the bottom of a cake pan with the leaves and remove them before icing your cake. Or put a good handful of rose geranium leaves in a fruit jar and fill it up with white granulated sugar and use the sugar for your apple pie, for instance. Mmmm.

My friends enjoy a *digestive* I make like this: heat the oven to 400, then turn it off and put a flat baking sheet full of fresh rose geranium leaves in it to dry for a minute or so. Put the leaves, along with finely chopped candied ginger and the sugar from the bottom of the jar, or box, or candy store sack, in a clean jar. Pour good bourbon over and close tightly, let sit a week, then strain through a cloth. I serve this either straight in *liqueur* glasses or with a splash of sparkling water in small wine glasses. Great burping agent after oniony and garlicky dishes.

GIN

Gin is a spirituous liquor distilled from cereals and flavored principally with juniper berries and the herb angelica, but, according to which distiller and which country, also on occasion containing cardamom, caraway, orange peel, lemon peel, cassia bark, cinnamon, orris (root of the common white Florentine iris), coriander and liquorice.

The name "gin" comes from an Italian word for juniper: "ginevra." The drink is also known as "geneva" but has nothing whatsoever to do with Geneva, although by logical error, the drink is often known in South America as "ginebra" from the Spanish form of the name of the Swiss city. Gin was first concocted in Holland in the late fifteenth or early sixteenth century as a medicine to quell the menstrual pains of nuns. Alone among the wines and spirits of this world, it does not take a flavor from its original source and does not improve with age. The Dutch gin is more often made of malted and unmalted rye, without wheat or corn, and often has a pale yellowish tint. Two of the principal brands, *Bokma* and *Wynand Fockinck*, have a delightful faint aroma of wet haystacks.

When the Dutch king William ascended the English throne, the introduction of gin was inevitable; it became an English standby, easy to make and a cheap binge in view of the increased duties on foreign wines and spirits. The English gin of the eighteenth century was real rotgut, often flavored with vitriol and sugar. Some workers were paid in gin! In poorer parts of London, one house in five sold gin, often from stalls outside. A famous sign read "Drunk for one penny, dead drunk for two, straw free." Sometimes children lay dead drunk in the kennels of the watchdogs. Ratings in the navy had a huge daily ration of gin. The situation grew so disastrous that the first licensing laws were created, and a purer product emerged.

Gin is not the greatest, most healthful or flavorsome drink, yet it is the most popular. More gin is drunk in the United States than whiskey, and five times more than all types of brandy. The world's largest manufacturer of London gin (which means unsweetened and is not a brand name) is in Peoria, Illinois. The special flavor of sloe gin, made in London and Peoria as well as Plymouth,

England, is due to the addition of either bruised blackthorn berries or wild plums, and is a useful and completely delightful addition to hundreds of punches, summer drinks, fruit compotes, sherbets, etc. Traditional to help children down bitter medicines too: a thimbleful of sloe gin, then the nasty stuff, then another thimbleful of sloe gin.

Gin is not often used in cookery, but has its place — and a greater place — in the still-room, for with a little imagination and some gin, one can manufacture all kinds of special cordials and digestives. Grated orange peel and very ripe macerated strawberries, along with sugar, a crushed clove and one or two crushed corianders, left overnight in good gin, then strained through cloth and chilled, served in chilled glasses with a frost of sugar on the rim, make a wonderful end to a summer meal. An ice-cold half wineglass of gin with a sugar lump and a splash of oil of anise is popular in some circles.

But you haven't lived until you've eaten the big green rather flavorless grapes soaked in gin with grated lemon peel and fresh mint. A green mayonnaise made with gin instead of lemon, then flavored with chives, tarragon, capers, parsley and a little grated fresh garlic, makes a sauce for cold boiled shrimp to make the angels sing.

GINGER
(Zingiber officinale)

Ginger is a pretty plant of the *Zingiberaceae* family, cousin of the orchid, and has yellow flowers touched with purple. The tuberous roots, known as "hands," and the fleshy young stalks are the parts used. It is most often sold in powdered form and alas, this powder is often adulterated with other spices or with turmeric powder to make it yellow. The fresh roots, available everywhere nowadays, and then dried, are the most fragrant and spicy to use. When one sweats after a curry, it is the ginger at work. This power to induce sweat made it an important ingredient for medicines against bubonic plague and many forms of fever, from the dimmest past.

Ginger has been used in China and India since before recorded history, and was one of the first Eastern spices to reach the Mediterranean world, long before Roman times. The Spanish brought it to the Americas; as early as 1537 great quantities were shipped home to Spain. In antiquity, Dioscorides and Pliny praised it highly; in the Middle Ages, St. Hildegarde, ahead of her time in so many of the remedies she prescribed, included ginger in countless remedies, including her treatment for cataracts. Nostradamus mentions a "tonic" confection of sweet almonds, egg white, sugar and ginger pounded together, as "excellent and very useful."

Ginger is often used as a substitute for pepper, and is very helpful in subduing the flavor of fishier fishes. It is sovereign against flatulence; perhaps that is why the stem ginger preserved in syrup is served at the end of Chinese meals, with their use of onion, garlic, cabbage, pork, radish, cress and all such gaseous ingredients. In the form of ginger ale it is a mild digestive and a useful burping agent for babies. Gourmets always serve candied ginger alongside peaches or any kind of melon. A marmalade made of oranges and ginger is a wonderful accompaniment to ham, pork or venison. Ginger is one of the most common pickling spices, too. Chicken roasted with sliced fresh

GINGER

ginger, green pepper, whole small onions, and chopped celery, is a completely delightful dish. Grated fresh ginger root added to mayonnaise, along with chopped parsley and basil, makes a grand sauce for cold boiled shrimp, crab or fish. Try adding powdered ginger to your favorite stews or your meatloaf, to your sausage patties. Or try these:

Ginger Ice Cream

6 egg yolks
1¹⁄₃ cups sugar
1 quart light cream
pinch salt
2 tablespoons vanilla extract
2 cups heavy cream

Beat egg yolks lightly in top of double boiler; stir in sugar, light cream, salt. Stir constantly over simmering water until custard coats spoon. Remove from heat, stir in vanilla, and heavy cream. Chill custard, then add ³⁄₄ cup finely chopped preserved ginger with about ¹⁄₂ cup of its syrup. Then freeze mixture, either in your hand-cranked freezer, an electric one, or in your freezer compartment. If the last, remove when mixture is frozen and beat it well in a chilled bowl, then return to freezer.

Sticky-Finger Gingerbread

12 ounces plain flour
6 ounces unsalted butter
5 ounces brown sugar
8 ounces golden syrup
8 ounces blackstrap molasses
2 large eggs
1 scant cup milk
1 teaspoon ground cloves
1 teaspoon powdered cinnamon
1 heaping teaspoon powdered ginger
1 teaspoon bicarbonate of soda dissolved in a very little hot water

Put butter, sugar, syrup, molasses, spices in a saucepan and melt over gentle heat. When all is dissolved, add milk. Pour into large bowl, add beaten eggs, and soda and mix well. Sift in flour and beat hard for about 2 minutes. Pour into a tin lined with well-buttered wax paper. Start in 300 degree oven, after ten minutes lower to 275, cook about 65 minutes.

That's an old and favorite recipe. Serve the hot ginger bread with whipped cream or plain yoghurt. This is very fine, too:

Mrs. Aquilla Arnold's White Gingerbread
(from Trade, Tennessee)

1 cup unsalted butter
2 cups sugar
4 cups flour
1 teaspoon soda
1 heaping teaspoon ginger
1 scant teaspoon cinnamon
1 teaspoon nutmeg
2 eggs, beaten
1 cup buttermilk
2 tablespoons white wine vinegar

Cream butter and sugar; add flour. Mixture will be crumbly. Put one half into a well-greased 9-by-13-inch pan; reserve other half. Combine soda, spices, eggs, buttermilk, vinegar. Pour over mixture in pan; top with remaining crumb goo. Bake at 350 degrees for 25 to 30 minutes. The perfume travels; neighbors will find a reason to call.

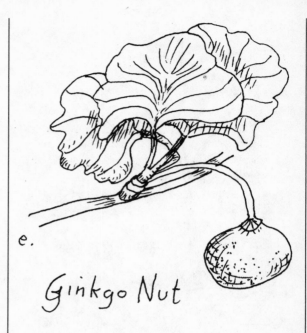

e.

Ginkgo Nut

GINKGO NUT
Maidenhair Tree
(Ginkgo biloba)

Considered a survival from prehistory, its form unchanged since the Triassic period, a kind of fossil tree, the lovely ginkgo, with its fan-shaped leaves which turn such a nice yellow tone in autumn, is heedless of polluted air and automobile exhaust, gets along with little water, and has been determined the best of all trees for urban landscaping. Native to China and Japan, it is a sacred tree planted in temple grounds. The male and female flowers occur on different trees. The nut, technically a fruit borne on the female tree, is encased in a particularly nasty smelling pulp, which is why the male tree is more often grown in gardens and on avenues. But once this pulp is removed, the nut has a special taste relished by most and occurs frequently as a flavoring in Oriental cookery. It is also roasted and eaten as a nut. Most Oriental food stores can supply this little-known item.

GOOD KING HENRY
All Good, Wild Spinach,
Lincolnshire Asparagus
(Chenopodium bonus henricus)

If ever there were a delicious green destined for home gardens, it's Good King Henry. It wilts within an hour of being picked, so it has never been nor will ever be a market item. Strictly for garden-plot-to-kitchen-pot. It has high nutritional value, has probably been cultivated since prehistory. The Romans brought it to Britain, where it went native. As the cultivated improved varieties of spinach took off, Good King Henry declined. Like spinach, Good King Henry belongs to the Goosefoot (*Chenopodiaceae*) family. It contains oxalic acid, so eating huge quantities or having it three times a day is not recommended.

It's called Good Henry in German to distinguish it from Bad Henry (*Böser Heinrich*) which is called dog's mercury in English. How the "King" got into the name is not clear, although it may be a joke about England's "bad Henry," Henry VIII.

The seeds are available in many American catalogues. The plant likes slight shade, a nitrogen-rich soil. If the bed is well-prepared before sowing, Henry can be left undisturbed five or six years. It appreciates a mulch of well-rotted manure every spring. Cut only a few stems the first year; never cut flowering stems. However, the shoots before flowering can be blanched under an upturned flower pot or such and are steamed just like asparagus. Delicious! Young leaves are used in salad, leaves and stems used like spinach. Cut just before cooking; keep in water. Good first course with butter, grated Parmesan.

GOOSEBERRY
(Ribes grossularia)

Many Americans have never tasted a gooseberry, and that's a big fat tragedy, to say the least.

Well, it *is* a sad tale. Most Europeans dote on gooseberries, especially the British. They make wonderful wines, jams, jellies, pies of the fruit, and, of course the British classic dessert, gooseberry fool. We find them in a fruiterer's bill sent to King Edward the First in the thirteenth century; Turner's *New Herbal* (1551) mentions more than one cultivated variety. In the nineteenth century the British Isles were really the Gooseberry Isles: gooseberry clubs, contests, festivals, and by 1831 some 700 named cultivars!

But when first brought to America they seemed vulnerable to mildew. So the European variety (*Ribes grossularia*) was crossed with a wild American plant (*R. hirtellum*) with happy results. Plant breeders at various state experimental agricultural extensions have produced wonderful hybrids but ... but ... but in the 1920s, the gooseberry was wrongfully blamed for the spread of a fungoid disease that attacked white pine and eventually the Federal Department of Agriculture banned gooseberries to the extent of ordering a general massacre and even sending agents into private home gardens to uproot and burn the poor innocents. Later, the culprit hosting the blister rust

Gooseberry

disease was determined to be European black currants and some of our wild *Ribes*, but it wasn't until 1966, some forty years later, that the ban was lifted.

The range of delightful gooseberry cultivars available to America is great: ranging from plummy sweetness to persimmon tartness, in color from greenish-white through pinks, yellows, rosy-gold to dark wine red. Something for everybody. All plump and with the little beak which gives them their name.

Gooseberries still haven't resumed the popularity they once had, but little by little they're creeping out of obscurity. Probably the best way to find how to acquire plants is to write your favorite gardening magazine. Here is the dessert which is to England what apple pie is to us. We often employ the phrase "Mom and apple pie." Perhaps, in England, they say something like "Aunt Gwen and gooseberry fool."

Gooseberry Fool

1 quart green gooseberries
¼ pound white sugar
1 pint heavy cream
½ pint water

Top and tail the gooseberries, cook them until tender with water and sugar in a jar placed in a saucepan of boiling water. Rub them through a hair sieve, add more sugar if necessary, and let the pulp become quite cold. Whip the cream stiffly, and stir it into the preparation a few minutes before serving. (Boiled custard may be used instead, if preferred.) Send to table in custard glasses or large dish. Sufficient for 6 or 7 persons.

That's Mrs. Beeton writing before World War I. In other and later cookbooks there are variants with suggestions for accom-

paniments such as "biscuits" (what we call cookies), etc., but that, above, is the classic gooseberry fool. In Mrs. E. Smith's battered 1729 cookbook preserved in the British Museum, there is a similar version using 6 eggs instead of cream, and with a splash of orange blossom water added for flavoring and 2 spoonfuls of spinach juice to heighten the green color.

HOLLY
Hulver Bush, Holm, Hulm, Holme Chase, Holy Tree, Christ's Thorn, Christmas Thorn
(*Ilex acquifolium*)

Holly is so much a part of Christmas decorations that it is difficult to remember its many other uses. The seasonal use of holly apparently comes from the ancient Roman custom of sending boughs of holly and ivy to friends along with other gifts, a custom adopted along with many others by the early Christians. At one moment of

history the Christians were forbidden to decorate with holly at the same time as the pagan Saturnalia, which commenced a week before Christmas. Yet in most old church calendars, Christmas Eve is marked *templa exornantur* (the churches are decorated). But the Druids had the same custom, believing that if they decked their huts with evergreens the sylvan spirits would enter and bring good fortune.

Dozens of legends in many countries and languages associate the holly with Christ, relating that the tree sprang up in his footsteps and is symbolic, with its thorny leaves and berries like drops of blood, of his travail on earth. Pliny writes that holly planted near a house protected it from lightning and witchcraft and repelled all poisons, and that the flowers can be used to make water freeze.

The leaves are particularly durable, remaining on the tree two and three years, and defying air and moisture when they fall, due to the highly durable nature of their fibers. In many parts of northern France, where holly proliferates and reaches greater heights than elsewhere, the young stems are gathered, dried and bruised and served with great success as fodder for cattle through the winter. The resulting milk is considered particularly healthful, and butter made of it of an especial excellence. In the Black Forest, holly leaves are used as a substitute for tea. Paraguay tea, used extensively in Brazil, is made from the dried leaves and shoots of another holly, *Ilex Paraguaensis*, while other hollies in South America are used for teas helpful in cases of cattarrh, pleurisy, colic, *I. Gongoha* and *I. Theezans* among them.

All hollies have been used in treating intermittent fevers and rheumatism, and modern laboratory science has corroborated the tradition by isolating a bitter alkaloid called *Ilicin* which occurs in the hollies. The berries are totally different, and even one or two induce violent vomiting and purgation. They should be kept away from children, who should be warned against them, although thrushes and blackbirds adore them and eat them with impunity.

There are many interesting forms of holly for the garden: some with yellow berries, others with variegated foliages or more curly or more prickly leaves, some almost thornless. Holly wood is very hard and even-grained, wonderfully white, and can take a high polish, hence its use in inlay work such as Tunbridge ware and many boxes, coffers, and altar fittings, and when stained, black holly often substitutes for ebony, in handles of tea and coffee pots, for instance. It is also used in manufacturing mathematical and scientific instruments, for the handles of whips, and for light walking canes. Old ballads abound with allusions to this tree. "Deck the halls" is proverbial. Another lovely one says:

"Christmastide comes in like a bride, with holly and ivy clad."

HONEY
Mellis, Miel, Miele

Honey, the chief sweet food of the world for countless centuries, is a sweet liquid manufactured in the sac of the worker bee from the nectar secreted by certain flowers. The carbohydrates in honey are a mixture of glucose and fructose. Honey also contains a bit of mannite, organic acids and fragrant ethers as well as that mysterious bee-glue called *propolis*, a resinous substance which makes up the walls of the cell.

HONEY

Honey varies enormously, according to location and the types of flowers common to each. Honey can be very thick or very thin. Tropical honeys are usually watery. The color runs a wide range: white, cream, brown, amber, red, purple, black, sea-green. There are between two and three hundred kinds of honey in the United States, clover honey being the most common. But honey connoisseurs crave the honey made of thyme or mother-of-thyme, the Narbonne honey derived from rosemary, and the resinous honey from pine forests as well as the Alpine honey made from countless wild flowers. Acacia honey is a favorite, and lovers of the rare and exotic fall over themselves trying to obtain a green honey in a red comb which comes from interior Africa.

Daily consumption of honey is universally linked with tales of astounding longevity, especially in the British Isles. One questions the authenticity of many of these tales, but some are so well documented that one cannot deny them. The one factor in common in all these accounts is that the subjects ate honey daily, and most of them consumed quantities of cider (no, not apple juice, yes, fermented cider).

Thomas Parr, who died in 1635 at the age of 152 years, sired a child at age 102. His amorous triumphs and venerable years were the subject of countless ballads, broadsides and books during his lifetime, and caused King Charles I to wish to meet him. He was invited to a tremendous feast in his honor; it proved too much for him. He died shortly thereafter and an autopsy revealed that his internal organs were as those of a youth. Cause of death was listed as "congestion."

Honey is part of many christening, matrimonial, and funerary rites in every civilization. Pots of honey were buried with the pharaohs. In 1932 a brave archaeologist sampled honey excavated in a 2000-year-old tomb, and stated that it was thin and slightly acid . . . but no different from the honey he had had for breakfast at the Mina House Hotel.

In ancient Egypt, marriage contracts stipulated that the bridegroom should supply a certain amount of honey every year of the marriage. Part of the ceremony required the young man to say, "I take you for my wife and bind myself to furnish you annually with 24 *hins* (about 32 pounds) of honey." Ancient Hindu wedding ceremonies were more elaborate and made much ado over honey. As honey was served to every guest, the bridegroom would kiss the bride and say, "This is honey, the speech of my tongue is honey, and the honey of the bees is dwelling in my mouth." At various moments of the ritual, the bride's forehead, lips, eyelids, and ear lobes were anointed with honey. Many attributed stimulating erotic powers to honey. In Morocco, the bridegroom still retires alone to eat honey before taking to the nuptial couch. For centuries, all love potions and elixirs have included honey alone with more exotic ingredients such as ground rhinoceros horn and dried powdered shrimp.

Honey, unlike common white cane sugar, is a genuine food. Sugar gives no nourishment. Recent studies suggest that sugar is addictive and see a strong connection between white-sugar consumption and hyperactivity, insomnia, irritation, nervousness, even crime.

Honey is an ingredient in hundreds of old recipes for cakes and candies, but nowadays cooks have forgotten how delightful it is for sweet-and-sour dishes, such as spareribs for instance. Or as a glaze for ham. There is no summer dessert more delicious than melon balls sprinkled with lemon juice and honey, or fruit salads of fresh fruit marinated in orange juice, honey, and a splash of Triple Sec or Grand Marnier or Cointreau. The following is nothing less than sensational:

Honey Mousse

6 egg yolks
1 pound strained dark honey
3 egg whites
16 ounces thick cream

Beat the egg yolks until pale yellow. Beat in the pound of dark honey. Put in a double boiler over hot but not boiling water and stir constantly, cooking until mixture thickens. Remove and chill. Beat egg whites stiff and fold into mixture. Whip the cream and fold in. Pack in mould or individual dishes or glasses and store in freezer until ready to serve.

HOP
(*Humulus lupulus*)

This delightful vine is found wild in most of the northern temperate regions, is easy to grow, and has, in the past, been used to make a screen for more delicate herbs and salad greens. The plant is first mentioned in Pliny, who informs us that the ancient Romans ate the young shoots in spring exactly as we do asparagus. But in most hop-growing regions, the young male flowers, too, are eaten as a vegetable, prepared with butter and cream, or as a garnish (*à l'Anversoise* — i.e., Antwerp style). But we know hops mostly as an ingredient for beers and ales. They supply an attractive bitterness as well as preservative qualities. An infusion of the catkins has been considered very helpful for rheumatic ailments since earliest history. In Sweden a fine white durable cloth is made from the fibrous stems, which soak a whole year before processing. Likewise, a fine white paper is also made from them.

HOREHOUND
(Marrubium vulgare)

This plant, part of the medicine chest since earliest antiquity, was considered by the Egyptian priests to be under the protection of the god Horus, who called it "Seed of horus," "bull's blood," and "eye of the star." The common name *horehound* is traced to this connection with Horus. The botanical name *Marrubium* comes from the Hebrew *marrob*, for this was one of the bitter herbs the Jews were ordered to take for the Feast of Passover.

It is a rather pretty plant which grows along roadsides and in dry fields, preferring the poorest of soils. It looks something like a curly mint, but the leaves are pale and covered with little whitish hairs. The whorls of whitish, sometimes faintly pink flowers are borne in whorls. The odd minty-musky smell is repellent to some, but fades in drying, and vanishes completely when the herb is kept.

For all chest problems — asthma, coughs, phlegm — and for the first symptoms of a bad cold, this herb has been used all over the worlds of Europe and the Mediterranean, whether as tea, or syrup, or made into beers and ales, or candied, or used to flavor sugar drops. Gerard, the famous herbalist, says: "A most singular remedy against the cough and wheezing of the lungs." The equally authoritative Culpepper says: "This I would recommend as excellent help to evacuate tough phlegm and cold rheum from the lungs of aged persons, especially those who are asthmatic and short-winded."

Horehound has always been cultivated in southern France, has always proliferated in a wild state throughout England, from whence it was brought to the United States by the earliest colonists. A delicious, refreshing, and healthy horehound ale is much consumed still in rural England. Horehound coughdrops are available in almost every country. For those who have known the distinctive flavor of these candy drops when a child, it remains a lifelong addiction.

Horehound Drops
(for coughs or just because you like them)

Put a handful of fresh leaves into 1½ cups of water. Let sit awhile. Strain. Add 4 tablespoons of this liquid to 2 pounds of brown sugar. Add 1 teaspoon honey. Add a very little grated orange and lemon peel if you like, perhaps ¼ teaspoon each. Boil mixture for 40 or 50 minutes. Candy is ready when a teaspoonful hardens when dropped into cold water. Pour the mixture onto a marble slab (let's hope you have one, for the usual necessities of pastry, etc.) or a baking tin or whatever, cut into squares when it cools. Dust lightly with powdered sugar and put into jars. (You can use this recipe with melissa or lemon mint, too, to make delightful candy drops.)

There is a plant called black horehound which cattle shun because it really stinks. It is of quite another family; properly known as *Ballota nigra*, it occurs in old Mediterranean formulas for worming animals, but is mostly shunned today. The white horehound we have been discussing has innumerable uses in repelling pests, and certainly should grow in every herb garden. A saucer of fresh milk with a few leaves of horehound in it can be placed in a spot swarming with flies. The flies partake of the milk and drop dead. Cheers! A sprig of horehound stuck into an anthill will cause the little dears to pack up and leave post haste. If you are infested with fire ants, avoid the strong, expensive commercial chemical insecticides which kill friend along with foe. Simply stick fresh sprigs of horehound into the hills and run. Later plant clumps of this helpful, flapproof plant in the vicinity. Most of all, bees love it to distraction, and flock to it, incidentally pollinating your melon, squash, etc., et al.

HORSERADISH
**Mountain Radish,
Great Raifort, Red Cole
(*Armoracia rusticana*)**

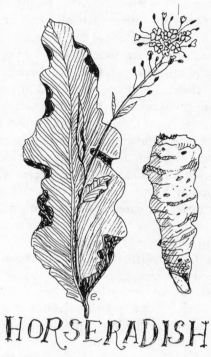

Next to the ever-mingling mints, ever reclassified, constantly producing new varieties, the most botanical confusion probably centers about the horseradish, a member of the mustard family and, like most of them, sharp, piquant, slightly bitter in flavor. The Parisians, not famous for botanical knowledge, call it *moutarde des allemands*, "German mustard," but seem to think it is the black radish, *Raphanus sativus niger*, while the more knowing French students of botany think it is undoubtedly the wild radish, *Raphanos agrios* of the ancient Greeks. Most scholars think it is one of the Five Bitter Herbs, along with coriander, horehound, lettuce, and nettle, which the Jewish people ate during the Feast of Passover. Some claim it was cultivated by the Egyptians, others claim it has been grown only in the last 2000 years.

Gerard, in his famous *Herbal* (1597), refers to it as *Raphanus rusticanus*, claims it grows wild in England. But almost all authorities agree that the form we know and use nowadays is native to Hungary, and spread to Finland, Russia and Poland, as well as to all the Mediterranean basin. Every province, every community almost, has an old name for it, and uses it both medicinally and gastronomically. (We might invent a local name and call it *Sophia's Sneezeroot*, perhaps.)

But the flavor is strong, tonic, delightful with seafood or red meat, and the "secret" ingredient of more sauces than you can shake a stick at. A charming myth attaches to the plant: Apollo went to the Oracle of Delphi to inquire the worth of numerous plants known for their curative values. The Oracle informed him that chard was worth its weight in lead, the turnip worth its weight in silver, but that the horseradish was worth its weight in gold. Considering the long list of remedies prepared from it, and cures claimed for it, this is altogether logical. It is a powerful stimulant to the digestive organs, so taken with oily fish or rich meat it greatly enhances digestion.

It has often been used exactly as was the universal mustard poultice, to relieve aching joints, rheumatic pains. It is used in remote parts of the world still to combat facial neuralgia, the fresh scrapings applied. An infusion of sliced horseradish in milk is the most ancient treatment for removing freckles or bleaching the skin. In the modern world, doctors in Europe still recommend large quantities to be eaten at every méal, to curb effectively the persistent cough which follows influenza.

The horseradish tree, also known as *ben tree* and *kren tree*, grows wild in the western Himalayas in India and Southeast Asia and . . . the southern United States. It grows proliferously in the West Indian islands. The chief value is in the nuts and the oil produced from them. The long pods have a meaty taste and are used in Indian curries. The "horseradish" in the name comes from the fact that the piquant root is sometimes used as a seasoning. The botanical name is *Moringa oleifera*.

Horseradish is one of the most delightful ingredients in dozens of sauces and delightfully spicy dishes. The English love their sauce of grated fresh horseradish with a little salt and a lot of fresh cream, with roast beef. A shrimp or crab or lobster salad is much improved by including this root. Devilled eggs become Something Else. Very ripe tomatoes dressed with sour cream and horseradish are very fine. A great dip for plain boiled shrimp is made of fresh cream, horseradish, dill, lemon juice, grated onion. Beet salad, roast chicken; there are dozens of dishes greatly improved by a dollop of horseradish. Look at this:

Roast Pheasant

3 pheasants
4 tablespoons butter
1 cup finely chopped green onions
6 slices bacon
1/2 cup brandy
2 cups chicken broth
salt to taste
1/2 teaspoon freshly ground black pepper
2 cups cream
1/3 cup of freshly grated or prepared horseradish

Melt butter in iron skillet. Add pheasants and onions and brown well. Put birds in smallish baking dish, cover breasts with bacon, secure with string or skewers. Pour warmed brandy into skillet, swish and swoosh the juices out and pour over birds, set on fire. When flames die, add stock, salt, pepper. Roast at 375 degrees for 30 minutes, basting frequently. Add cream and horseradish and a dash of mace to sauce, cook 15 minutes longer. Serve on heated platter with watercress. Cook longer if birds are big; test by pricking thickest part of creatures; when juice is golden instead of pinkish, then the thing is cooked. A dish of Brussels sprouts and chestnuts is good with this, too.

Horseradish is best fresh (and better for you: it has over 80 milligrams of vitamin C to a quarter pound) and why not have it fresh, it grows like a weed. In fact, it'll take over the garden if not controlled. An old half-barrel or an old tank or whatever works just fine. Any piece of root about 6 inches long with at least one bud will start a jungle. Many fruit trees are assisted greatly by an interplanting of anti-pest horseradish. You can keep the roots in a box of damp sand in a cool place or just leave them in the ground till you need them.

There are many brands of prepared

horseradish in jars, some vastly better than others. Sample! There are dozens of variations of horseradish sauce to go over roast beef in the English style or as sauce for shrimp, crab or whatever. This is an all-purpose sauce:

Horseradish Sauce

¹/₄ cup plain yoghurt
3 tablespoons mayonnaise
1¹/₂ tablespoons minced onion
1 teaspoon dried dill
2 tablespoons prepared horseradish

Mix well and serve.

Variations: cream instead of yoghurt, added turmeric for color and flavor.
Pink Sauce: ¹/₂ cup mashed cooked beets and juice, ¹/₂ cup heavy cream, 3 tablespoons prepared horseradish, 2 teaspoons tomato ketchup, pinch salt.
Sauce for fish fillets: 1 cup plain yoghurt, 2 tablespoons prepared horseradish, ¹/₂ teaspoon each of dried dill, celery seeds, 1 tablespoon grated lemon peel, few drops of lemon juice.
Curry Sauce: same as fish fillet sauce but with 2 teaspoons curry powder instead of dill, celery, lemon peel.

Devilled Eggs

6 boiled egg yolks, mashed well
1 tablespoon prepared horseradish
2 tablespoons mayonnaise
1 tablespoon minced mild onion
1 tablespoon minced inner celery leaves
1 heaping teaspoon chopped capers
AND, according to your taste, one of these:
  1. *minced anchovy fillets which have been soaked in milk.*
  2. *canned herring fillets, washed in warm water, mashed.*
  3. *2 tablespoons chopped shrimp, dash Tabasco.*
  4. *2 tablespoons chopped crabmeat, pinch of dill.*
  5. *2 tablespoons chopped dried beef (chipped beef).*
  6. *devilled ham, drop of tomato ketchup.*
  7. *half cup of minced chives and shallots, Tabasco.*
  8. *minced prosciutto ham, chopped capers.*

No matter which version, sprinkle with chopped parsley or cilantro when you've stuffed the whites heaped high, then put a rosebud of mild paprika in the middle of each stuffing. Or a radish slice dusted with paprika.

Experiment! Horseradish has a nice way of heightening flavors, stimulating taste-buds, and opening the sinus. Horseplay! Horseradishplay!

HYSSOP
Hysope, Joseph, Ezob
(Hyssopus officinalis)

"Cleanse me with hyssop . . . ," says the Biblical phrase, and for many people, their acquaintance with this charming little perennial herb ends there. A little over a hundred years ago doctors and scientists tended more and more to regard all early plant and herbal medicinal lore as purest superstition, but since World War II, when so many scientists have studied this lore with new respect, the hyssop has been given a very high rating in the list of nature's remedies. In ancient times, lepers were forced to cleanse themselves with this herb before contact with non-lepers. Now the laboratory workers tell us that the mould

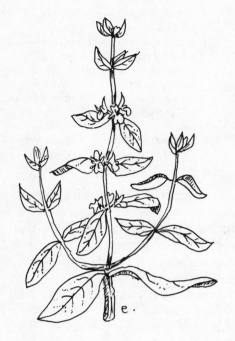

e.

Hyssop

which produces penicillin grows on the leaves of hyssop. This seems to settle another centuries-old scholarly controversy as well, where Biblical scholars are about evenly divided on whether to translate the *ezob* of the Old and New Testaments as a variety of savory (*Satureia thymus*) or as hyssop.

Hyssop is a compact plant with pretty blue (sometimes pink or white) flowers growing along one side of the flowering stems. It grows easily from seed, sprouting in just two or three days. This herb needs sunshine, and is not happy in even partial shade. Although not a principal cooking herb, it is so valuable in the garden that everyone should plant it. Bees adore it. Cabbage butterflies won't go near cabbage if there are hyssop plants in bloom at the other end of the lot. A little hedge of hyssop around vegetable plants has been found immensely valuable in actually cleansing the soil, and keeping soil pests away. It improves the yield from grapevines and fruit trees if planted beside them, especially in poor soil that is difficult to work. But don't plant near radishes; they'll lack flavor. A poultice of bruised hyssop leaves and sugar has been used for wounds or cuts since time was. Hyssop does miracles in dealing with a black eye or other skin discolorations due to bruises or insect bites.

Put a small bunch of hyssop in a bit of clean cotton cloth, immerse in boiling water a minute. Then place on the eye as hot as it is bearable. Repeat the treatment every thirty minutes; the results are surprising. A strong tea made of hyssop has long been used for lung, nose and throat congestion, any catarrhal complaints, while an infusion of hyssop, mint, and horehound will nip a cold in the bud nine times out of ten. Concentrated oil of hyssop is blended with other fragrances for well-known *eaux-de-cologne*; the herb is part of many "secret" formulas for digestives and liqueurs. If thrown onto the coals for barbecue or in smoking meats, hyssop imparts something very special to the "smoked" taste. You will find something about the fragrance of the flowers familiar therefore, even when you smell them for the first time.

It is little used in cookery, but should be more explored in this respect. Any bland vegetable such as the little ubiquitous yellow squash benefits by a dollop of bacon fat and a sprinkle of hyssop leaves. I have often used hyssop along with thyme, bay, dill, basil in flavoring a meat loaf or pâté, with interesting results. Or try a Dutch hotch-potch:

Dutch Hotch-Potch

Dice some celery (including the inner leaves), carrots, onions, cabbage, a few mustard greens or watercress, baby turnips or a parsnip, squash or zucchini, one or two potatoes.

Put 2 tablespoons unsalted butter, 2 tablespoons pure olive oil into your pot. Toss in vegetables and sauté over moderate heat for a few minutes. Then add 1 tablespoon cornstarch, an ample cup of beef or chicken stock, a scant handful of hyssop leaves, salt to taste, freshly ground black pepper, dash of cayenne, then cover and cook over medium heat about 5 or 6 minutes.

DON'T OVERCOOK; vegetables should be crisp and chewy. Sprinkle with chopped parsley before serving. This, with cornbread and some pork sausage, makes a great meal for a dismal rainy evening. Follow with a platter of sliced apples marinated in lemon juice, a variety of cheeses, crystallized ginger.

JERUSALEM ARTICHOKES
Sun Root, Canadian Potato, Girasole, Girasol
(Helianthus tuberosus)

They're not in any way related to the artichoke, they didn't come from Jerusalem, you've seen them all your life, and chances are you haven't tasted them.

It's a native American sunflower with a tuberous edible root and grows all over the North American continent. The roots were a staple of diet for the Indians, especially in the eastern half of our country.

California growers have started calling the root "sun choke," which doesn't help

Jerusalem Artichoke

one bit! Personally I'd call it "crunch root." But when it went to Spain and Italy from the New World, it was called *girasol* and *girasole;* the English ate it in Spain and Italy, asked its name, heard "Jerusalem" instead of "girasole" and so it became.

The roots don't keep well. Dig as needed. Don't wash until you're going to use them. The skins are thin, and much of the taste is in the skin. Raw, the texture is crisp, with a sweet taste. You can use them in any way you use potatoes, but since Jerusalem artichokes are totally starchless they can be served to diabetics and dieters. Raw, they're not unlike water chestnuts, good in salads, in thick slices good with dips, and can be pickled like cucumbers. High time we begin to "dig" them.

JUNIPER BERRIES
(Juniperus communus)

The juniper branch of the vast cypress family ranges from the dwarf juniper of the

JUNIPER

Alps to quite large trees in warmer countries. The berries take two or three years to ripen; they are a nice silvery-blue color. The resinous, sweet-sharp flavor of the berries is a stimulant for the appetite, while an oil from them is important medicinally for treatment of kidney and digestive complaints. They are, of course, a principal flavoring for so many gins, and account for the "clean" taste which pleases so many. In France, Sardinia and Corsica, the juniper berries are as important in the kitchen as garlic, while in Germany they go into sauerkraut and cole slaw and into *latwerge*, an aromatic chutney-like conserve to eat with cold meats.

We seldom use them in America, save in sauerkraut, and usually have only a ghostly acquaintance with them in our gin drinks, but these berries are strongly aromatic, cleanly astringent, mingle well with other herbs, and if used judiciously with garlic and celery can change the opinion of many people who won't eat anything wild or gamey, such as mallard ducks, for instance. With any pork dish they are superb, fragrant and appetizing. Seven or eight berries to a dish are usually sufficient, mashed with the back of a wooden spoon. If you buy dried commercial juniper berries, you might have to use one or two more. But ponder these recipes, dear friends:

Juniper Chicken

2½ to 3 pound chicken, rubbed inside and out with
lemon
2 ounces soft breadcrumbs
2 teaspoons herbs: parsley, thyme, fennel, marjoram,
bay, etc.
9 to 12 dried juniper berries
½ pint white wine
2 carrots sliced thin
2 green onions, sliced thin
butter and salt
freshly ground black pepper
a little grated lemon rind

Combine the breadcrumbs, herbs, slightly smashed juniper berries, salt, pepper, lemon rind. Stuff chicken with this mixture. Slather the bird generously with butter, place in baking dish, pour wine over, then add carrot and onion. Cover with foil and cook at 375 degrees for about 1½ hours, lowering heat a bit halfway through cooking. Put chicken on a hot plate. With wooden spoon scrape up all pan juices, adding a little more wine if you need; heat this sauce and pour over chicken. Potatoes baked in their skins are good with this; green salad afterwards. (Yes, I said "baked" potatoes; potatoes sealed in tinfoil are "steamed" potatoes which are something else again.) Cook a duck like that but use sage instead of mixed herbs.

Veal Provençal

2 pounds veal fillets
2 large chopped onions
2 chopped garlic cloves
4 ounces unsalted butter
1 pound sliced Gruyère (or Swiss) cheese
some soft breadcrumbs
salt to taste
freshly ground black pepper
about 12 crushed juniper berries

Gently fry the onion and garlic in butter until soft. Add the crushed juniper, a little salt and pepper. Place in baking dish, lay the fillets on top, add slices of cheese. Sprinkle thickly with breadcrumbs, bake at about 350 degrees for 45 minutes.

Sauerkraut comme il faut

Okay, you think, sauerkraut is boring? You haven't lived! Consider this:

1 big tin, about a pint, of sauerkraut
1/2 pint stock
1 chopped onion
1 or 2 chopped garlic cloves
1 chopped tart apple
2 ounces unsalted butter
1 cup of yoghurt or heavy cream
5 to 8 crushed juniper berries
1 scant teaspoon celery seeds

Put butter in pan over low heat and gently sauté onion, garlic, apple. Add juniper, sauerkraut, celery seed and stock. (I often use dry white wine instead of stock.) Simmer together a few minutes, then put in covered dish in 300 degree oven for 45 to 60 minutes. Before serving, stir in yoghurt, cream, or even sour cream, as you prefer. Serve with grilled pork or ham slices and some nice spicy grilled sausages.

Cajun Cabbage

1 pound well-seasoned pork sausage
1/4 pound salt pork (cut rather small)
a bit of chopped parsley
1 bay leaf
dash thyme, marjoram
a few chopped celery leaves
some crushed peppercorns
1 medium head cabbage, shredded
salt to taste
freshly ground black pepper
dash nutmeg
3 or 4 crushed juniper berries
1 cup good chicken stock

Cook the salt pork in boiling water with herbs and peppercorns. Take out the salt pork, cook cabbage in the water for about 10 minutes. Drain well. Mix with salt, pepper, nutmeg, juniper. Grill or fry the sausages to remove as much fat as possible. In ovenproof dish place half the cabbage, lay in sausages, cover with remaining cabbage, pour in stock. Cover, cook in 350 degree oven about 1/2 hour. (The salt pork and sausage fat, along with a red pepper pod, goes into your next soup or white beans or boiled greens.)

KETCHUP
Catchup, Catsup

First, the name. It derives from an ancient Chinese sauce called *ke-tsiap*, and in various eastern countries one finds all manner of sauces called keo-tsiap, kitjap, ketjap, etc. They all have a fish brine base and innumerable combinations of sweet-and-sour ingredients. In the early 1800s, English cooks recreated a Malaysian fish sauce called *ki chop*; the idea crossed the Atlantic and the Shakers made ketchup with cucumbers,

KETCHUP

gooseberries, and apples. The Mexican tomato spread little by little through the American continent (the "love apple", as it was called, was at first thought to be poisonous or at least unhealthful), and cooks in Maine, in the first third of the last century, added it to their ketchup sauces with happy results. In 1867 Henry John Heinz brought out his first bottle of *Heinz Catsup*, the name now reverting to a more correct *ketchup* and selling some 300 million bottles a year.

Both Worcestershire sauce and ketchup are descendants of the old Roman *garum*, which was fish entrails and white wine left in the sun to reduce it in volume to a strong liquid employed exactly as its modern counterparts. In the Deep South, in the eighteenth and nineteenth centuries, the three great ketchups were oyster, mushrooms, elderberry, then later pecan and tomato. The pecan ketchup was a southern version of the wonderful green walnut ketchup enjoyed in the British Isles. Ideally ketchup, no matter what the ingredients, is not so much sweet-and-sour as it is sweet-and-sharp or sweet-and-tangy and I enjoy this kind of sauce on many seafoods, with spareribs, and cer-

tainly with thin, crisp french-fried potatoes. (What we call "french-fried" are simply "julienne" in France.)

Now we hit a snag. For a great many serious eaters, serious gourmets, dainty pickers, all schools of the table, ketchup has become a symbol. It seems to represent the very worst of the fast food and greasy-spoon traditions, and the sight of a Ketchup bottle often brings open scorn. It became a national issue, and caused hoots of laughter and derision when President Nixon admitted that he liked best for lunch cottage cheese with glops of bottled ketchup.

I can understand both sides. The home-made ketchups are surely the best of sauces, whether straight or as basis for other accompaniments. However, I stock Heinz on my kitchen shelves. I like crisp-fried catfish fillets alongside a dipping bowl of Heinz to which I have added vinegar from the caper bottle, some chopped onion, some Dijon mustard, some chopped inner leaves of celery and a bit of syrup from the preserved ginger. I call this *Sauce Barbare*. My friends usually say "Mmmm, what's this?" but some, having a built-in prejudice toward the commercial Heinz, just sneer, "stage blood."

Here's the traditional Deep South tomato ketchup and the other classic varieties.

Tomato Ketchup

Cut up about 8 pounds unpeeled tomatoes, 2 sweet red peppers, 6 or 7 onions, 2 to 6 garlic cloves, according to your taste. Cover with water, boil until all is soft. Add a good dash of cayenne, 2 bay leaves, 1 tablespoon each of mustard and celery seeds, dash of mace and cinnamon, a little grated lemon peel. Boil all this together 20 minutes, then strain. Boil down the juice to half, stirring constantly. Add ½ cup brown sugar, ½ cup honey, 2 cups of best white wine vinegar. Simmer until thickened as much as you like. Seal in hot jars or bottles which have been sterilized. This makes about 5 quarts. Great!

Elderberry Ketchup
(*Poulac Ketchup* in some old books)

Strip ripe berries from their stalks and cover with white wine vinegar allowing ½ inch on top. Put in 350-degree oven for an hour to extract juice. Strain while hot. Boil this liquid with cloves, mace, crushed black peppercorns, a few cracked juniper berries, a few shallots and 6 or 8 of best Portuguese or Scandinavian anchovies to each quart of liquid. Boil until anchovies are dissolved and liquid reduced; it should be fairly thick. When cold, bottle in small sterilized jars, seal tightly.

Oyster Ketchup

Open 48 good oysters, saving liquid. Wash, bone, and pound 6 to 8 ounces of best anchovies, add to oysters with half a sliced lemon, pinch of powdered mace. Pour 1½ pints of dry white wine over mixture, bring to a boil, simmer 20 minutes, then strain through muslin. Add 1 teaspoon each of cloves and nutmeg. Boil ten minutes then pour over an ounce or so of sliced shallots. When cold, bottle as is.

Klosky's, Mobile's famous Royal Street eatery, always served this with omelets or scrambled eggs.

Mushroom Ketchup

Windermere ketchup, of Victorian cookery books, is the same recipe given here, with the addition of a good quantity of grated horseradish and a little grated lemon peel. Wolfram ketchup is, again, the same formula, with the addition of anchovies, and ale instead of sherry or brandy.

Put layers of sliced fresh mushrooms (about ½ inch deep) in pickling jar or earthen pot, sprinkle each layer with salt, freshly ground black pepper, and powdered allspice. Leave in a cool place for 5 or 6 days. Press to extract juice. Strain. Add a good quantity (say 1 wineglass to each pound of mushrooms) of either dry sherry or brandy. Season with thyme, bay, ginger, marjoram, and a little tomato paste. Simmer long, until reduced to good ketchup consistency, then cool, strain, bottle in sterilized jars. (The discarded mushrooms can go into pickle, be added to meat loaf, or salad.) This is delicious with cold roast or turkey, or over hard-boiled eggs.

This last is an oddity of Gulf Coast origin, imitating the Walnut ketchup common in Europe and America in the nineteenth century.

Pecan Ketchup

Crush well 100 fresh pecans (i.e., not seasoned, but as they come from tree), then place them in a jar with 6 ounces of chopped shallots, a head of garlic, minced, 2 quarts of white wine vinegar, and ½ pound salt. Let all this stand for a fortnight, then drain off liquid and put into a pan with 2 ounces of anchovies, 2 ounces whole peppercorns, ½ ounce cloves, ¼ ounce mace, then boil, skimming constantly. When no more scum rises, strain it all. When cold, pour off carefully so as to leave any sediment. Cork down closely in small bottles. Store in a cool, dry place.

Pecan ketchup was often heated with fresh cream as a sauce for fillets of veal, fillets of turkey breast, or the oilier fish, dill added in the last case.

Mrs. Beeton's Walnut Ketchup

(Adapted by Miss Melanie Marx)

100 walnuts, gathered green, chopped
handful salt
1 quart vinegar
1 heaping teaspoon each: mace, nutmeg, cloves,
ginger
1 tablespoon freshly ground black pepper
good glop prepared horseradish
¾ cup anchovies (soaked in milk, drained, pounded)
1 pint port wine

Let walnuts, vinegar, salt marinate a week, stirring every day. Drain, combine with all other ingredients, bring to boil, turn down heat, simmer half an hour. Strain it or not as you prefer. If you have put in 2 or 3 bay leaves, as most Southern cooks do, remove them. Taste, add if need be more port or more vinegar. Store in sterilized jars.

KIWI
Chinese Gooseberry, Monkey Peach
(Actinidia chinensis)

No two people agree on defining the flavor of anything. But there is one delicious fruit which draws a unanimous taste reaction. The greenish brown wooly fruit known nowadays usually as "kiwi" since it seems to have reminded New Zealand farmers of their little local bird, but which might pass in my eyes for the eggs of such a chimera as the duckbilled platypus, makes almost everybody who tastes it think of a combination of strawberry and banana with a hint of either watermelon or pineapple.

Actinidia chinensis (from *aktin*, a ray,

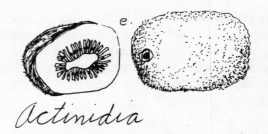

Actinidia

referring to the spoke-like radiations seen when the fruit is sliced) originated on the banks of the Yangtze and has been cultivated since antiquity in China under the name of "monkey peach." There are about forty members of the *Actinidia* family, many with delicious fruit, but the one we deal with here seems to have been preferred always for flavor, ease of cultivation, and high yield of fruit. Many Chinese aristocrats over the centuries also planted two other varieties in their garden because of their unusual attractiveness to cats, whose "erratic and frivolous" behavior upon contact with the vines mightily amused the sovereigns and their courts. The English naturalists who brought the first plants to England in 1900 were reminded, because of the green color of the ripe flesh, of the gooseberry. Introduced into New Zealand in 1906, it became a cash crop very quickly and was nicknamed kiwi, under which name we encounter it in shops and markets today.

They are easy to grow. One needs a trellis or arbor on which one lets the female vine ramble, with a male vine, kept trim close by. One male and three or four females will put you in business as purveyor of kiwis; they fruit about three years after planting.

And they are, purely and simply, delicious, sweet and succulent, perfect dessert after a heavy meal. Simply peel and slice them. Or cut in half and spoon them out of their skins like little melons. Each fruit contains more vitamin C than a big orange, as well as many useful minerals, especially a fat load of potassium, and almost no calories. An enzyme in the fruit makes it a fantastic meat tenderizer. Simply rub your steaks or stew meat with a halved kiwi and let sit for a half-hour. But try these, too:

Monkey Peach Pie

1 baked 8-inch pie shell
4 to 6 kiwi fruits
2 egg whites
4 tablespoons sugar
few drops orange juice
tiny pinch powdered mace

Preheat oven to 400 degrees. Peel and slice your kiwis, then arrange nicely in pie shell; put few drops of orange juice over them. Beat egg whites until stiff. Add mace to sugar. Beat sugar into egg whites until meringue is thick and glossy. Spread evenly over fruit, so that it touches sides perfectly. Bake about 8 minutes until top is just golden brown. Serve immediately.

Actinidia Cream

3 kiwis, simmered in water 10 minutes, peeled, puréed
1 fresh kiwi, kept aside for garnish
1 cup scalded milk
¼ cup heavy cream
2 eggs, separated
1 tablespoon cornstarch
½ teaspoon vanilla extract
½ cup sugar
little salt

Beat egg yolks with cornstarch, vanilla, and good pinch salt until smooth. Stir in milk; cook over moderate heat until thickened, stirring with wooden spoon constantly. Stir in ½ cup sugar. Beat egg whites until stiff. Add rest of sugar. Fold whites into egg-yolk mixture along with whipped cream and kiwi purée. Pour into bowl and garnish with kiwi slices. Chill well.

A wonderful hors d'oeuvre for a summer meal is slices of spicy Italian salami or sausage with peeled slices of kiwi sprinkled with lemon juice and accompanied by fresh watercress, or lettuce hearts, dressed with yoghurt and dill.

Or use any favorite sherbet recipe and make a sherbet of kiwis. And watch out for that "erratic and frivolous" behavior!

KUDZU VINE
Mile-a-Minute Plant
(Pueraria lobata)

The kudzu vine, in the hundred-odd years since it was introduced into America, has generated more strong opinion, folklore, pros and cons, than even the mint julep, Boston baked beans, or Tallulah Bankhead. It was grown and shown in the Japanese pavilion at the Philadelphia Centennial

Kudzu   e.

Exposition, later was the source of much ado at the New Orleans Exposition in 1883. It was considered a pretty, sweet-scented flowering shade plant for trellises, verandas, pergolas. The name quickly was changed to Mile-a-Minute Plant, when it was noted that the kudzu could, indeed, grow a foot a day. It was quickly seen that horses, cattle, chickens, goats all loved to eat the plant. It soon was demonstrated to be a remarkable agent for controlling erosion and revitalizing worn-out soil in a South where sterile burnt-out farms were the rule, ruined after decades of careless repetitive planting of corn, cotton, tobacco. The huge, deep roots of kudzu are a fantastic fertilizer, pumping nitrogen into the soil, bringing up mineral elements from deep down in the earth. During the Depression years there was a veritable kudzu cult in the South, a Kudzu Club with over 20,000 card-carrying members, all preaching that the vine would save agriculture in the South.

But the forestry service began to be disillusioned when the vine toppled telephone and power poles, whereupon the electrical and communications monopolies began an anti-kudzu publicity campaign. James Dickey published his famous anti-kudzu poem in the *New Yorker* in 1963 at the height of the anti-kudzu feeling, with lines like "smothered . . . by green, mindless, unkillable ghosts." Patience, James!

Now, less passionate and more reasonable souls are proposing, in every agricultural college, in every farm bulletin, that with the astronomical costs of chemical fertilizers, cattle feed, etc., kudzu might still be the savior it was claimed to be when introduced.

What is kudzu? Why do we include it here with herbs, spices, and flavors?

Un peu d'histoire: the plant originated in China, where it has been a part of the culture since 2000 years, as fodder, as human food and medicine and as source of fibers for textiles. For at least 300 years, commentators have pointed out that if the early Chinese had understood the properties of kudzu, there would be no Gobi Desert.

The plant grew even better in Japan. A poem of about 600 A.D. speaks of the young leaves as a delicious green vegetable. But the root supplies a starch like our arrowroot, common in most oriental cookery. This powder can also be used to gel things in the manner of gelatine or agar, also to make a lovely shiny glaze on sweets. All of the plant has strong medicinal qualities. It is used to give quick relief from intestinal and digestive disorders, any kind of upset stomach, acid indigestion, etc. But it is highly helpful for colds, hangovers, fevers and many more serious ailments.

Kudzu fibers supply the weavers who manufacture a naturally waterproof fabric of them. But a more refined and highly durable silklike fabric, *kappu*, is made of these fibers, which is styled into the elegant *katsui* (kudzu kimono) made by the master weaver, Tsugio Odani, in Kyoto, never selling for less than $500 nowadays.

Kudzu fibers are made into a fine quality paper used especially in fine art books. Japanese basket makers find their chief raw material in the flexible young vines. Bits of root fiber have been the reinforcements for plaster walls in China and Japan for at least 1000 years. The leaves of the vine are an easily harvested fodder, rich in protein and chlorophyll. Dried fibers are used to stuff mattresses, cushions, chairs. The flowers are a great bee flower, especially delicate honey. The dried leaves, burned, are a powerful insect repellent. The green leaves are a particularly rich mulch, or compost.

Called *kuzu* in Japanese, the powdered root is the basis of a huge galaxy of sweet dishes of unbelievable variety.

What occasioned this entry? The realization that hundreds of decorators and fancy shops in the United States spend a fortune importing the Japanese wallpapers in natural colors which are derived totally from kudzu fibers. The number of natural food shops AND fancy food shops selling confections based on kudzu root powder. Our very own health/gourmet shops carry *kuzu* powder.

Recently I read a bulletin from the Georgia Agricultural College with fantastic ideas about new kinds of insulation, cultivation, etc., suggesting that with the rising costs of fossil fuels, fertilizer and so forth, we should look to natural local usages. The best idea consists of planting kudzu in barrels on roofs to make a quick insulation and cut down on air conditioning costs. Pretty, too!

So let's stop bellyaching about kudzu and get some clever Japanese technicians over here to help start up paper factories, textile mills, food processing plants, wallpaper manufacturers, basket weavers' combines, all that. We are griping about one of our best natural resources.

So, on a moonlit night in summer (green) or in fall or winter (grey-brown), when you glance out over the landscape and see the forms of strange grey-brown shackled tree forms, lumpy shapes of rocks, camelopards, crumbling towers, grimordines, grimauldines, hunchback giants, all that, think UP not DOWN.

As this book goes to press, a courier from Opelika, Alabama, informs us that some Serious Citizens have formed a group to bring over Japanese specialists. Together they'll deal Seriously with the kudzu.

LAVENDER

LAVENDER
(*Lavandula vera, L. stoechas, L. fragrans, L. delphimensis, L. spica*)

The Bible is full of references to spikenard and nard, referring to a very costly oil or ointment, deliciously fragrant, now known to be derived from a tree of northern India called *Nardostachys Jatamansi*. But lavender, common in the western Mediterranean, was often used to imitate or adulterate spikenard, so nard sometimes means lavender. Lavender takes its name from the Latin word *lavare*, "to wash," and was widely used by the ancient Romans and Libyans to perfume their baths and their persons. One form they knew was *Lavandula stoechas*, which grew plentifully on the islands of Hyères, which the Romans called the *Stoechades*. It is smaller, has deeper purple flowers.

In some medieval herbals, lavender figures as *Pseudonardus femmina*, in others as nard or *nardus*. Only in the late Middle Ages did an accurate description of the plant in its varieties appear, in an herbal compiled by Abbess Hildegarde at a cloister near Bingen on the Rhine. For most people lavender means sweet English lavender (*Lavandula vera*), which is the basis of so many soaps, perfumes, toilet waters; French lavender means the aforesaid *L. stoechas*; or *L. spica,* which has a coarser rather rosemary-ish aroma, but is widely used in cheap soaps in Europe. Two forms of lavender occurring in France were lumped together as *L. officinalis,* and only in the last century were identified and labelled as *L. delphimensis* and *L. fragrans*. A white form growing in the Alps is an albino form of *L. fragrans;* Queen Henrietta Maria loved this and grew hedges of it in her palace gardens, but nobody in England has made white lavender flourish since. Some catalogues list pink lavender but it is a dirty pinkish-mauve, nearly grey, and not worth the trouble.

L. stoechas and *L. vera* are the types to grow in your herb garden. They can be started from seed or cuttings. Lavender is the greatest of bee plants, and honey with a faint whiff of lavender flowers in it is totally delightful.

Oil of lavender was much used in both World Wars in front-line hospitals, as an antiseptic and to overpower foul odors. A drop of the oil on the temples relieves nervous headaches in record time; it is an essential element in smelling salts.

Mrs. Grieve, the distinguished modern herbalist, writes: "It is agreeable to the taste and smell, provokes appetite, raises the spirits and dispels flatulence. The dose is from one to four drops on sugar or in a spoonful of milk. A few drops of essence of lavender in a hot footbath has a marked influence in relieving fatigue. Outwardly applied, it relieves toothache, neuralgia, sprains, and rheumatism. In hysteria, palsy, and similiar disorders of debility and lack of nerve power, lavender will act as a powerful stimulant." But she neglects to mention one of the best qualities of oil of lavender: it is a powerful insect repellent. A few drops on face, wrists, and ankles and nothing flying or crawling will come anywhere near you.

In earliest times lavender was used in perfuming vinegars and desserts, but these culinary uses have slipped out of fashion. Queen Elizabeth I was inordinately fond of a conserve made of pears, honey, and lavender flowers. "Lavender snow" occurs in English cookery books right up to the turn of the last century. Heavy cream in which lavender flowers had been steeped was beaten with sugar and egg whites to make a froth which was served on bare lavender twigs, coming to table in little pots and looking like snow-covered bushes.

If you want to try something different, let lavender flowers remain in sugar in a closed jar for a week, then sift out the flowers and use the sugar to sweeten a compote of fresh fruit. Very Good.

LEEK
Poireau, Porro
(Allium porrum)

Once, the leek was widely cultivated in the Gulf Coast regions, but since World War II it seems to have vanished from the scene. Leeks don't travel well, since they become strong and bitter very soon after being pulled from the ground. They are the sweetest and mildest of the *Allium* clan, which includes chives, onion, ransoms, garlic, shallots, and so forth, and are very easy to grow. Leeks make a nice vegetable dish simply boiled and buttered, or boiled and served cold with a vinaigrette sauce. One of the glories of the dining room at that old hotel at Coden was an oyster stew thick with leeks and tender celery.

The leek is so much a part of human history that no one can determine its origins. It was grown in ancient Egypt; the Romans esteemed it highly, and probably brought it to England. Many varieties are cultivated, varying from the gigantic ones grown for farm fair competitions in Scotland, through the smaller varieties popular in Holland, France, and Italy especially.

Size is not the first consideration in choosing leeks, freshness is the prime aspect. And whiteness. The more white section you see, the milder the flavor. Leeks are difficult to clean. In heaping earth about them to blanch them, a little always gets in between the leaves. Always wash them upside down, so that you don't send the fine earth deeper into the leaves.

There are many recipes which call for both onion and leek, since there is a subtle difference in the flavors. Like onions, leeks take on a different flavor when browned, and are part of many broths and court bouillons. In central Europe, leeks are part of the flavorings for cooking pork or lamb. Leeks are never eaten raw, save in parts of Tibet and Africa. Faced with the difficulty in finding good fresh leeks, which are not yet part of the mass production vegetable farms, a society has been recently formed in this country, called *The National Society for the Elevation and Propagation of the Leek.* (I haven't found the address yet, but I'm seeking.)

Here is the classic European dish:

Leek Soup

About 6 small or 3 large leeks
1 tablespoon butter
4 cups chicken stock
1 cup breadcrumbs
4 tablespoons grated Parmesan cheese
salt to taste
freshly ground black pepper

Wash and slice your leeks. Put butter into pot and turn leeks until well-coated, then cover and cook on very low heat about 15 minutes. Don't brown. Stir frequently. Add stock and seasoning; simmer until leeks are tender. Taste for seasoning. Add crumbs and cheese before serving.

The leek is the national emblem of Wales and from those parts comes this great stew:

Welsh Lamb Stew

2 pounds bone shoulder of lamb
10 leeks
1 cup diced carrots
1 cup diced turnips
12 small new potatoes
1 cup cooked peas
2 tablespoons bacon fat or butter
2 tablespoons flour
1 mashed garlic clove
pinch mace
few pinches brown sugar
salt
freshly ground black pepper
bay leaf
some marjoram
few celery leaves
1/2 teaspoon grated lemon peel

Meat should be in good hefty bite-size pieces. Brown meat on all sides in fat or butter with salt, pepper, brown sugar. Add flour, stirring well until it is lightly browned. Add warm water slowly. Put in flavorings, stirring constantly. Meat should be covered by liquid. Cover, simmer 1 hour. Remove meat (remove and discard bay leaf) and skim off as much fat as possible. Return meat to liquid, add all vegetables save peas. Simmer 30 minutes, then add peas and cook about 12 or 15 minutes longer.

LEMON
(Citrus limon)

This is another of those ordinary every-day things about which we know absolutely nothing. The *Encyclopedia Britannica* says that the lemon was unknown to the Greeks and Romans . . . yet it is depicted in both mosaics and frescoes at Pompeii. Virgil described it quite precisely, calling it a "Median apple." Almost all botanists think it is a hybrid which occurred spontaneously, perhaps a hybrid of the citron and the lime . . . but where? Most scholars today agree that it must have originated in the Indus Valley, but no identifiable fossil seeds have been found. It's a pretty spiny tree anywhere from ten to twenty feet high, with white flowers tinged with mauve or pinkish purple. One usually sees fruit and flowers together.

Everything about it is paradoxical. One of the most important commercial food crops on the planet, it is seldom eaten alone (although in India and Morocco whole pickled lemons are served as accompaniment to other dishes). The lemon tree likes lots of water but doesn't like to get wet! Which is why Florida with its rainfall can't compete with dry Sicily and California. Two quite distinct flavorings come from this fruit: the acid juice and the volatile oil in the skin. I repeat, two distinct flavorings. The juice, squeezed on fish or vegetables, used in a classic salad dressing, in Italy even squeezed over steak, added to countless dishes, heightens flavor, points up other seasonings apart from serving as a starting point for legions of sweets.

Since we are constantly faced with the disgusting first-course salad plopped down in front of one in a restaurant, on a plate much too small, and smothered in some unspeakable blop of undoubted coal-tar derivation, whose only virtue is to disguise the tastelessness of the well-traveled iceberg lettuce, the whole abomination the reasoning of fad dieters, thinking by the first course ruse to destroy the appetite for the rest of

Lemon

the meal, this originating in California, source of so much oddity, as for example the Guyana Kool Aid and Christ cult (we know how *that* ended; the first course trash salad is no less perverse), we might sit a moment and define salad.

Basically, it is a dish of the freshest possible, tenderest possible garden or field greens (the choice is infinite) dressed in a combination of good oil and an acid agent, with salt and usually some fresh ground black pepper. The best salads contain about two-thirds good wine vinegar to one-third lemon juice. (Lemon juice has the more satisfying acidity, but the vinegar adds flavor.) Salad usually comes after the meat or most important course to cleanse and refresh the palate. Serving it along with other dishes destroys the flavor of what accompanies, either by the sharpness of the acid content or the palliative effect of the oil.

Lemon peel, either grated or in the form of what the French call a *zest de citron,* which is a fingernail-size paring of lemon peel added to various dishes toward the end of cooking, is the secret ingredient of most oriental or Mediterranean cookery. Try

adding some grated lemon peel to your next beef stew, your next sparerib sauce, to your gumbo, your shrimp cocktail. If you haven't done so before, you'll be agreeably surprised. The lemon is the favorite flavor for desserts, beating all competition. Recipes for lemon pies are legion. Lemon sherbet outsells orange and lime by far in the United States. Here are some lesser known recipes:

Lemon Consommé

Wonderful first dish on a cold day. Simply add finely grated lemon peel and a generous flavoring of freshly ground black pepper to a good strong beef consommé or broth. Heat the soup bowls, put a tablespoon of good dry sherry in each one, send the tureen to table piping hot.

Wally Windsor created a real furor at her Paris luncheons with an old southern recipe:

Shrimp in Lemon Cups

Use biggish lemons. Cut off a bit at one end so they'll sit straight. Cut a bigger lid off other end, then, with grapefruit knife, remove flesh and pith without piercing skin. Squeeze to obtain juice. Dress your boiled, peeled baby shrimp (or crabmeat) with a bit of lemon flesh, lemon juice, prepared horseradish, finely chopped sweet green pepper, a little grated onion, some pure olive oil and a dash of tomato ketchup, salt to taste, and some freshly ground black pepper. Fill your lemon cups and place on bed of ice with garnish of watercress or parsley or inner leaves of celery. (This is also good with crabmeat, flaked white fish, even canned white tuna.)

An old Virginia favorite since the seventeenth century is:

Lemon Syllabub

2 lemons
¹/₈ pint best brandy
6 ounces sugar
1 pint heavy cream
³/₈ pint sweet white wine
lady fingers

Pare off skin from lemons without any white pith. Squeeze juice, place in bowl with brandy and lemon rind and leave overnight. Strain then stir in sugar until it dissolves. Whip the cream until fairly thick, but not buttery, then gradually add lemon juice mixture, whipping away merrily the whole time. When all liquid has been added to cream, the cream should stand in peaks and remain so. Pile into chilled custard glasses and serve with lady fingers, or *langue de chats,* or any thin, subtle, crisp "finger" cookie.

LEMON BALM
(*Melissa officinalis*)

Lemon balm might better be called by its proper botanical name, *Melissa officinalis,* since it is often confused with barm (yeast), lemon verbena (citronella, that is: *Verbena tryphilla*) and bee balm (*Monarda didyma*). *Melissa* is the old Greek word for bee, and in the ancient Mediterranean world, quantities of this herb were planted around hives to guide the bees back home, and to attract homeless bees to join them. It was the holy herb of the bee priestesses, who cleaned their altars with it. It has always been considered a "cheerful" herb, and medically is recognized as helpful to circulation and in relieving tension, when the leaves are infused into a tea.

A number of Englishmen who have lived well past 100 all took lemon balm tea sweetened with honey for breakfast. This member of the mint family is the basis of the *eau de Melisse* made for centuries by the Carmelite nuns in France, a digestive drink credited with curing headaches and neuralgia besides cheering up the despondent. The medieval "scholar's tea," taken on the eve of examinations as an aid to memory, is just an infusion of dried melissa leaves.

Modern organic gardeners claim that they get a much greater yield of tomatoes, cucumbers, eggplants, apples, peaches, when their gardens include a good patch of melissa. The Latins already knew this; the herb is their *apiastrum.* And bees literally are mad about melissa and come from miles around, incidentally pollinating everything in the garden.

A favorite Renaissance stuffing for duck, which breaks down the fatty texture of the bird but is also delicious, is this: pierce all the fatty parts well, stuff the bird with a mixture of tart apples peeled and coarsely chopped, stoned but uncooked prunes and a good handful of melissa leaves, chopped, with a pinch of salt and some freshly ground black pepper.

Melissa was once used in everything where now we use the lemon, which has only in recent times been easily available. Melissa is wonderful in salads, chopped over cucumbers, mixed with dill and chives for an omelet, to flavor jellies and gelatine desserts, in marinades for pickles and fish, in wine cups, and a sensational variant for mint in a julep. An easy-to-grow perennial, it likes full sun, space and plenty of water in hot summer.

LEMON GRASS
(Cymbopogon citratus)

This plant is a long-leaved tuft of grass looking not unlike a smaller pampas grass, but it has a bulbous root. Common in all

Southeast Asia, where it figures in hundreds of dishes, it is now cultivated in Africa, South America, and Florida because of the essential oil *citral,* widely used as a substitute for real lemon in perfumery and dozens of commercial food and household products.

It is delightful in both appearance and scent and should be in every garden, and, as with lemon verbena, delightful used dried in storing clothes or linens. The combination of whole black peppercorns (which can later go into the mill) and dried lemon verbena or lemon grass is so much nicer than mothballs for storing woolens in winter.

LEMON VERBENA
Herb Louisa
(Lippia citriodora)

This perennial woody shrub, with its intensely fragrant lanceolate leaves arranged in threes, and its inconspicuous white or mauvish flowers, is not to be confused with vervain, although they are of the same plant family.

Lemon verbena appears under many names in old books. Although *Lippia citriodora* is most often given nowadays as the botanical name, the plant is still referred to as *Aloysia citriodora, Verbena triphylia,* and *Lippia triphylla.* In many eighteenth-century books, it is Herb Louisa. The French call that other herb, vervain, by the name *verveine:* confusion begins by their calling the lemon verbena *verveine olorante* or *verveine citronelle.* Lemon verbena is *hierba de la Princesa* in Spanish, *cedrina* in Italian. Most of the *Verbenaceae* family are tropical, generally South American in origin. Lemon verbena came to the Gulf Coast by way of the Caribbean isles; it reached New England by way of the British Isles, where it was introduced in 1784. Before the common lemon was available, the leaves of this plant, with a very high amount of volatile oil of strong lemon flavor, was much used in cookery: with fish, as a flavor heightener in stews and ragouts, in sherbets and jellies. The lemon sherbet which was commonly served between two meat courses in eighteenth-century gorge-orgies was more often made from lemon verbena than from lemons.

The flavor is powerful and must be used with caution, since some people are reminded of dime-store lemon soap, which,

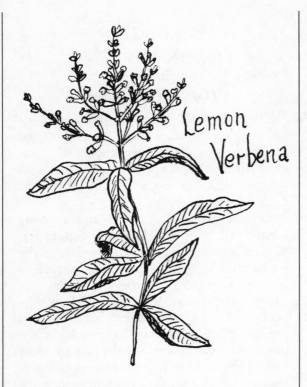
Lemon Verbena

enhair fern fixed in them. A fabulous sherbet is made of white corn syrup which has been heated with lemon verbena steeped in it, and buttermilk. Or, in recipes where white sugar is required, lemon flavor can be obtained by tightly packing layers of lemon verbena leaves and sugar in a jar and letting it sit for a month. The dried leaves are delightful in linen and clothes, used just as lavender.

LIQUORICE
Spanish Juice, Black Sugar, Réglisse, Arozuz, Regaliz
(Glycyrrhiza glabra)

Liquorice (also licorĭsh, and licorice) root is still listed in the official British and American *Pharmacopoeias,* but you'll play hob trying to find it, although ole-fashioned pharmacies still carried it up to World War II.

The plant is a small perennial of the legume (pea and bean) family. Very pretty, too, with its mauvish blue flowers and pinnate leaves. Rather fussy about soil and climate; difficult to grow and not worth the fuss for most family herb gardens. It grows wild in southern Europe and all across the Middle East as far as Afghanistan. The ancient Chinese knew and used it; it was well known in classical antiquity. We still use the name bestowed on it by Dioscorides: from the Greek *"glukas,"* sweet, and *"rhiza,"* root. It was introduced into England, probably, during the last Crusades, and flourished as a commercial crop in Yorkshire, where the Black Friars seem to have taken it. A community called Pontefract was/is famous for a sweet called

in fact, until fairly recently was flavored with . . . lemon verbena. All, but all, of the perfumes or *eaux de cologne* labeled verbena or *verveine* or *citronelle* or *acqua cedrina* are made from lemon verbena. Like the coral vine, the Grand Duke jessamine, the Mexican lilac, lemon verbena once flourished in all Gulf Coast gardens; like them it has simply vanished.

It is not only easy to grow, but most accommodating as to soil, and location, and is bane to all insects, especially mosquitoes. A few dried pyrethrum and lemon verbena leaves, burning in a dish, will rid a wide area of such pests. Any pot of apple or plum jam or jelly is vastly improved by the addition of a few lemon verbena leaves. In the last half of the last century, ladies often gave pots of clear jellies as gifts, with a little bouquet of lemon verbena, rose geranium, and maid-

"Pontefract cakes," still exported to points around the globe.

In recent years, large commercial plantations of liquorice have been established in Spain, Italy, Turkey, and especially in the U.S.S.R., where the study of natural medicinal plants and the age-old applications of traditional remedies has interested research workers in the field more generally than it has in other countries.

Liquorice root is the part used, and in its simple dried form is available everywhere in Europe, less noted in our country. This root has always been given to teething babies, who relish the slightly acid, sweetish taste. But it speeds the healing of gumboils, inflamations of the tongue, swollen gums. We all meet up with it more often than we think, for it goes into many mouthwashes, into many cough mixtures, tablets, pastilles, many remedies for quinsy, bronchial troubles, persistent coughs, often to sweeten (without sugar) more bitter or acrid mixtures. And, of course, those who love liquorice sticks or the brightly colored candies from England called "Liquorice All-Sorts" have a fond addiction for the flavor.

In the last decade, all over Europe and the Middle East, liquorice has found a very modern application: it has helped many people to shake the smoking habit. Instead of popping a candy into your mouth, reach for a bit of liquorice root when you have a nicotine fit. It has a smooth sweet presence which reduces your tickling yearn for the old coffin nail. And, if you're making up a tea of mixed herbs, include some liquorice root to sweeten it naturally, without sugar.

LOVAGE
Love Parsley
(*Levisticum officinale* or *Ligusticum officinalis*)

Garden lovage was once one of the principal sweet herbs cultivated in the late medieval gardens. The roots, leaves and seeds were used in numerous medicinal and culinary preparations. In recent years, with the interest in garden herbs and a more varied cuisine, lovage has slowly returned to favor, as is only right, for it is easy to grow, is a handsome plant, and has many uses in our modern kitchen.

A tea brewed from the leaves has a highly attractive aroma; it is good for upset stomachs following overeating, against flatulence, and for relief of the symptoms of the common cold. The seeds are delightful sprinkled on rolls or biscuits, very good on crackers made to go with cheese. The stems can be candied like angelica, or blanched like celery and eaten as a vegetable. The leaves are often added to stocks or broths to give it a more meaty taste. For centuries in England, an after-dinner cordial called "lovage" was much enjoyed; it took its flavor as much from tansy and yarrow as from the herb we're discussing. But a wonderful

Liquorice

cordial is still made at home in the Mediterranean world as well as in the British Isles: nothing more than lovage steeped in good brandy for a week or so, then strained through cotton cloth.

The flavor is quite different and hard to describe. Claire Loewenfield says lovage reminds her of "Yeast and Maggi soup." Tom Stobart says it is like "a pleasantly musky-lemon-scented celery." It does look rather like a gigantic celery with yellowish green flowers and any nearsighted creature could easily mistake the plant for any of the other members of the *Umbelliferae* family: fennel, dill, alexander, etc. Another form of the plant, known as Scottish lovage, grows in the north of Britain and in the Carolina highlands of the United States. It is eaten as a cooked green or in salads, is known under an old Caledonian name as *shunis.*

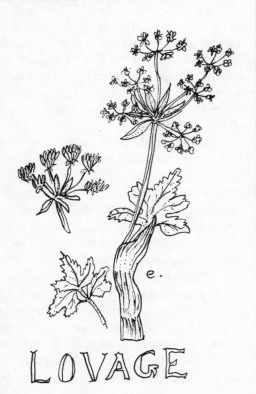

LOVAGE

The plant is easy as nothing to grow, is perennial, likes full sun and lots of moisture. I like the stems boiled and buttered with a little salt as a side dish to pork chops. The younger leaves are unexpected, fresh, and delightful in salad. Sometimes I take Limburger cheese when it is almost *too* ripe and mix it with Philadelphia cream cheese, then sprinkle lovage seeds over the pot. Thin biscuits liberally sprinkled with a mixture of dill and lovage seed are very good with any sharp cheese. Best of all are ripe red tomatoes served with lemon, oil, salt, pepper, and a good sprinkling of chopped lovage leaves and little stems. Tomatoes and basil are classic, but the use of lovage makes a tantalizing change.

Homemade mayonnaise to which is added a very little chopped parsley, one or two capers chopped fine, a little chopped shallots, a little extra lemon juice, a bit of horseradish AND a good handful of chopped lovage leaves makes a sauce for boiled shrimp or boiled fish which will make people sit up and take notice. Carrots and lovage stems braised in butter are another surprise, very nice with turkey or roast. An unusual salad is comprised of paper-thin cucumbers which have been soaked in cold salt water and lovage stems simply dressed with lemon, oil, salt, pepper. In a white fruitcake, candied lovage stems work like the usual angelica but add a sweet muskiness of their own.

MACE
(Myristica fragrans)

The name mace comes from a medieval word for "nut," and implies "valuable in ointments or salves." Mace is a lacey outer

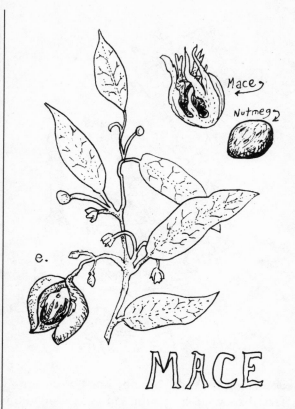

Mace

Nutmeg

e.

MACE

covering of the seed of a fruit which looks rather like a small smooth yellow pear with a longitudinal furrow. The seed itself, of course, is nutmeg. Most of the world supply comes from the Banda Islands by way of Java and Sumatra. The trees reach about forty feet, are evergreen, with smooth dark green leaves and insignificant flowers. Mace and nutmeg are similar in flavor, but mace is much more subtle, and much more expensive. The aril of the nutmeg ("aril" is the proper name for this flaky seed-covering) is bright scarlet when taken from the fruit, dries to a warm brown.

Mace of good quality has a warmish color; beware of cheaper forms from less desirable species of the nutmeg, for the flavor is simply not the same. Buy powdered mace of a known brand; otherwise you will

get adulterated powders. Mace has always been used as a tonic, stimulant to appetite, and aid to digestion. In small amounts! Both mace and nutmeg, taken in excess, lead to over-excitement, increased circulation, increased body heat.

No doughnut or pound cake is worthy of its name unless containing a pinch of powdered mace, valued for its yellowish color as well as its delightful aroma. All of the classic clear soups—turtle, for instance—all of the great beef stews, marinades, etc. include a "blade" or so of mace. It has a way of pointing up the other flavors involved. One of the most delightful dishes to accompany pork, duck, any rich or fatty main platter (I like it with turkey) is individual onions baked in foil. You take big onions, cut off a lid, scoop out the flesh and chop it fine and mix it with plenty of unsalted butter, powdered mace and freshly ground black pepper, a few pounded fennel seeds, pinch of salt, then pack this back into the onion shell which you've buttered inside and out, and wrap each onion in foil, poking one small steam hole on top. Bake an hour at about 350 degrees, or until fork goes easily through onion. This and sautéed celery are wonderful with the rich holiday dishes. Perfect complements to the turkey stuffing, too.

Any fruit jelly is immensely improved by a bit of powdered mace. A plain old apple jelly, for instance, becomes Something Very Special if cooked up with a rose geranium leaf and some blades of mace (both discarded before bottling). Try marinating fresh strawberries in sweet sherry flavored with a little lemon juice and powdered mace. This does wonders for some of the oversize not-quite-ripe fruit offered in stores. Pears baked slowly in red wine and honey, flavored with mace and cinnamon, are very good indeed, and nice alongside fried ham and eggs for breakfast.

If you want to make a delightful cordial to sip after a rich meal, try soaking orange peel, blades of mace, a nutmeg or so, and a few sugarlumps in a bottle of gin for a week. Strain and serve very cold in thimble glasses. Or vodka. But the angelica and juniper taste of the gin adds something. Chocolate sauces are improved by a pinch of powdered mace, cookie recipes without exception gain, and if you want to pass as a subtle continental-type with-it cook, simply mix over boiling water a little melted unsalted butter, some dry white wine, two or three drops of lemon juice, a good dash of powdered mace, a few tarragon leaves, with a pinch of salt and a dash of freshly ground white pepper and serve over plain boiled fish. And smile knowingly. You might say, "Oh, it's something Julia taught me, the dear." Or "This is how Waverley likes it." Or if you get enough praise, just boldly lie: "Alice B. always did it this way."

MAIDENHAIR FERN, CAPILLAIRE
Cheveux de Venus, Adranthe, Culantrillo
(Adiantum capillus-veneris)

This pretty fern, which grows wild in much of the southern half of the United States, is rare in England, and up until the last decade of this century, was a favorite greenhouse plant there. The leaves, boiled with water and sugar, make the delicately green syrup known as *capillaire,* which,

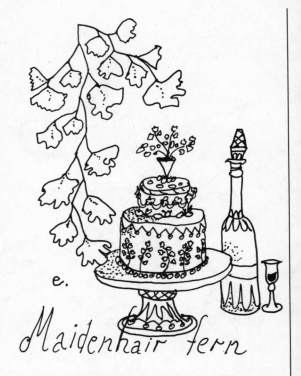

Maidenhair fern

according to André Simon, was "often preferred to wine by young ladies . . ." in the nineties of the last century. It is reported that Dr. Johnson liked to add a splash of this syrup to his port. A jelly with an odd distinctive taste was often made of this fern, flavored with angelica, lemon rind, or other aromas. But the glory of the maidenhair fern was in its use to decorate fancy cakes and desserts in much of the late eighteenth century and throughout the nineteenth, right up to the twenties. Candied flowers, such as small roses and violets, but many others as well, were combined with fresh maidenhair leaves and garlands and swags of colored icing and crystallized fruits cut in fancy shapes to form fantasies of wildest culinary baroque. And pretty they were! Some of the old French and English cookery books of the nineties have colored prints of these triumphs. Worth reviving today.

Candying flowers is not all that difficult. Gather in early morning, coat with beaten egg white, then with sugar crystals, dry in an oven which has been heated to 400 degrees, then fire turned off, with door ajar. Nothing to it. Gather your maidenhair fern, wash well, dry with clean dishcloth. If you have a moist icing, the fern leaves can simply be pressed against it. Almonds covered with silver leaf add much, too.

MANGO
(Mangifera indica)

For some six thousand years the mango has been cultivated in India, for some hundreds of years in various other tropical zones, yet it is likely that most of the inhabitants of temperate zones have never tasted what is called "the king of fruits," "the apple of the tropics" (it's the most eaten fruit in warm countries, whether raw, pickled, or cooked), "the most delicious flavor of this earth," etc., and generations of writers and commentators have twisted themselves into pretzel shapes trying to describe the unique lusciousness of this fruit.

There are many varieties, all with different uses in African, Asian, Caribbean cookery. At best the flesh is firm and succulent and the color rather like canned peaches. The taste? Ah, the best I can do to describe a really good fresh ripe mango is to say that it's like eating a perfect ripe peach while smelling a pine grove in spring. BUT a pine grove filled with flowering yellow jessamine. They are best chilled (they'll keep a week in the fridge), and lovers of mangoes greedily eat the flesh then suck the last bit of fiber from the stone. Messy behavior done

just like the lovers of boiled shrimp outside or on a porch.

In India, since recorded history, the mango has been used to make jams, sherbets, puddings. The varieties used are the plump, golden Alphonso, the thinner green Langra and the pink and yellow Romani which looks like a peach. Lesser varieties, more fibrous, are employed in hundreds of chutneys and pickles. Emotional arguments and even knife fights are common in Indian families over the "right" mango to use in whichever recipe handed down from grandmother Leyla. Monkeys love mangoes, so do birds. Hanuman, the Monkey God, is often depicted holding a mango. The mango groves (they're big shady trees) are natural bird sanctuaries, the delight of ornithologists.

Mango

In Malaysia there is a whole repertory of pickles called *atjar,* which accompany huge meals. To make a mango *atjar,* the flesh is sliced from the stone, soaked in salt water for several days, then dried. Garlic, fenugreek, turmeric and hellfire red peppers are cooked in oil, curry powder added; this mixture is spread between layers of the mango and put up in jars. Other more complicated versions include baby turnips, carrots, cauliflowers, whole lemons and a kind of light-skinned tangerine called a *naartje.*

Mangoes were growing in Florida in 1825, but not until 1889 when the Department of Agriculture began experiments in grafting did anybody take the fruit seriously as a possible commercial crop. This was the moment of history when sweet mango chutney, introduced into the West by British subjects returning from India, became a faddish taste everywhere. Here's an old Florida recipe from the turn of the century:

Key West Mango Chutney

3-4 pounds mangoes (mixed green and ripe)
1 pound currants
1 pound white raisins
1 pound brown sugar
3 or 4 pieces fresh ginger root
2 or 3 cups cider vinegar
¹/₄ ounce ground cloves
4 large toes garlic
¹/₄ ounce salt
3 onions
crushed red hellfire pepper to taste

Peel mangoes, slice into large cooking pot, add other ingredients; cook to desired consistency. Put into jars. This is delicious beyond belief, I mean it.

MARINADES

The original sense of the word *marinade* is "to pickle in brine," and referred to the fish preserved in this fashion. But since early times there have been precooking baths of wines or oils with various herbs or spices employed. Sylvia Humphrey, the well-known food editor, says, in an essay on this tradition: "Marinades, the beauty baths that touch up cheap cuts of meat and leftovers, have become popular when there are no longer any cheap meats. But the principle works even with expensive meats. Although marinades will make nearly anything tender, they also season foods in a most pleasant way. The most expensive of meats, the fillet of beef, can profit from a marinade, not to tenderize this tender-as-butter cut of meat, but to enhance the flavor of one of the most tasteless."

Basically, a marinade is a mixture of oil, acid (lemon, wine or vinegar), and spices and/or herbs, in which meat or fish soaks for a few hours or overnight. The acid breaks down the fibers, tenderizing the flesh, while the oil carries into it the savory seasonings.

Usually the marinade is strained and used to baste the flesh when it is later cooked, or at the end, to make gravy. However, in South America, the Caribbean, Charleston, and the Scandinavian countries, there is the seviche, prepared with corbina, bass, or salmon, where the marinade serves to "cook" the fish employed. The fillets of fish are simply put to soak in lime juice with paper-thin onion slices, or lemon, or a combination of lime, lemon and orange, or white wine vinegar, overnight. Dill goes with the salmon, cracked white peppercorns into most of the fish marinades. Wine is the essential ingredient in many of the baths for cheaper cuts of meat, but goes into dozens of marinades for different purposes. Left-over roast beef soaked in a good dry red wine before going into a stew with onions, celery and carrots, has a new and delightful flavor, nothing like yesterday's spare roast. Here is a classic *cooked* marinade:

Cooked Marinade for Venison

1 pint oil
1 cup minced onion
1 cup minced carrot
2 tablespoons minced shallots or green onions
1 crushed garlic clove
10 whole peppercorns
1 pint vinegar
2 bottles dry white wine
3 quarts water
3 or 4 stalks parsley
2 sprigs rosemary
2 sprigs thyme
2 bay leaves
2 cloves
2 tablespoons salt
4 tablespoons brown sugar

Heat the oil and sauté the vegetables a little, then add vinegar, wine, water, salt, peppercorns and sugar. Cook 20 minutes, let sit for a quarter of an hour, then strain and let it cool before marinating the haunch of venison or any very big cut of meat. The strained liquid is used to baste the cooking meat, afterwards with pan juices or drip-pings, it makes the gravy. The great Escoffier recommends for a leg of mutton such a marinade, but adds 1 tablespoon of juniper berries, 1 quart less water, 4 more cloves of garlic.

The consensus of opinion among great cooks everywhere is that seafoods require very little time in a marinade, delicate fish are actually precooked in this way, so that you can cut down the actual cooking time. Meat should be soaked in a pot close to its own size, with a weight employed to keep the meat submerged. The bigger the cut, the longer the soaking time. A 10-pound roast needs overnight. Remember that the strength of the vinegar increases with time, use much less for a long marinade. Wine is better. But *remember* that red wine often *darkens* pale meat or fish.

Yoghurt is another good tenderizing agent: marinate mutton or lamb chops in yoghurt with some garlic and dill. A won-derful marinade for a leg of lamb is thus: make slits all over the leg and insert slivers of raw garlic and onion. Smear the meat with a mixture of Dijon or Creole mustard, dry red wine, freshly ground black pepper, rosemary, a bit of brown sugar, a little salt, about 2 tablespoons pure olive oil. Turn and turn the meat in this mixture. Roast in hot

oven, basting with (unstrained) marinade. When meat is done, keep hot, and scrape up all the gunk in the pan, adding more wine and dash of bitters. Reduce to make your gravy. Have lots of crusty bread for dipping.

A wonderful hors d'oeuvre: Brussels sprouts cooked till just pierceable in water with sugar and salt. Cool, cut precisely in halves, sprinkle with lemon juice, and let sit a few minutes while you mix some yoghurt, prepared horseradish, dill, pinch of salt and pepper. Mix altogether and let stand. Sprinkle with chopped parsley or chives or both when ready to serve. A good French dressing can be employed to marinate any leftover cooked vegetables to transform them completely.

A welcome change from our usual tomato-y Creole barbecue sauces is this mixture for big shrimp, crayfish, lobster, and great for salmon: 1/3 cup soy sauce, 1/3 cup light oil such as safflower, 1/3 cup sherry, 1 tablespoon minced mild onion, 1/4 teaspoon ground ginger, pinch of mace, several pinches of dill. Marinate the seafood about half an hour at room temperature. Salmon takes 2 or 3 hours. Broil or grill. A whole salmon should be turned on the spit. Delicious.

Don't forget dessert marinades. Ripe peaches marinated in white port, chilled, served with either a sprig of mint or a slice of crystallized ginger, is a perfect sweet course. But after pork or lamb, try surprising your guests with tart apple slices soaked in lemon juice, sweet white wine and crème de menthe. The color is outrageous, the taste reassuring. If you really want to scare your in-laws, soak the apple slices in a blue-colored *triple sec,* or the purple liqueurs made from passion vine fruit such as *parfait amour.* Well, dears, have a good soak!

MARJORAM, OREGANO
Marjolaine, Dittany of Crete, Wurstkraut, Amaraco, Rigano, Persa, Persica, Mairan, Mejoran
(Origanum vulgare, O. marjorana, O. dictamus)

The botanical name of the family of plants known variously as sweet marjoram, wild marjoram, oregano, origan, and dittany of Crete—the most widely used of all culinary herbs, along with garlic, onion, and basil—is *Origanum* from the Greek *oros* (mountain) and *ganos* (joy) and, indeed, one of the English names for wild marjoram is Joy of the Mountains. A Latin myth describes Venus wandering on Mount Ida plucking wild marjoram to heal Aeneas' wounds, and how fashionable ladies took up the use of the herb, reserving it for care of the eyebrows and hair.

Well, myths aside, it is plain medical history that marjoram is highly antiseptic, inside or out, and that if your hair is coming out in clots in your comb, the best remedy is an infusion of marjoram patted into the scalp after a shampoo. It is a tonic for the scalp and perfumes the hair with a fresh, balsamic aroma.

The *origanum* family is native to the Mediterranean and has been used medicinally and as a culinary flavoring since before recorded history. Sweet marjoram, or knotted marjoram (from the knotted appearance of the terminal flower buds) has a thyme-like flavor, but is much more delicate (for which reason it is usually better added to cooked dishes toward the end of cooking) and the young leaves give a wonderful savor to green salads. But then it goes into marinades, stews, is sprinkled on grilled steaks, has endless kitchen uses. In its natural state in dry foothills and on rocky slopes of its native Portugal, the plant is a woody grey-green shrub often knee-high. Farther north it is more green, more tender. The flavor varies from location to location. The vivid marjoram, a slightly different botanical form is, in its strong-flavored Sicilian and South Italian manifestations, the powerful salty *oregano* which is part of every pizza and every tomato dish in the peninsula. To confuse cooks, there are some ten forms of *rigani* grown in Greece, especially *Origanum dictamus,* known as dittany of Crete, which flavors many a Greek grilled meat or fowl dish. Turkish, Greek, Italian, Spanish cooks often fling handfuls of dried leaves onto the coals when preparing such dishes: a thought for our own barbecuers. A jar of dried *origanum* is an ancient and inexpensive substitute for smelling salts. If you feel faint or have the vapours, just open the jar and inhale. Presto! All is well again.

For a superb vinegar, stuff a bottle with sweet marjoram leaves, boil up some white wine vinegar and pour over. When cool, cork. On first spring lettuce hearts, with a little pure olive oil, oh my! Or a salad of cooked first green beans. A truly great treat is to cook some steak fillets in butter in a heavy frying pan, turning once. Pour a half cup of good brandy over and set on fire. When flames die out, put steaks on hot dish, pour the pan liquids over, dust with salt, freshly ground black pepper, and a nice handful of marjoram leaves. Or try filling a baking dish with new potatoes in alternate layers with chopped fresh shallots, marjoram leaves, and pats of butter. Top with buttered breadcrumbs and bake slowly at 350 degrees for about an hour. Top with Parmesan cheese if you prefer.

One of the best picnic sandwiches I know is brown bread spread with cream cheese and a good sprinkle of chopped fresh marjoram leaves. In the garden any of the marjorams help cleanse the soil, repel pests, attract bees. Goats and sheep love marjoram, horses accept it, cows loathe it.

MELILOT
Sweet Clover, Trebol Dulce, Honigklee
(Melilotus officinalis)

This grows wild all over the United States and much of Europe. It is a rangy, untidy tall plant, with yellow pulse-like flowers. When dried, this herb has an altogether attractive smell of new-mown hay, and has been used to flavor herb beers and in certain colognes. It is related to Greek hay, or fenugreek, and has something in common with it. It is always used in dried form. Melilot is much used in wrapping, stuffing,

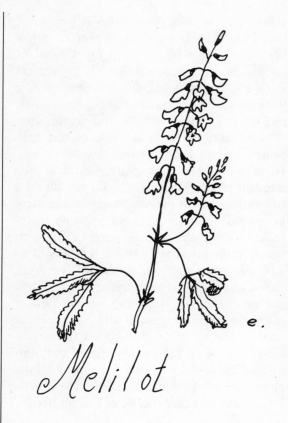

Melilot

or in marinades for rabbit meat, as well, giving a delicious flavor.

A blue flowering form, *Melilotus coerules,* is cultivated in the region of Glarus in Switzerland, and around New Glarus in Wisconsin. It is jealously guarded, not sold to the public. This is used to flavor *Schabzeiger* and in herb mixtures for other flavored cheeses, harvested before it flowers. The yellow melilot described above is often steeped with mints, bergamot, and other aromatics to make a herbal tea to treat colds, coughs, any bronchial discomfort. Yes, a common name for the plant is sweet clover, although not resembling what we know as clover.

THE MINTS
Several thousand varieties
(Mentha)

In a Greek myth, Menthe was a lovely nymph, daughter of a river god. Pluto saw her dabbling her feet in the stream and became enamored. His wife Proserpine promptly changed the nymph into the mint plant, to be trampled underfoot. The oldest known herbal, a Chinese compilation of some 5,000 years ago, mentions mint for many medicinal purposes. The Eber Papyrus, much older than the Book of Exodus, shows mints as one of the most important medicinal and culinary herbs. The Greeks liked to rub their arms with it after bathing, but in the myth of Zeus and Hermes going about disguised on earth and testing people for their sense of hospitality, when they dine with Philemon and Baucis, Baucis rubs the wooden table with mint before setting out supper.

Many an herb and culinary plant have fallen into disuse, especially since the industrial age, but mint has always kept its place. It gives the botanists fits. Mint cheerfully hybridizes and produces new varieties all over the globe. Roughly 2,000 have been described. The most remarkable is the minuscule plant known as crème de menthe: Mentha requieni is a plant about ½ inch high with white flowers the size of a pinhead. Crushed, it gives out a strong aroma of mint. All the many mints are used in cooking all over the globe, although the family of "horse" mints is more favored in the Orient than in the Occident. Peppermint *(Mentha piperita)* alone is not used fresh or dried: it is the source of oil of peppermint which flavors candies and other sweets. This oil is strong in menthol which causes a cooling sensation in the mouth. Peppermint, too, is an untraceable hybrid, probably, the offspring of water mint and spearmint. One of the most delightful mints to plant in your garden is *Mentha citrata,* which appears in plant catalogues as *eau de cologne mint,* orange mint, lavender mint, bergamot mint and St. Lawrence's mint. It has an orangey flavor, is delicious in tea or fruit cups, or just to rub and smell.

The ancient Romans invented the mint sauces for the rich meat course; in the third century they brought the idea to England, and there it is highly unusual to serve lamb or mutton without mint sauce. The French, staunchly suspicious of all which is not French, scorn the English mint sauce. Listen to Louis Lagriffe, a delightful Provençal writer on herbs and spices: "Very dear to the English, who consider it one of their glories, this sauce is so strong that it astonishes the palate and disconcerts the stomach of those who are not of the British Isles." He exaggerates, of course, and very good it is:

Mint Sauce for Lamb and Mutton

This is made in no time at all: put 2 tablespoons chopped mint or 1 of dried into a jar with sugar, vinegar, and hot water. Or use honey for sugar, lemon juice for vinegar. Lots of mint added if not thick enough after being shaken and left an hour. This is even better:

Mint Jelly

3 tablespoons chopped fresh mint
5 heaping tablespoons sugar
6 teacups best white wine vinegar
7 tablespoons water
1 packet of gelatin (or enough to make 1 pint of jelly)

Soak gelatin in 3 tablespoons heated water, add sugar, over this pour boiling vinegar and rest of water, add chopped mint. Pour into small glass jars to keep.

Mint Tart

This, cold, is one of the best hot weather dishes ever invented. Serve with cold ham or beef and ice cold beer, salad alongside or after.

1/2 pound cream cheese
6 eggs
3 tablespoons mint chopped fine
1 thinly sliced cucumber (don't peel)
short pastry

Line a pie-dish with a thin layer of pastry, then spread with cream cheese you've softened with a little cream or milk. Arrange cucumber slices. Break the eggs onto this, adding some freshly ground black pepper, a hint of cayenne, pinch of salt. Sprinkle the mint on top. Bake about half an hour at 350 degrees or until eggs are set and pastry golden.

And here's a delightful dessert:

Crystallized Mint Leaves

Choose clean perfect mint leaves. They must be perfectly dry. With a fine paintbrush, coat them with slightly beaten egg white, then dust all over with sugar. Put on wax paper in warm oven to dry, leaving oven door half open. Turn occasionally. When quite dry and glistening, put away in airtight container between wax paper. These are wonderful to decorate cakes, to put on top of a sherbet or ice cream, to serve along with crystallized ginger as part of the melon course. Both mint and ginger make all the *cucurbitae* (cucumbers, melon, squashes, etc.) digestible for people who have trouble with them.

MIRLITON
Vegetable Pear, Christophène, Pepinello, Choko, Chocho, Chayote
(Sechium edule)

This species of squash was a basic item of diet for the Aztecs and Mayas. It is a rampant vine which produces a heavy crop of large, pear-shaped, often ridgy fruits, some forms with prickly hairs. There are four main types, ranging in color from white to dark green. The flavor of the whitish flesh is very delicate and blends well with many other ingredients. The Spaniards took it to Spain, from whence it spread throughout the Mediterranean world. It is much appreciated in the South of France, on the Gulf Coast of the United States, in Algeria, Australia, Italy, and in recent years has become an important commercial crop.

Mirliton is the French name for a toy known in years past in the British Isles and America as a "kazoo" or "Tommy Talker." (A tube with a membrane over each end, and two holes on the cylinder; one hummed into one of the holes, a comical version of the sound came from the other hole.) A small reed flute also goes under this name. But a mirliton is also a kind of French pastry. Several species of climbing summer squash rejoice in the vague appellation "vegetable pear," as does one kind of cucumber. Probably the name *chayote* (derived from Aztec *chayotl*) is the easiest for universal recognition, BUT this squash has always been known in the South as *mirliton,* so there you are.

All of the plant is useful: the young shoots are boiled and served like asparagus, the leaves boiled up to make delicious greens, the enormous tuber looks and tastes like a yam. Our local shops have had them lately, piled up near avocado pears or guavas and usually with no identifying label, only a (high) price tag. They are imported from California or southern Florida. But they flourish right here. If you leave a ripe mirliton in a sunny window it will sprout, then you simply set it out in a sunny place and stand back. Unfussy about soil, tolerant of drought and flood, it is a much-neglected and completely delightful plant.

The best way to first taste them is to peel them, remove the big seed, slice thin and sauté in unsalted butter with a pinch of salt and some freshly ground black pepper. Or done the same way with sugar instead of salt, powdered mace instead of pepper, and a sprinkle of sugar. If you want to be fancy, heat a little cognac, set it on fire, pour over your sliced, sugared, sautéed mirlitons; a nice dessert. You can use them instead of apple or pear for a lovely pie. The Cajun style of stuffing them with shrimp is wonderful, although often too hotly flavored for my taste: I like to be able to taste some of the delicate flavor of the mirliton. I like to cut them in half, boil until pierceable, remove seed, dig out flesh, leaving layer of flesh inside skin, then mix cooked flesh, some chopped onion and green pepper sautéed until soft, cooked shrimp, bread crumbs, a little butter, a little cream, dash of mace, black pepper, salt to taste; stuff in mirliton, sprinkle a little Parmesan cheese on top, run into a 350 degree oven for a few minutes. Chill that dry white wine.

Here's a dessert from the Caribbean:

Chayote Relleno

3 large mirlitons
3 lightly beaten eggs
³/4 cup sweet sherry or white port
1¹/2 teaspoons ground nutmeg
1 cup seedless raisins
1 cup sugar
4 cups finely crumbled fresh pound cake or sponge cake
¹/2 cup slivered blanched almonds

Cut mirlitons in half, place in cold water, bring to boil, turn heat down, cook about 25 minutes. Drain. Cool. Remove seed, spoon out flesh, leaving a thin layer next to the skins. In mixing bowl, beat flesh until smooth, then beat in, little at a time, eggs, sherry, nutmeg. Add raisins, nutmeg, cake and beat again. This filling should have consistency of mashed potatoes and hold its shape. If need be, add more cake crumbs. Set oven at 350 degrees. Fill mirliton shells, heaping and rounding up the filling; top with almonds. Bake in low dish until tops

are golden, about 15 minutes. A delightful dessert. You can use macaroons, or you can add a little chopped candied ginger if you like.

A completely delectable summer first course is chilled cooked cubes of mirliton dressed with horseradish and fresh cream, salt and pepper, served in a lettuce heart sprinkled with lemon juice and slivers of baked ham. Another good cold dish: cooked mirliton halves filled with chopped cooked beef and a little crumbled bacon, with a mustardy mayonnaise.

Here's a dish from South Alabama which is sometimes known as North Haiti:

Mirliton Balls

4 mirlitons
¹/2 cup minced onion
¹/2 cup chopped green pepper
1 tablespoon vegetable oil

1 egg, slightly beaten
¹/₂ cup shredded cheddar cheese
1 garlic toe
³/₄ teaspoon ground cumin
a few rosemary leaves
1 tablespoon lemon juice
¹/₂ cup seasoned breadcrumbs
¹/₂ cup flour
dash salt
dash freshly ground black pepper
vegetable oil for frying

Cover mirlitons with water, simmer 30 minutes until tender. Drain. Remove seeds, dice and drain. Sauté onion and green pepper in oil until just tender. Mix well the egg, cheese, spices, lemon juice, crumbs. Put in mirlitons and mash with potato masher. Shape into balls the size of a small hen's egg. Now mix flour, salt, pepper. Dredge the balls. Put 2 to 3 inches of oil in Dutch oven or *sautoir,* heat well, fry balls until nicely browned. Drain on paper towels. If you like, sprinkle with chopped parsley, dill, or cilantro.

MISTLETOE
Birdline, Cross Wood, Mytyldene
(*Viscum album*)

This is an evergreen, truly parasitic plant, although members of the same plant family include normal trees and shrubs. When one of its sticky berries comes in contact with the bark of a tree, usually through the agency of some bird, especially certain thrushes who dote on these berries, it sends out a thread-like root which has a little flattened point at the end. This point pierces the wood and firmly roots itself. The Druids worshipped the mistletoe and at the beginning of the year, according to certain phases

Frankincense, Myrrh, Mistletoe & Merry Merry.

of the moon, the priests went to gather it with a golden sickle. They held that mistletoe protected them from all evil; their respect included the rare oak which harbored it.

The parasite is seldom found on oaks, never on pear trees, is common on apple and nut trees according to all botanical authorities, but our Gulf Coast mistletoes scoff this, and seem to prefer live oaks. The leaves and young twigs, collected before the berries form, and dried, have been used since before Christ as an anti-spasmodic, tonic, and narcotic, especially for treating epilepsy, and many nervous complaints.

In Norse mythology Balder, the God of Peace, was killed by an arrow made of mistletoe wood, but all the gods together restored him to life and placed mistletoe under the protection of the Goddess of Love, ordaining that anyone passing under it should receive a kiss. Little do some of our locals know that, in our holiday brawls, we are reenacting scenes from Scandinavian mythology. Don't tell everybody! There are *some* who might be made nervous! Kiss me!

MUSTARD SEEDS
(Sinapis alba, Brassica nigra, Brassica juncea, Brassica alba)

Mustard greens are a tasty dish and a great winter tonic in the South; the thin bread-and-butter sandwiches with mustard-and-cress seedlings are one of the glories of British food (these and a raised beef and kidney pie are enough in themselves to silence forever the carping about British food). But we're talking about mustard seeds now, a completely delightful seasoning almost unknown in our American cookery. Since there is much confusion about the names of the mustards we'd better stick to the botanical appellations.

The *Sinapis alba* is the plant of mustard-and-cress and the greens we love. (Even here, we forget to add a few *young* leaves to a salad of such as, say, the dreary iceberg lettuce, to sex it up.) In the States, this is called yellow mustard, everywhere else, white mustard. *Brassica nigra* is the strong mustard, the black mustard. *Brassica juncea* is the brown or Indian mustard, not nearly so pungent as the black, but a smaller plant easier to harvest mechanically, so it has replaced the black as a commercial crop. They all belong to the *Cruciferae* family (so-called because their blooms all have the typical four petals which resemble a Greek cross), a highly interesting plant group in that this is one of the rare orders which contain no poisonous members. Cousins of the mustards include sweet alyssum, candytuft, wallflowers, woad, the cresses, horseradish, and cauliflower.

Which takes me back to my theme: instead of making some gloppy cheese sauce next time you serve cauliflower or broccoli, try sprinkling them with lemon juice, pure olive oil, salt, freshly ground black pepper, and a good handful of mustard seed. So good! Try boiled turnip roots OR greens dressed this way. Whole mustard seed is not hot at all, just a nice nutty crunchy pungent thing, an aid to digestion, and delightful combined with other spices or herbs to dress any one of thousands of dishes. Try very thin cornbread cooked in an iron skillet with a generous sprinkle of sesame and mustard seeds on top. With leftover beef or mutton or ham, or as a side dish to anything curried, try this:

Lemon and Mustard Seed Chutney

4 medium onions, sliced
5 big lemons, seeded and chopped up
1 ounce salt
1 pint apple cider vinegar
1 ounce mustard seeds
¼ pound seedless raisins
1 scant teaspoon ground allspice
1 pound sugar
dash mace
1 or 2 cracked black peppercorns
plus a pinch of cracked coriander, if you like

Sprinkle the salt over the onions and lemons and leave for 12 hours. Add remaining ingredients, bring to boil, then simmer on very low fire for about 45 minutes. Put into sterilized jars and seal when cold.

A Surprising Fish Meunière

Put almost a quarter pound of butter in baking dish. When it's sizzling, put in fish fillets dipped in milk and coated with a few fine breadcrumbs. Sprinkle with very little salt, 2 teaspoons mustard seeds. Bake for 40 to 60 minutes at 350 degrees. If they get dry, toss in more butter. When serving, pour the butter over fish. Garnish with big peeled and seeded grapes.

The use of mustard in poultices is ancient and universal. A tea made from the infused seeds has universal praise for soothing persistent bronchitis and rheumatism.

For simple prepared mustard, NEVER make up your mustard powder for the table with vinegar! Use water! The volatile oils will be destroyed otherwise. That's why if you are using mustard in a cooked dish, it should be added last.

If, as I, you find pineapple on baked ham bores you silly, try taking the ham from the oven toward the end of cooking and removing the skin, scoring the fat, and (forget those cloves just one damn time!) smearing the thing with a thick *impasto* of freshly prepared mustard, brown sugar, a generous splash of Angostura bitters, and some powdered cloves, then mix in 1 small grated onion and heavy cream. Serve either hot or cold.

Be brave! Face up to the challenge . . . I mean, the joy . . . of the almost scorned mustard seed. Invent! Have fun!

One of the most delightful relishes on earth is this fresh tomato relish. It is an old Southern recipe and goes well with cold chicken or meat. But best of all, smear one slice of bread with homemade mayonnaise, the other with this relish (pile it on!). Then put in one lettuce leaf and some ham slices.

Press the sandwich well to make the relish penetrate the bread. Definitely Three Star, or rather, Three Yum.

Fresh Tomato Relish

Clean and dice a big green pepper, slice thin 1 sweet red or purple onion, ditto 1 big cucumber. Fling all into boiling water for five minutes, then blanche and drain. Mix ½ cup apple cider vinegar, 2 teaspoons salad oil, 2 teaspoons water, 2 teaspoons mustard seed, good dash cayenne pepper, good dash mace. Mix all well, then add 4 large ripe tomatoes diced, and mix well again. Chill before using.

Here's another forgotten Southern dish; so good:

Ham and Sweet Potato Pie

1½ pounds ham
1 pound sweet potatoes
1 big onion
½ pint onion soup
2 teaspoons mustard seed
2 tablespoons brown sugar
blop of butter
pinch salt
freshly ground black pepper

Slice ham, cut into pieces, put into baking dish. Peel sweet potatoes and onion, slice thin, arrange in layers over ham, sprinkling each layer with mustard seeds, salt and pepper. Pour in onion soup, sprinkle brown sugar on top, dot with butter, cover and bake at 350 degrees for about an hour. (Cold beef or lamb can also be used thus.)

Mustard is so easy to grow, the seed so easy to harvest, that any home gardener

mustard Seed

might find no better amusement than toying with the various blends and types. *Brassica alba* seeds are easy enough to find. Study the seed company catalogues; write your favorite gardening magazine. Plant them from late February to early April; put them in some corner of the garden you can control—they tend to take over.

Remember the young leaves, even a few, to liven up a green salad, but don't take too many. The mature leaves boil up for greens, or can be added to turnip, beet, kale or any other greens for a savory mess.

Black mustard needs more space; it grows three or four feet tall. White mustard stops at about a foot and a half. Once they flower, watch for the seed pods. Black's are smooth, only half an inch long, with some twenty rust-colored seeds. White's are curved and hairy, over an inch long with fewer seeds. The pods develop in roughly ten weeks. They pop open when ripe, so watch them: harvest when they are about to let go, and spread on a cloth to ripen in the sun. When

they are brittle, open the pods and collect the seeds.

Now is when the fun begins. You can do hundreds of different prepared mustards, according to what dishes you are serving or what follies fuzz your head that day. I use mortar and pestle and elbow grease to grind mustard seeds, but a nut and spice grinder or an electric blender will serve nicely. The prepared mustard powder we buy has the husk of the seed removed and the kernel milled. But I like the flavor and grittiness of home-ground mustard better.

When you mix up the powdered mustard, hot liquids kill off some of the volatile oils, giving a sweeter mustard. Cold liquids help retain the more pungent flavors. With roast pork or pork chops I like, for instance, mustard powder mixed with a little ruby port wine and a handful of seedless white raisins and served like that, or used to flavor a salad of tart apples. If your mustard comes out too hot in taste, add a pinch of sugar, some olive oil and one clove of grated garlic.

A good prepared mustard for boiled meat, cabbage and potatoes (an underestimated meal, served with the right garnishes) is made with beer as the liquid, a little ground mace and cayenne to flavor. Make a green mustard for boiled shrimp by mixing your powder with white wine and adding chopped tarragon, parsley and capers with a small pinch of sugar. Or mix your mustard powder with red wine vinegar and flavor with thyme and a dash of bitters. Make up your private fantasy mixtures in small quantities; they begin to fade in flavor after about two weeks. But you can always add what's left to soups, sauces, stews, pickles . . . and some of the best salads ever are based on cleaning out the icebox and the last of an herb mustard.

A few formulas:

Herb Mustard

Grind together 2 tablespoons mustard seed with 1 teaspoon each of chervil, parsley, tarragon. Add 1 tablespoon pure oil and 1 of cider vinegar. Mix well into paste, let sit an hour before using.

Hellfire Mustard

Mix ½ cup ground mustard seeds with 3 tablespoons cold water; let hatch for 15 minutes. Mix in ¼ teaspoon each of allspice, cayenne pepper, salt; 1 teaspoon freshly ground black pepper, 1 tablespoon black molasses, 3 tablespoons cider vinegar. Mix well; let sit a bit.

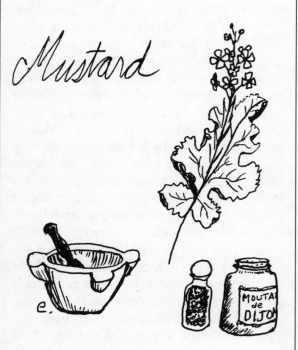

Wine Mustard

Put ¼ cup whole mustard seed in ¼ cup wine vinegar and ¼ cup white wine. Steep overnight. Then put in 2 teaspoons tarragon, 1½ teaspoons salt, good dash freshly ground black pepper. Blend in blender until seeds are coarsely chopped. Or, to put cooked beets into another category, mix up some mustard powder with a bit of white wine, add a pinch of salt, powdered mace and a dot of powdered cloves, then mix in 1 small grated onion and enough heavy cream to make a thick sauce for the beets. Nice color; serve hot or cold.

Try mustard seed on buttered new potatoes and make your guests guess what they are. Add a few seeds to any green salad. Crack a few and mix with mayonnaise for sandwiches. Sauté hard apple or sand pear slices in ham or bacon fat and sprinkle with mustard seed to go with grits, fried grits, waffles or pancakes alongside sausages, bacon or pork chops.

MYRRH
(Commiphora myrrha)

Myrrh is a pleasant natural incense and we all have smelt it in church censers or in perfumed church candles. It is obtainable in little lumps for use in sachets and to burn as incense, but also in powdered form for use in many poultices, gargles, ointments, and tooth powders. The Biblical myrrh is quite likely a derivative of a wholly unrelated plant, the rock-rose (*Cystis*). If you want to whip up a sublime incense for your Christmas party, blend together 2 ounces myrrh, 10 ounces frankincense, and 5 ounces of benzoin and burn on charcoal embers.

NASTURTIUM
Indian Cress, Peruvian Cress
(*Tropaeolum majus*)

Here we have another entry for the Department of Total Confusion, equalled only by such a case as the confusion between the pot marigold *(calendula)* and the *tagete*, called marigold: the first is used to color and flavor various stews and cheeses most deliciously, the second is inedible and quite stinking. But with watercress and nasturtium the confusion in nomenclature is not so deadly, for they have almost identical flavors and can be used in much the same way.

The proper botanical name of watercress is *Nasturtium officinalis*, derived from the Latin *nasus tortus*, or "convulsed nose" from the pungent sinus-clearing flavor of the plant. The common garden flower known as nasturtium is thus known because it smells and tastes like watercress (proper *Nasturtium*), but this red, yellow, orange favorite is really botanically known as *Tropaeolum majus*, a name bestowed by Jesuit botanists who brought it from Peru in the seventeenth century, and imagined it as a "trophy of arms" — the buds like spears, the leaves like shields, the flowers like helmets, the seeds like calthrops. This New World exotic quickly became known as nasturtium because of its flavor, and we'll call it that for the rest of this essay.

It is one of the least fussy of plants, actually preferring poor soil. Overly fertilized, it produces fewer blooms. Every bit of the plant is edible: stems, leaves, flowers and seeds. But you must find the old-fashioned single form of the flower, with its single flowers and peppery smell. There are double-ruffled, double-puffled, doubly-obscene modern hybridized forms in which sweet scents have been bred: to hell with them! If you pry a bit, you can still buy seeds of the culinarily acceptable older forms. The pickled green seeds have, since the eighteenth century, been used as a substitute for capers, but the taste is really different, and just as delicious.

Pick the green seeds before they're too hard, wash them, dry them, put them into strongly salted vinegar. Pungent and good with salads or in a sauce for any of the mild white fishes. If you wish a milder flavor, say to put into an omelet, then pickle the flower buds in the same way. There's no prettier salad than one of garden greens (not the indestructible iceberg variety) and nasturtium flowers simply dusted and blown off and plopped right into the bowl, with

e.

Nasturtium

classic dressing of oil, lemon, salt, pepper: no glop, thank you. If you want a treat of rarity comparable to nightingales' tongues, allow each dinner guest a single thin piece of bread spread with Philadelphia cream cheese on which is sprinkled the nectar-bearing spurs of the nasturtium flower. Don't laugh; try it.

A highly delectable vinegar is made by packing nasturtium flowers into a bottle, then covering them with a vinegar flavored with a little shallot, garlic, red pepper and salt. If you want an unusual and good tea sandwich, chop together nasturtium stems and the delicate inner leaves of celery and put on bread spread either with Philadelphia cream cheese or a homemade mayonnaise flavored with onion or garlic juice.

The flowers are pretty as edible garnish with any summer dish, nice with sliced cucumbers or chicken salad. But we have not spoken of another of this agreeable plant's virtues: it repels many insect pests, and if you plant it in a circle around your roses, tomatoes, or fruit trees, you'll find it highly effective. If you edge your vegetable beds with nasturtiums, chives, marigolds *(tagetes)* and basil, you'll be quite amazed at the absence of pests.

NOYAU
Seeds of various small fruits

Noyau is a French word meaning the stone of a small fruit, and the after-dinner drinks which make up the class of *crèmes de noyaux* are infinite, manufactured from cherry, peach, apricot or almond pits. Europe produces a great many; Martinique

some of the best. The kernels are pounded and steeped in powerful alcohol, then redistilled to get rid of the cyanide. If not done properly, the resulting cordial can be very harmful in quantity, as are so many nice things in this life.

Old cookbooks up to World War I often called for *noyau* or *noyeau*, especially in recipes for cookies, cakes, candies, sometimes in marinades or for sweet-and-sour dishes. The flavor is often similar to almond essence, but much more delicate and interesting. If I were trying an old recipe calling for this, I'd use almond essence with a few drops of pure rose water and two or three drops of lemon juice.

NUTMEG
(Myristica fragrans)

The *myristica* is the only case of two major spices produced from the same source. This beautiful, slow-growing, big evergreen tree only flowers when eight years old, produces an apricot-like fruit containing a seed wrapped in a brilliant scarlet husk. The husk dries to a yellowish brown color and falls into fragments known as "blades of mace." The seed kernel, dried, is the nutmeg.

Both flavorings were known to the ancient world but came comparatively late to Europe and the West. During the sixth century A.D. the Arab traders brought it to Byzantium (Constantinople), and by the end of the twelfth century, mace and nutmeg were much appreciated in Europe. Luxury products, naturally, for the wealthy.

Ferdinand Magellan set out in 1519 to

discover a direct route to the Spice Islands (Moluccas) under the patronage of the Spanish crown. But he was killed on an island which is now part of the Philippines, and only one out of his five ships, with a handful of crew, returned over a year later. The emaciated sailors, toward the end, ate the leather bindings and knots in the riggings and gnawed at the nutmegs which were part of their cargo. They discovered that huge quantities of nutmeg made them "high" and led to hallucinations, but also brought on headaches and stomach discomfort. Four centuries later, we read in *The Autobiography of Malcolm X*, how prisoners in jail with him ate quantities of nutmeg for the same reasons. To get "high"; put their problems out of their minds.

The *myristica* tree seems to grow well only in the Moluccas, but in the period from 1796 to 1802 when the British were occupying the Moluccas, an Englishman managed to smuggle a few seeds to the island of Grenada, the only other place on earth it flourishes.

Producing mace and nutmeg is a long and problematic process. Only after seven or eight years is the tree productive. A male plant will fertilize up to twenty females but nobody can tell a male from a female until they flower. So, at a certain point, dozens of male trees are cut down, after being nurtured for almost a decade.

"I have a little nut tree / Nothing will it bear / But a silver nutmeg and a golden pear . . ." says a children's rhyme: the silver nutmeg probably refers to the little pocket grater with compartment for a nutmeg that fashionable English lords and ladies carried in the eighteenth century, fashioned in ivory and/or silver, some decorated with brilliants.

La mode, snobbism, the perversities of fashion! Connecticut was long known as the Nutmeg State because the Yankee peddlers who came south in warm weather spent their winters by the fireplace whittling imitation nutmegs from a kind of pine knot which had a perfume called *pinene*, which might lead the innocent to think their fake was really a nutmeg. In 1974 a lady in Beaufort, S.C., cleaned out an old cupboard belonging to her family since time was. Lodged behind a drawer she found a Yankee peddler fake nutmeg, so had it mounted on a silver chain to wear as a conversation piece.

We know the nutmeg mostly as a flavoring for sweets of all kinds: cookies, cakes, puddings, sherbets, etc., and, of course, sprinkled over the ubiquitous eggnog, but nutmeg is a kind of secret ingredient in many Italian sauces, in meat and vegetable dishes in many cuisines.

Nutmeg is less adamant than most spices and so can perk up hundreds of dishes with its gentle muskiness. Try a meat loaf made of ground beef and pork, containing chopped parboiled onions and sweet peppers and a nice dash of nutmeg.

Or boiled brown rice with dried apricots soaked in wine, a bit of garlic, white raisins, and a nice sprinkle of ground nutmeg. Good with chicken or ham. Any cooked apple dish screams for nutmeg, and pears baked with honey and nutmeg are very fine. Personally I wouldn't eat a turnip root unless it is diced, steamed, dressed with unsalted butter, a grain or two of salt, and a kind sprinkle of freshly ground nutmeg.

Like pepper, nutmeg must be ground at the moment of use. The dead dust sold in tins and bottles is just that . . . dead. I keep close to the stove a glass jar with a little hand grater and four or five nutmegs at all times.

PAPRIKA
Pimentòn, Piment doux d'Espagne, Piment de Hongerie

There are two families of plants which are known in English as "pepper." The vine which produces black pepper, white pepper, and green peppercorns is not our subject here. Nor is the new craze among French chefs: pink peppercorns. *These*, not peppers, are from a third unrelated family of plants and we shall discuss them later. Paprika is of the family of annual plants which includes the bell pepper, the Tabasco pepper, the cayenne pepper and the yellow Nepal pepper.

This *Capsicum* family originated in South America. Many varieties still grow wild there, but botanists are undecided about the ancestors of the cultivated peppers, since they were cultivated long before Columbus hit these shores. Many experts think all of them are descended from one simple original wild species, which became, in cultivation in different localities and by selection, a complete gamut.

Most people are not acquainted with any of the peppers, whether the black or red variety, for most ready-ground powders offered in shops are the deadest of dead dust. Paprika became the national spice of Hungary once introduced there; it is the basis for all their famous goulash and spiced chicken dishes. India nowadays produces well over a quarter of a million tons of red peppers, whether the paprika or chili type. As Tom Stobart says in his great book on herbs and spices, "One wonders how they managed in former days."

Paprika (the name is Hungarian) is a bright red powder made from a pointed variety of pepper which is pungent but not as fiery as chilis. The brown powder often sold under this name is just plain-out stale. Spain produces a great deal of *pimentòn*, a kind of paprika which is naturally less red and more brownish, but it is nothing like the real Hungarian product, which has a sweetish and mild bitterness unlike anything else. It contains an amazing amount of vitamin C, far more than any citrus fruit.

The Hungarian Nobel Prize winner, later naturalized American, Professor Albert Szent-Györgyi, discovered in paprika a new group of substances called bioflavonoids, which contribute enormously to the health of the capillary system. If you want to taste the delights of red paprika, which comes in a piquant and milder form, you can write to *Paprika Weiss*, 1546 Second Avenue, New York City, and get a catalogue from one of the most remarkable food shops on earth, for they import it and do mail orders. Keep paprika in the icebox; a multitude of little beasts love it, too, and will breed in it.

Here is a good introductory dish:

Stuffed Flounder Fillet

2 pounds flounder fillets
1¹/₂ pounds crabmeat
4 slices bread
¹/₂ cup milk
3 tablespoons unsalted butter
¹/₂ cup chopped onion
1 clove minced garlic
¹/₂ cup chopped celery
1 teaspoon paprika
2 lightly beaten eggs
salt and freshly ground pepper

Soak bread in milk; squeeze dry. Melt butter over moderate heat and sauté onion, garlic and celery. Add bread with remaining ingredients to skillet. Stuff your fillets, sandwich style, fix with toothpicks. Bake about 25 minutes at 350 degrees, basting with ¹/₂ cup melted butter, ¹/₄ cup lemon juice, ¹/₄ cup minced parsley and more paprika to your taste.

Welsh rabbit is Something Else if you toss in a scant teaspoon of paprika, or rub your roast with the spice before putting in the oven: People Will Talk. Ditto chicken and turkey. If you give out of ideas for Sunday night, cook up seven or eight ounces of flat noodles and dress them with unsalted butter, 1 teaspoon grated lemon peel, a scant ¹/₂ cupful of raisins and one heaping teaspoon sweet paprika. Cover with grated Swiss cheese and bake about 23 minutes at 350 degrees or until top is nicely browned.

This is a classic favorite:

Veal Paprika

2 pounds cubed veal
4 tablespoons unsalted butter
2 cups sliced mild onions
¹/₂ cup dry white wine
1 tablespoon hot paprika
1 cup sour cream
fresh dill or, in extremis, dried
freshly ground black pepper
salt

Heat butter in skillet till it froths up, add onions and veal. Cook about 15 minutes, stirring casually, or until veal loses pink look. Add wine and paprika. Cook, covered, over modest fire, for some 45 minutes. Add other ingredients. Salt to taste. Sprinkle with dill before serving. Babs, where's my drooling bib?

PARSLEY
(Petroselinum crispum, P. hortense, P. sativum)

Poor old parsley! The most familiar, the most used, the least eaten. The pretty curly leaves decorate countless plates, only to be pushed aside rather than nibbled, yet often the parsley has more value than the dishes being decorated. Parsley is poisonous to most birds, and lethal to the parrot tribe, but it is wholly beneficial to the human race and other animals wise enough to eat it. Both wild hares and domestic rabbits seek it out and devour it avidly. Sheep like it; if they eat enough, it prevents foot rot. Parsley is as rich in vitamin A as most grades of cod liver oil, contains three times as much vitamin C as oranges. The valuable element of parsley, apiol, was discovered in 1849; it is highly valuable in treating malarial dis-

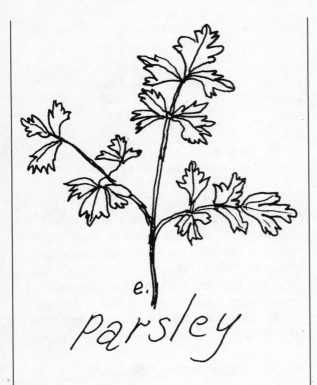

e.

parsley

There are many varieties of parsley, some curly, some flat-leaved. Around the Mediterranean, cooks feel that the flat-leaved variety has more flavor, although the curly leaved is also grown for decoration. One reason that English and American cook-gardeners prefer the curly has to do with one of Mother Nature's nastier little jokes. That poisonous weed, Fool's Parsley, has a remarkable way of turning up in beds of parsley: it looks just like flat-leaved parsley, although slightly darker, and gives out a nasty odor when crushed. So better have curly, and the difference is clear. Another form of parsley is grown in southern Italy, and has thick stems which are eaten like celery. Most European cookery is unthinkable without parsley. It goes into many famous sauces: *tartare, vinaigrette, ravigote, maître d'hotel* butter, etc.

One of the great secrets in French cookery, the thing which adds that special something to unnumbered soups, for instance, is the addition of a *persillade*—finely chopped parsley and shallots—toward the end of the cooking. What is called Japanese or Chinese parsley, please remember, is the green leaf of the coriander plant, nothing to do with the parsley tribe. Also known as cilantro.

Parsley seed is notoriously slow to germinate. Soaking the seed in warm water before planting is a help. So is pouring a kettle of boiling water over the ground where you are going to plant seeds. Plants must be so spaced that one does not touch another. In warmer climates it is best to plant one lot in April, one in September, to assure a year-long supply. Once dedicated to Persephone, parsley was later attributed to St. Peter, who succeeded the pagan Charon as guide to the souls of the dead.

orders, any ailment of the kidneys; apiol is a part of many remedies for dropsy and jaundice.

Parsley has been revered since the dimmest past. The Greeks considered that it sprang from the blood of the hero Archemorus, the forerunner of Death (his nurse carelessly placed him in a bed of parsley where he was devoured by serpents). Regarding it as the "herb of oblivion," they decorated tombs with the herb. But there were happier uses. Homer tells us that the warriors fed their chariot horses on parsley. Theocritus writes:

At Sparta's palace, twenty beauteous maids,
The pride of Greece, fresh garlands crown'd
* their heads*
With hyacinths and twining parsley dress'd,
Graced joyful Menelaus' marriage feast.

PEANUT
Goober
(Arachis hypogaea)

Known under several hundred names, including arachide, cacahuete, earth almond, earth pistachio, Erdnuss, gedda, goober, goober pea, grass nut, ground nut, mani, monkey nut, nguba, pindar, and turrabele, etc.

In the United States, the peanut is thought of as a snack (whether roasted or as peanut butter) or as component of sweets, but in many parts of the world it is a highly important part of everyday diet, because of its high protein content (26 percent of its weight; it is topped only by the soybean, with 36 percent) and because of its high yield per acre.

As in any discussion of flavor, individual taste and smell varies to an unlikely degree. Alexandre Dumas, the gourmand author of *The Three Musketeers*, claimed that peanuts taste like liquorice (and bring on headaches and a sore throat). The legume originated in Brazil; Portuguese slave traders introduced the peanut into West Africa in the early 1500s, from there it made its way to Charleston in the early eighteenth century. The Portuguese describe peanuts as tasting like almonds.

A French gastronomic dictionary says they taste like toasted *brioche* and says peanut butter should be used to spread on gingerbread! India grows the greatest quantity, but West African cookery boasts the greatest variety of dishes prepared from the legumes. Rachel Carson, in *Silent Spring*, adds a sinister note about peanuts grown in the South, where they are often raised in alternation with cotton, which is treated with a carcinogenic chemical, benzene hexachloride. The subsequent crop of peanuts absorbs the toxic chemical. If you find peanuts with a musty and unmistakable chemical taste, spit 'em out quick!

The Egyptians love *foul sudani*, a peanut soup. In Indochina and Malaysia there are countless dishes using whole nuts, ground nuts or peanut butter. The late great inventor, Dr. George Washington Carver, once demonstrated the peanut's versatility to a group of Alabama businessmen when he served a grand banquet based entirely on peanuts: peanut soup, ersatz "chicken" made of peanuts, peanuts used as a vegetable, salad with peanut oil dressing, a peanut "cheese," peanut ice cream, cookies, and at the end, coffee made of roasted peanuts.

The Democratic convention which nominated Jimmy Carter displayed huge signs: "Make the peanut our national tree," revealing a highly erroneous knowledge of natural history on the part of the conveners. The peanut is a legume, and might be mistaken for a bean plant in its early stages. But the way it fruits is unique in the plant world. Five to six weeks after it's planted, flower buds appear. They are perfect (that means having both pistil and stamens; they are self-fertile) and pollination occurs *before* the flower has opened. The flowers wither soon after opening and the ovary develops a long tendril called a "peg" which bends toward the earth and buries itself. The embryo on the tip of this tendril becomes two or three nuts encased in a thick fibrous pod. In the fall, the whole plant is dug up and turned upside in the sunshine to dry. When the nuts rattle in the pod they are picked, and the pods stored in mesh bags for two or three weeks' curing in a warm, dry place.

There are some fifty varieties, with wide variation of size, number of nuts or pods, and color, which ranges white to cream to brown to red to variegated. All the great gourmets of the world use *huile d'arachide* (peanut oil) for fried dishes where a neutral flavored oil is required. For preparing some of the delicate mushrooms, for instance, the taste of olive oil would be all wrong. For certain salads, the great French chefs prefer peanut oil to olive oil. Peanut oil is practically flavorless.

In the United States we have been notoriously and abjectly neglectful of the peanut in cookery. Yet one of the most delightful dishes on earth is chicken marinated in lemon juice and garlic, then thoroughly dried, dipped in a mixture of bacon fat and unsalted butter, then in coarsely ground peanuts before deep frying or roasting on the barbecue. Most cookbooks carry a peanut soup recipe. If you want something very good try an Indochinese version of kebabs, which may be of lamb or beef. This is the sauce:

Satey Sauce

Melt about ½ stick of butter, then add a scant 2 tablespoons of cider vinegar and 4 bouillon cubes (3 chicken, 1 beef). Mix well over low fire until all is melted. Add a scant tablespoon of dark brown sugar little by little, tasting as you go. You don't want to make it too sweet; you want to keep the salty taste. In this case, the ideal is sweet-sour-salty. Add one finely minced big onion, two minced garlic toes, a very very small pinch of thyme, a nice pinch of powdered ginger and of flaked red hellfire peppers. Cook until onion is soft, then remove from fire and add one cup of peanut butter, mix-

ing all well. Pour in any drippings from meat you are serving, if there is any. Heat gently, then pour this sauce over your chunks of kebab meat and serve with plain boiled rice to which you've added lemon juice. This is very fine.

PENNYROYAL
(Mentha pulegium)

Here we have another example of a pot herb which has almost completely lapsed in usage. Serious herb gardeners include it in their collection of mints, but save for certain old-fashioned cooks in Provence and rural England, few use it in flavoring stuffings and sausages or in marinades for pork or lamb. The plant is the *Menta romana* which goes into the famous Roman artichoke dish, *carciofi alla romana*.

I tried it in the spirit of research, using a few leaves, with thyme, in sausage patties, and with celery, bacon, and marjoram to flavor a stuffing for chicken, and thought it delightful and novel. A tea of pennyroyal with honey has been considered a cure for whooping cough since antiquity, and it has often been cited as a great relief for asthma sufferers.

Walafrid Strabon, the Abbot of Reichenau in the Middle Ages, loved the mint family and recognized its polymorphous character, with its more than one thousand hybrids and countless intermediate forms. He wrote that to know all the mints would be the same as knowing how many fish there are in the Red Sea and how many sparks when Mount Etna is in eruption. But in his own garden list he put pennyroyal first, under its French name of *menthe pouliot*, also known as

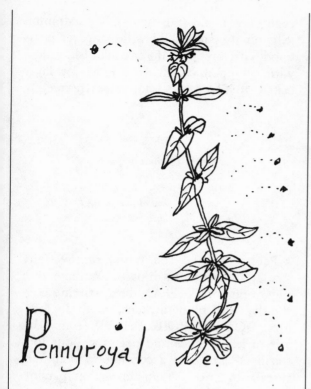

Pennyroyal

St. Lawrence's Herb, as *fretillet*, and as marsh mint. The English common name is Pennyroyal, though country folk still call it Run-by-the-Ground and Lurk-in-the-Ditch. Pudding Grass, too, referring to its old use in savory puddings to accompany roast goose.

A famous stuffing for suckling pig was made of pennyroyal, pepper, and honey. For most gourmets, nowadays, the flavor is too pronounced; it is the strongest flavored of all the mints.

It was Pliny who named the plant *pulegium*, from its power of driving away fleas, and this aspect of the plant's usefulness has been employed unabatedly since remotest times until now. Some village churches in rural England have beds of pennyroyal near the church door so that churchgoers can take a few sprigs to rub their ankles during services, especially in the hotter time of summer when the fleas proliferate.

When woolen carpets are taken up for summer, a sprinkling of cracked black peppercorns and pennyroyal leaves will protect them from moths, fleas and whatever beasts, as well as make them give off a delightful perfume when they are relaid in autumn.

Pennyroyal is a creeping mint with smallish leaves and purple flowers, slow to establish itself, but sturdy and prolific at last, especially if kept watered and if in a good rich soil. Easy from cuttings. It will grow well in shade or half-shade. If you are one of the increasing numbers who distrust chemical sprays, you might soak pennyroyal and horehound branches in water to make a simple spray against fleas, ants, etc. And try a tiny pinch in an omelet with onions and green pepper, or in meat loaf or sausage patties or in a stuffing for fowl. You'll be surprised.

PERSIMMON, DATE PLUM
(Diospyros)

The botanical name comes from *Dios*, Jove, and *pyros*, grain, alluding to the edible fruits. The persimmon, of the ebony family of trees, is a large genus of some two hundred evergreen and deciduous trees and shrubs. In China and Japan, the kinds with large edible fruits have been cultivated for at least a thousand years.

Introduced into Europe in the early eighteenth century, they have been important food crops in southern France and in Italy since early in the nineteenth century. The wild American variety, so beloved of opossums, was first described by English naturalists in 1699. The Southeast American Indians employed the wild forms in many sweet dishes; the larger cultivated Oriental form was introduced into the southern states about 1870 and is usually grown in home gardens. The wild form is seldom cultivated, but vast quantities are harvested from wild trees. *However,* from 1863, one Logan Martin, an enterprising young southern Indiana farmer who took buckets of wild persimmons to market in Louisville, Kentucky, had such success with them that he began to raise the fruit commercially.

For over forty years "Persimmon" Martin shipped 2,000 to 2,500 gallons of wild persimmons from his hometown to big city markets, including New York City. There is even a persimmon festival now in Mitchell, a town not far from Martin's farm. Mrs. Dymple Green, nowadays, processes every year 25,000 cans of persimmon pulp for customers throughout the nation. I feel I should inform you that her business is called Dymple's Delight and is located at Rt. 4, Box 5, Mitchell, IN 47446.

The Indians taught the early settlers to make persimmon bread and persimmon beer. John Bradbury, an Englishman exploring the Missouri territory in 1809, described being entertained by an Osage chief who served him a delightful "gingerbread" which turned out to be a concoction of yellow corn meal and wild persimmon. Persimmon loses its distinctive taste when cooked, but imparts to breads or cakes a wonderful quality and texture. When the Grand Duke Alexei of Russia turned up in Topeka, Kansas, in 1872, the locals got together and served up a grand banquet with 109 dishes, and it is reported that the one the Grand Duke most preferred was roasted year-old 'possum with persimmon jelly on the side. This following recipe is good with any 'possum or pork dish, mixed with whipped cream as a filler for layer cakes, or served over vanilla ice cream:

Persimmon Jam

3 cups persimmon pulp
2 cups sugar
1 tablespoon fresh lemon juice
1/2 teaspoon grated lemon rind
slight dash mace and powdered ginger

Peel and seed the fruit, remove any stringy filaments, mash pulp. Combine with sugar and cook over low heat, stirring constantly, until pulp thickens, about 15 minutes. DO NOT BOIL. Remove from heat. Stir in lemon juice and peel and pour into sterilized jars, seal according to manufacturer's directions. Remember that persimmon must always be cooked in stainless steel, glass, or enameled ware, since the tannin in the fruit tends to turn it black in any corrosive metal.

Persimmon Pudding

2 cups persimmon pulp
2 cups flour
2 teaspoons baking powder
2 teaspoons cinnamon
1/4 teaspoon baking soda
2 cups sugar
2 well-beaten eggs
1/2 cup melted unsalted butter
1 cup cold heavy cream
pinch salt

Heat oven to 350 degrees, have ready a floured pan about 2 by 9 by 13 inches. Sift flour, baking powder, cinnamon, salt, and soda together. In a big bowl, mix together the fruit pulp, sugar and eggs. Add dry ingredients and stir until well blended; stir in melted butter. Pour batter evenly into pan. Bake about 40 minutes, or until center of pudding springs back when pressed. Beat cream in chilled bowl. Cut pudding into squares and serve warmish or at room temperature with whipped cream, which you can sweeten to taste.

'Possum's Passion

2 cups persimmon pulp
3 tablespoons sugar
3 tablespoons fresh lemon juice
pinch powdered ginger
pinch powdered mace
1½ cups heavy cold cream

Combine fruit pulp, sugar and lemon juice. In chilled bowl, whip cream until peaks form, fold into fruit mixture. Pour into 1-quart mold and freeze. Remove from freezer a good half hour before eating. (The delicate flavor of the persimmon is intensified if this cream is left a few days in the freezer.) Very thin crisp lemon wafers go well with this.

The persimmon is winey-sweet and truly pleasing when ripe; before, its acid quality puckers the mouth and puts lots of folks off it forever. The truth is, this fruit takes longer to ripen than any other. Long after the leaves have fallen from the boughs, the fruits are there waiting for the autumn sun to sweeten them. The myth says they are ready after the first frost. No. They're ready when they drop from the tree. That's why, in old Southern gardens, on a chilly November morn, you'd see Gramps shaking trees while the grandchildren held the corners of a sheet to catch the beauties that fell.

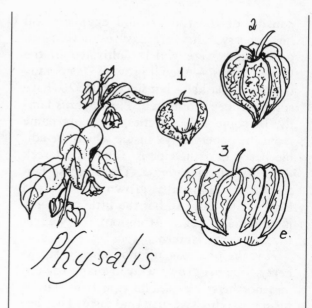

Physalis

PHYSALIS
Bladder Cherry, Cape Gooseberry, Jamberberry, Tomatillo, Husk Tomato, etc.

When are green tomatoes not green tomatoes? When they're tomatillos, widely grown in Mexico and Central America to make "green tomato" sauce, and tomatillo sauce.

When are cherry pies totally devoid of cherries? When they're made of the delicious ground cherry.

When is strawberry jam as remote from strawberries as the Moral Majority from Versailles? When it's made of strawberry tomatoes.

When is a Chinese lantern neither Chinese nor lantern? When the bladder cherry is grown for its ornamental bright red calyx beloved of dried flower arrangers.

What we're talking about is a fascinating family of edible fruits, mostly annuals, cousins of the tomato and eggplant and huckleberry. They are easy as nothing to grow, once were widely cultivated in the United States — they'll grow in every state, but not in Alaska — but since the 1920s have somehow been forgotten. The *Physalis* family, of some 100 varieties, takes its name from the papery calyx inside which the edible berry or fruit ripens. From the Greek word for bladder, *physa*. The Chinese lantern form is usually grown for the red lantern-like calyxes, but the little red berry is edible and good. Attention: DON'T eat the calyx, the lantern.

Physalis pruinosa (ground cherry, strawberry tomato) grows wild in many eastern and northern states. The ripe fruit have a most satisfying sweetish acid taste. They are wonderful raw, as is, without anything, good as accompaniment to strong cheeses (Gorgonzola, Limburger, etc.), and people who eat this fruit in pies, jams, preserves, in sweet-sour sauces for spareribs, in chutneys or ketchups to go with game become quite addicted. The taste is finally somehow between the ripe tomato and ripe strawberry. *Physalis ixocarpa* is the tomatillo beloved by our Latin neighbors who use it to make their famous *salsa verde* (not to be confused with the Italian sauce called the same) and to can it as "green tomatoes." This form can be eaten raw, when it is yellow, soft, and of a rather bland flavor. Much better used green. You grow them just like any tomato.

Salsa Verde

2 mild green chilies,
fresh or canned, seeds removed
4 medium tomatillos, husked
1 peeled crushed garlic toe
1 sprig of cilantro
pepper to taste

Place chilies in heavy pan over medium heat, turning now and then until skins begin to blister. Put them in a closed brown paper bag for 10 minutes as skins loosen, thus insulated.

Peel, remove pith, rinse under running water. Simmer tomatillos in a little water until tender. Either with masher or blender, reduce chilies, tomatillos, garlic and pepper to coarse consistency, not purée. Heat 2 tablespoons best oil in skillet. Add sauce, stir a few minutes, turn down heat, simmer until thickened to your taste.

Add the minced cilantro if you like. This makes a good dip, good spooned over hard-boiled or scrambled eggs, spread on hot corn bread or tacos, with meat, with duck, etc. Keeps in fridge about a week.

Physalis peruviana (Cape gooseberry) is one of the most important cultivated fruits of South America and has been cultivated elsewhere for 200 years. The ripe fruit of this variety is rather less sweet than other forms, but still has the attractive slightly acid flavor. *P. pruinosa* and *P. peruviana* are forms which make unforgettable "cherry" pie. (Good with dry cereals, too, or with sugar and heavy cream.)

Ground Cherry Pie

4 cups husked, ripe ground cherries
2 cups sugar
2 tablespoons flour
1/2 teaspoon cinnamon
pinch mace
2 tablespoons melted unsalted butter
2 tablespoons lemon juice

Combine all ingredients, stir till well-mixed, pour into unbaked 9-inch pie shell. Top with remaining crust, cut steam vents. Bake at 350 degrees for 45-55 minutes or until crust is golden brown. (Brush a little milk on top crust in last 10 minutes of cooking, if you want a darker brown.)

You can order *P. pruinosa* from Stokes Seeds, Inc., 737 Main St., Box 548, Buffalo, NY 14241; while *P. peruviana* seeds are available from George W. Park Seed Co., Hwy. 254 N., Greenwood, SC. 29647.

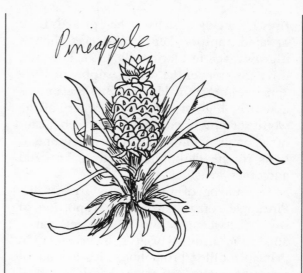

PINEAPPLE, KING-PINE
(*Ananas comosus*)

Most people associate the pineapple with Hawaii so adamantly that it comes as a surprise to know it was introduced there only in the 1880s. It was Christopher Columbus' crew who first reported the pineapple, in Guadalupe in 1493. Native to the Caribbean, Central and South America, the pineapple aroused great enthusiasm among early explorers and writers. The first description we have is by Gonzalo de Oviedo y Valdes, who wrote in 1535 that the fruit, known as *piñas*, combined the flavors of melons, strawberries, raspberries and pippin apples. Sir Walter Raleigh, in 1595, reported delightedly on the "great abundance of *piñas*, the princesse of fruits, that grow under the Sun, especially those of Guiana . . ." All who tasted the fruit raved; the exception was Charles V, King of Spain as well as Holy Roman Emperor, who refused to taste it for fear of being poisoned.

The fruit had reached China early on, was in cultivation there by 1594, even earlier in the Philippines. Louis XIV was anti-pineapple because, when offered the first he'd seen, he greedily bit into it without peeling it and cut his lips badly on the fruit's sharp "eyes." Louis XV, on the other hand, ordered a special hothouse built for pine-apples and spent 1000 francs a year on the culture of this delicacy. George Washington accompanied his brother Lawrence to Barbados in 1751, wrote home that of all the exotic fruits he'd tasted, "none pleases my taste as do's the pine."

Caribbean and Central American Indian boys, for initiation rites, were forced to run between close parallel lines of pineapple plants. Modern hybridizers, now, however, have all but eliminated the prickles, to help the harvesters. The Indian custom of hanging a pineapple over the entrance door to indicate that they were at home to friends, that food and wine were being dispensed, took hold quickly in Europe: the pineapple became the very symbol of hospitality. Soon the fruit was carved, painted, wrought, cast, on sideboards, serving dishes, overmantles, cups, punchbowls. On beds, too, but we'll discuss that another time. The usage still remains: one new local restaurant has a handsome big black tin pineapple over the entrance.

Pineapples remained unknown to most of the United States until well into this century. The fruit has to ripen on the plant; once ripe, it quickly goes bad when picked. Lack of rapid transport kept it rare, even though it grows well in Florida. By 1951, however, three-quarters of the world's supply of pine-apples came from Hawaii. But the unions asked the highest agricultural wages in the world for pineapple pickers, so the big can-ning companies moved much of their opera-tions to the Philippines, Kenya, Thailand and other areas.

The flavor of the fruit is irresistible. Pineapple contains a strong proportion of sugar (between 15 and 20 percent), citric and malic acids, as well as a fermentation principle called bromoline, plus a kind of vegetable pepsin. This makes it an ideal digestive dessert for any meal featuring heavy meat dishes. Most people can't be bothered with cleaning a fresh pineapple and resort always to the canned, but oh, my, how good the fresh. The classic French way of serving it after a big meal is simple and the best of all: the sliced fresh fruit is mari-nated in the clear *eau-de-vie* of cherries called *kirsch*, then topped with a few can-died violets. Both Dumas and Balzac, how-ever, were wildly fond of pineapple fritter, and wrote at length of them:

Pineapple Fritters

You must have thin slices of the fruit. You can use canned, but fresh is 100 percent better. Sugar the slices very lightly and put to soak half an hour in either *kirsch* or white rum. Then dry the slices thoroughly and coat them with a very thin layer of apricot jam. Stick pairs of slices together and dip into a light batter. Fry in deep fat, serve at once in a napkin.

The following is a delightful Caribbean dish:

Chicken Barbados

Cut 2 or 3 small chickens into serving por-tions. Melt a nice lump of butter in your heavy skillet, along with some ham or bacon fat. Nicely brown the chicken pieces, then place them in a lidded pot with sweet onions peeled and cut in half, 1 pineapple, sliced, 2 or 3 green peppers cut in strips, a generous sprinkle of freshly ground black pepper, a drop or so of Tabasco, and 2 cups of white wine, salt to taste. Simmer, covered, until chicken is tender, adding more wine if nec-essary. Arrange chicken on platter, dump pineapple and vegetables over, with what-ever liquid. Plain boiled rice on the side.

Pineapple Upside-Down Cake

One of the perennial Southern favorites is this cake, although the first published ver-sion of the recipe seems to be in the great Fannie Farmer's 1906 Boston cookbook. But pineapple sherbet and this cake were recorded in manuscript family cookbooks in Mobile and New Orleans already in the 1870s. So good! Especially with black N'Orleans coffee with chicory.

12 tablespoons unsalted butter
1 cup dark brown sugar
1/4 cup pineapple juice
5 sliced pineapples
1/2 cup milk
1 egg
1 1/2 cups flour
2 teaspoons baking powder
scant 1/2 teaspoon salt
1/2 cup white sugar
good pinch powdered mace
hint powdered cloves

Preheat oven to 400 degrees. In your iron skillet, melt 4 tablespoons butter, stir in brown sugar, dissolve over low heat. Remove from heat, add juice. Arrange your pineapple slices in skillet and set aside. In another pan, melt remaining sugar, remove from heat and stir in milk and egg, beating well. Mix flour, baking powder, salt, white sugar in a bowl, add milk-egg mixture and beat in till smooth. Pour batter over pineapple slices in skillet, and bake about 35 minutes or until toothpick comes out clean. Let pan sit to cool about 10 or 12 minutes, then turn out on plate with pineapple on top. For the more baroque tastes, whipped cream flavored with Cointreau can be served alongside.

The best Southern breakfast of all consists of scrambled eggs to which a little fresh cream has been added, and a nice pinch of dried dill, with spicy pork sausage patties and sliced fresh pineapple cooked in the skillet with the sausage. Hot grits, naturally.

If you'd like to honor that first meeting of Columbus and his men with the pineapple you might serve this:

Antilles Custard

1/2 pineapple, peeled, cut into small hunks
1 cup sugar
2 large eggs plus 4 more yolks
1 scant cup of flour
2 cups scalded milk
1 teaspoon vanilla extract
1 cup heavy cream
1/2 cup dark rum
1/2 cup blanched almonds, slivered and toasted
3 cups powdered sugar
1 tablespoon grated orange rind

Beat the granulated sugar and egg yolks for about 10 minutes, then add the whole eggs and flour and beat some more. Pour in pan over low heat and stir constantly until lukewarm. Boil milk in another pan, then whisk into egg mixture. Cook, stirring, until it becomes smooth and custardy. Take off fire, stir in vanilla, cream, rum. Strain into big bowl. Pour half into buttered baking dish and cover with pineapple chunks. Cover with remaining half and strew orange rind, almonds, and confectioner's sugar over top. Brown under broiler for about 90 seconds.

PINK PEPPERCORNS
(but they're not pepper!)
Rowan Berries
(Sorbus aucuparia)

In the last year or so those fancy New York/Paris chefs have *oo-la-laaed* and acted as if possessed of arcane secrets over *le poivre rose* (pink peppercorns). It's only a decade since green peppercorns were the news of the day, but they really *are* peppercorns, the unripened form of our familiar black pepper. But pink peppercorns are something else again. Paris and New York import them from the Isle of the Reunion, a dear little speck in the sea east of Madagascar. They needn't! But they do, and our Federal Department of Agriculture, a charter member of that vast American conglomerate of bureaucracies better known as the *Stop the Motion Club*, began sniffing about and decided to ban the importation of these pretty little rosy-red berries (they look like beads from a child's rosary) on very vague grounds. Now, my personal theory is, that some congressman discovered exactly what they are and, if he came from somewhere in the Appalachians, realized that his mountain acres were loaded with them and he could put them in jars as easily as the

SNIFF! SNIFF?

e.

Pink peppercorns?

Rowan berries have a delicious, astringent flavor which is nigh perfect with game and wild fowl, but wonderful when added to apple or peach pies or chutneys. And they definitely have a peppery taste. The aftertaste for an instant suggests apple peel. A good sirloin rubbed with crushed rowan berries and sautéed in sizzling unsalted butter, and afterwards sprinkled with a little orange juice mixed with 2 or 3 drops (no more) of soy sauce, is practically a religious experience. But cracked rowan berries, excuse me, pink peppercorns, added to marinades for pork ribs, are delightful. If, by chance, you have access to fresh berries, make jelly to go with duck, pork or venison. Boil up the berries with enough water to cover until the juice is quite red. Strain through a jelly bag and boil up again with one and a half pounds of sugar per pint of liquid until it jells. Age for two years.

Fresh rowan berries can be made into a wine, using your elderberry wine recipe and adding slightly more sugar.

The berries are often added to homemade wine to liven it, and Pepys, in the *Diary*, mentions that ale he had brewed with rowan berries was the best he'd ever had. And I say that baby turnips, peeled, simmered until just pierceable, buttered with unsalted butter, a nice glop of heavy cream added, and then a *hint* of nutmeg, and a nice pinch of ground pink peppercorns is . . . well, how shall I say . . . I mean . . . *ooo-la-laa!*

POMANDER
Scent Balls, Stink-Killers, PuzzaToy

Pomanders, or scentballs, are an apple, an orange, a pear, a lemon, whatever, stuck

dears on that island. So he complained to the FDA. That's my theory.

Pink peppercorns are nothing on earth but the berries of the rowan or mountain ash tree. In the British Isles they have been making them into wine, pickles, jelly and delicious sauces for venison since the Middle Ages. The early settlers in America recognized the only slightly different American form of the tree (*Sorbus americana*) and happily employed it in their kitchens. The only noticeable difference between the American and British forms (the tree grows all over Northern Europe, too) is that the American one has rather gummy buds in spring. They are all related to the service tree, the white beam and distantly to the hawthorn and azerole.

with spices and dried. They have, at various times in history, been carried in globes of gold filigree ornamented with precious stones, worn on a ribbon about the neck, worn as a pendant to a gold chain, and even made in miniature to dangle as ear pendants. There is evidence that the Egyptians made great use of them. Boy, you bet they'd have to do so, what with open sewage in a hot climate.

The English name, *pomander*, is a transliteration of the French name for them, *pomme d'ambre* ("amber apple"), since the most common pomander on the continent, in ancient times, was an apple stuck with spices and rolled in powdered ambergris as a preservative. In the Middle ages pomanders went into every linen or clothes cupboard, were as common as aspirin tablets today. Since they repel moths and many insects, the custom is still viable. Henry VIII gave his daughter a "bauble to containe ye pomander" which is described in household accounts as a precious golden globe ornamented with twelve emeralds. In modern usage, oranges have almost universally replaced apples in making pomanders, since the delightful orange odor adds greatly to the total effect.

There is no more pleasant Christmas tree decoration on earth than small lime or lemon pomanders hanging on bits of gold cord. Pomanders have been used as finials for drapery pulls, on top of lamp shades (where the heat of the bulb sends the perfume eddying about the house), and as pendants swinging from the chandelier.

Many herb shops and specialty shops sell pomanders today, but what fun to make your own.

Take a healthy fresh citrus fruit (even grapefruits if you want to be more MGM)

Pomander

or apple or pear or quince and stick it all over with cloves, crowded together. Place this fruit in a dish containing a mixture of orris root powder and other ground spices such as cinnamon or sandalwood; I love the subtle presence of mace and you can easily mix up your personal melange, drawing, for instance, on star anise, ginger, true anise, fennel, sassafras, cedar, musk, allspice, cardamom, what you like.

Leave the pomander in the dish with powder for a few days, rolling it over every time you pass it by. Then hang it up to dry in an airy spot. When it's dry, tie a ribbon to it and it's ready to use. Or have your jeweler run up a globe of gold filigree with a few precious stones, and affix your pomander bauble to a good heavy solid gold chain and wear it to the opera or the dog races.

POMEGRANATE
Grenadier, Melograno, Malicorio, Cortezade Granada, Solomon's Apple, Fever Apple
(*Punica granatum*)

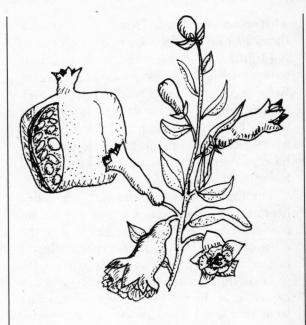

POMEGRANATE e.

The pomegranate, originating in the semitropical regions of Asia, was so early naturalized in the Mediterranean (it was cultivated for four thousand years in Persia) that the ancient Romans assumed it was native, and assigned it the name *Punica granatum*. That *Punica* refers to Carthage, or Libya, as its habitat.

In both Oriental and Christian art and religion, the fruit has always held an emblematical and symbolical importance. Because of the myth of Persephone, who must spend part of the year in the underworld with her husband Pluto, before being allowed a visit to her mother, Demeter, protector of cereal crops, the pomegranate is symbolic of death, fertility, the returning growing season and the cycle of the year. In Christian myth the fruit represents hope. Solomon sings of it.

That extraordinary Spanish lady who was Queen of France, Anne of Austria, wife of Louis XIII, chose it as her personal emblem and had it stamped in gold on her bookbindings, embroidered on her linens and gloves and scarves. On her bed-draperies the image of the pomegranate was coupled with the motto: "My worth is not in my crown." She referred to the little pointed "crown" which is the calyx of the blossom which remains on the bottom of the fruit as it develops. Since she guaranteed the royal succession (among her progeny was Louis XIV) and

was a political whiz kid, her choice of motto was apt.

In all warm climates the pomegranate tree is grown for its shiny foliage and striking scarlet flowers (there are white and pink forms, single and double), but in most of the Near Eastern and Oriental countries it is an important food crop. Bark, peel, buds have been important medicinally since earliest times, especially in treating diarrhea and as a vermifuge. In India, Iran, Turkey, these folk remedies are still much used. There are three kinds of pomegranates: one yielding a very sour juice used as verjuice in cookery, another sweet, one very sweet indeed. The last two are a favorite dessert when split open, sprinkled with sugar and rose water.

The juice, sometimes boiled down to a kind of paste, supplies a fruity sweet-sour element which is universal in many meat, fish, mixed vegetable dishes in the countries whereof we speak. In the Islamic countries, where alcohol is forbidden by their religion, there is a whole world of syrups made of roses, mint, pomegranates, which are poured into cold water to make the long summer drinks the men sip in cafes.

Our familiar grenadine is still used in confectionary and in many mixed drinks. Pink lemonade is properly colored and flavored with grenadine, and in antebellum southern cookbooks, both printed and manuscript, there occur dozens of "ladies'" drinks such as Saratoga Punch (Saratoga Springs, N.Y., was a favorite resort for Southerners escaping the heat, and enjoying the horseracing in that high altitude town. Robert Hillyer has a delightful poem about that time and place called "The Square Piano." ". . . those summers / When the Danube still was blue / At Saratoga Springs . . ." he writes.), Ladies' Punch, Racetrack Lemonade, etc. These were all lemonade made with sparkling spring water, *generously* laced with white rum, colored and flavored with grenadine.

One of the most suitable of summer desserts is very ripe peaches, splashed with lemon and grenadine and well chilled. Ditto melon balls. But grenadine sherbet is an almost forgotten Southern classic:

Grenadine Sherbet

Mix 2 cups buttermilk with 1/4 cup lemon juice, 1/2 cup sugar, 1 1/2 cups white Karo syrup (corn syrup), freeze until mushy, then place in chilled bowl and beat smooth, mixing in 1/2 cup of grenadine. Return to freezer until firm. If you have any pomegranate blossoms you might alarm the timid by placing one perfect bloom on top of each serving. Or very pretty is a borage flower. If all else fails, use mint leaves.

Turkish Baked Bass with Pomegranate Seeds

You'll need a 4- or 4 1/2-pound bass. Wash it under cold water and dry well. Sprinkle inside and out with salt and lemon juice. In a baking dish big enough to hold the fish, pour same amount of oil over. Let this sit for a while as you prepare the stuffing. In a heavy skillet, heat about 1/2 cup pure olive oil and put in 1 cup finely chopped onions, 1 1/2 cups finely chopped green peppers, 1 cup shelled and crushed walnuts (you can also use pecans, but walnuts are better). Cook these a few minutes, then off fire add: 3 tablespoons pomegranate seeds, 1/3 cup chopped parsley, a scant 1/2 teaspoon very finely chopped lemon peel, lots of black pepper.

Fill the fish with this stuffing, close the opening with skewers. Bake in preheated 400-degree oven for 40 to 50 minutes, basting every quarter hour. Don't overcook! When fish feels firm and "just right," grab it out of that oven and spread evenly over it a sauce made of plain yoghurt mixed with a little cream, a pinch of salt, and more pomegranate seeds and chopped parsley. Garnish with sliced lemon.

POPPY
Coquelicot, Corn Rose, Mawseed, Papavero
(Papaver)

The common red field poppy is one of the French *tricouleur* of field flowers, often used as a symbol of France or of the world of French agriculture (they occur in all cultivated fields as volunteers). They are the

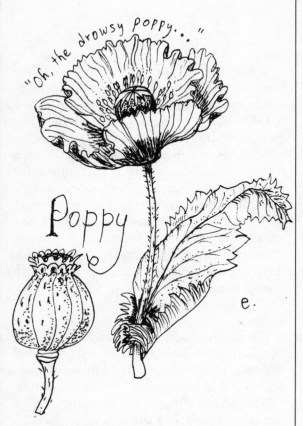

"Oh, the drowsy poppy..."

Poppy

e.

The white poppy, or opium poppy (*Papaver somniferum*), occurs in all shades from the purest white to a purplish crimson. The most common form, very pretty, has pale mauve petals with a red-purple splotch on the base of the petals. The botanical name, *somniferum*, means "sleep-bringing." The milky juices of the unripe seed pods are the source of opium (from the Greek word for "juice") and its derivatives morphine (from Morpheus, the Greek god of sleep), codeine (from the Greek for "poppyhead"), and laudanum. This last is a name which Paracelsus applied to a medicine with which he effected remarkable cures. His published recipe (1658) lists as ingredients goldleaf, unperforated pearls, and other fanciful items, but it has long been suspected that it was only some distillation of the opium poppy.

Although horror tales of drug addiction cause most people to quiver imperceptibly at mention of poppy derivatives, they have been used since the cave age medicinally, and are unexcelled as hypnotic and sedative, to relieve pain and calm excitement. The astringent qualities make them useful in cases of diarrhea, dysentery, and persistent coughs. In many remote parts of the world of eastern and central Europe, many horsemen share small portions of opium and morphine with their jaded horses, since small quantities serve as nerve stimulants and add greatly to powers of endurance. Four thousand years before Christ, the poppy priestesses of Crete cultivated the pods and prepared syrups and distillations to alleviate both pain and sorrow.

But for us, in our ordinary daily life, the totally non-narcotic type poppyseeds are what interest us, for their completely delightful nutty flavor, which adds immeasurably to many kinds of breads, cakes,

coquelicot (red field poppy), the *bluet* (cornflower), and the *marguerite* (common daisy). But this red poppy, having only small traces of the alkaloids and acids of its more famous cousin, the opium poppy, is much cultivated in France, the Lowlands, and parts of Germany for the seeds which are used in many dishes, even more so for the oil derived from them, an exquisitely flavored salad oil known as *olivette*. Not to be confused with a cruder poppy seed oil used in oil painting! The leaves have been used in place of spinach in hard times, and until fairly recent history the petals yielded a red coloring used in inks. "In the red . . ." (This flower is also known as corn rose, corn poppy, *flores rhoeados*, and headache.)

cookies and salad dressings. Our favorite cheese straws, for instance, become Something Else Again when liberally sprinkled with poppy seeds. Or try this dressing:

Poppy and Mustard Salad Dressing

2 tablespoons powdered mustard
1¹/₂ tablespoons poppy seeds
¹/₄ cup sugar
juice ¹/₂ lemon
1 tablespoon white wine vinegar
1 cup purest olive oil
3 tablespoons very finely chopped onions
1 teaspoon salt

Blend your mustard with a little warm water and let "hatch" for a quarter hour, then dump everything together in a mixing bowl, beat up with a rotary beater until thickened. Put in jar and use as needed.

A summer salad of fresh sliced ripe peaches with a little celery and some lettuce dressed with this is delightful. Even the hateful iceberg lettuce is transformed. Or curly endive and crisp apple. If you want to *épater les bourgeois*, take some baby turnip roots, peel and slice thin, soak in cool water with salt and sugar, drain, then serve with inner celery leaves and this dressing.

If the kiddies are fretful on the morning of a non-school day when it pours down rain, try this: whip up your usual batch of biscuits. When they are nearly done, take them out of the oven and smear with unsalted butter, honey, a dash of cinnamon, plenty of poppy seeds, then run them back into the oven for a bit. Put a roll of paper towels on the table when you serve the Gorgeous Stickies and say, "Children, take two or three of Mama's best double-damask napkins, and lean over your plates."

PURSLANE
Porcelain, Kulfo, Porcellana, "Pussley"
Green Purslane *(Portulaca oleoracea)*
Golden Purslane *(Portulaca sativa)*

This is one of the commonest weeds on the Gulf Coast, indeed, all over the United States. It grows wild in India, where it has been eaten for thousands of years. It is cultivated in the Middle East, was introduced into England probably in early Tudor days, and was a favorite salad or cooked green in Elizabethan days. It has long since gone wild in North and South America, since the seventeenth century, undoubtedly. In the Carolina mountains, it's the much enjoyed salad green "pussley." It pops up in every garden patch, out of sidewalk cracks.

It has fleshy, usually rosy red stems, neat little shiny long oval leaves, tiny yellow flowers, in June and July, which last until noon. It is pure child foolishness to pull it up as a weed. Let it grow and use it. Since long before Christ, it has been considered sovereign as a hot weather dish, soothing all pains in the head due to "the heat, want of sleep, or the frenzy." It has very little aroma or taste, like so many greens. But it has a

PURSLANE

delightful succulent consistency, and is very good raw in salads, boiled as a side dish with bacon fat, or pickled in vinegar for winter use.

The golden variety can be grown in the herb garden and is ready in six weeks. Vast fields are grown in Holland as a winter salad. Pigs go thoroughly mad over it; they can't get enough. Recent researches find it very helpful for dry coughs, for inflammation of mouth and gorge, for gumboils. American Indians used a slightly different form of the plant for "journey food," finding small quantities very sustaining. The seeds, bruised and boiled in wine, are one of the most ancient vermifuges for children, mentioned in the oldest Chinese and Indian *materiae medicae*.

In Italy it is one of the wild herbs included in the endless varied and delicious tonic winter salads, dressed with lemon, oil, garlic, salt, pepper. The name "purslane" is nothing but a transliteration of the French word *porcelain*, and refers to the shiny look of the green leaves and rosy stems. Some seed companies supply developed varieties for the garden. Once, in the south of England, near Chipping Camden, I saw a vegetable garden with beds edged with this charming plant. Very pretty and appetizing. (You can get seeds of golden purslane and many other herbs from: J.A. Demonchaux Co., 827 N. Kansas St., Topeka, KS 66608.)

RADISH
(Raphanus sativus)

Cumin and caraway and then anise and dill and then lemon and lime: in the great

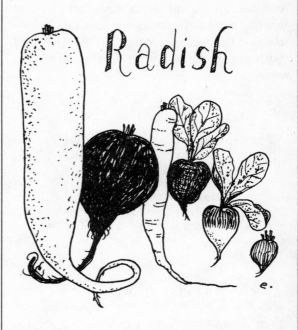

galaxy of flavors some *can* be confused for each other. The radish, no. *Perhaps* a dulled palate *might* take a baby turnip for some kind of radish, but not many would. The sweet, spicy flavor of the radish family and all its diverse members is something else again. The human race has enjoyed and grown the radish for so long that its geographical origins and historic stages are lost in prehistory. They come in all shades of red and pink, some are black and white. The size varies from rosebud through the white "icicles," to golfball (the black), to the bludgeon-like white Japanese *daikon*. The simplest European farmer and the great French gourmet both like the same thing to start a meal in spring or early summer. A plate of radishes fresh from the garden, leaves and roots left on, accompanied by a pat of unsalted butter, a little mound of sea salt and fresh crusty bread. Nothing is more amusing than to watch a tableful of Frenchmen served with such an hors d'oeuvre: one will dip his radish in salt, then eat buttered bread. One will eat his radish as is, then salt his buttered bread. One might butter his radish, then dip it in salt, follow with a chunk of plain bread.

Radishes are perhaps the easiest food plant to grow. If you dig your bed deep, thin them after they are up an inch or so, water if there's no rain. They will keep up to a week in the fridge if in a plastic sack. They are always improved by being soaked in cold water before coming to table. The young leaves are delicious and it's just plain silly to remove them. Take off older or yellowed leaves, of course, and the messier looking roots, but leave the leaves. The radish begins to deteriorate the moment the leaves are cut off, so don't clean them until shortly before eating.

If you plant a few seeds every week you can have the little dears all season. The day you see the flower stem appear from a radish, though, don't eat it. The root becomes much too hot and tough as the stem develops. If you are very wise, you'll let a whole bed of them go to seed and gather the green pods (rather like mustard pods) and pickle them. This is one of the most delicious pickles on earth.

There are hundreds of kinds of radishes and a bouquet of four or five different kinds makes a beautiful, eye-catching, tasty first dish. Or with some cream cheese as a salad of course. If you are one of the under-privileged and are forced to use the dismal Californian invader, the hateful and flavor-less iceberg lettuce, you could do worse than to chop up some radish and bitter dandelion leaves to give your salads character. Next time you serve hamburgers, you can cause comment and exclamation by serving this pretty pink relish with the meat:

Radish and Horseradish Relish

1 cup grated horseradish (fresh, if possible)
1 cup grated red radishes
1/4 cup white wine vinegar
1 teaspoon sugar
pinch powdered ginger
pinch powdered mace
1 tablespoon minced fresh parsley

Mix all save parsley together and keep in fridge overnight, tossing occasionally. Stir in parsley just before serving.

Keep a roll of radish butter in your fridge and whack off a round or so to melt over hamburger, steak, chicken or to completely transform a simple baked or broiled fish.

Radish Butter

1/2 cup grated red radishes
1 clove garlic
1/4 cup fresh chopped parsley
1/2 cup unsalted butter
2 teaspoons Creole or Dijon mustard
1 tablespoon lemon juice
1/4 teaspoon sour salt
1/4 teaspoon freshly ground black pepper
a dash Tabasco

Chop garlic and parsley very fine or do in blender. Add butter and mustard, blend until very smooth. Stir in remaining ingredients, mix well. Pack in a crock or shape into a log. Cover with plastic or foil. Will keep in fridge a week; frozen will keep up to a month. For variety this can be flavored with other elements: minced anchovy or fresh dill, or minced green scallions.

Now, if you want something very good indeed, boil up some quartered baby cabbage (steam in only an inch of water) after soaking an hour in water (to cover) with sugar and salt and take 2 heaping tablespoons of above radish butter, add a pinch of dill, a pinch of mace, a splash of white wine vinegar, and ³/₄ cup dry white wine, then whisk together over medium heat (mustn't boil). Pour over your cooked cabbage and sprinkle lightly a few celery seeds and some freshly ground black pepper. My!

One of the best soups imaginable is simply chicken broth with sliced red radishes, chopped inner celery with leaves, a bit of fresh ginger root (instead, you can put a pinch of ginger powder or even curry) and at the end of 30 minutes cooking, add a nice dollop of yoghurt or sour cream and serve.

ROCKET
Rughetta, Rugola, Roquette, Ruccola, Land Cress, Pepper Cress, etc.
(*Eruca sativa*)

Travellers to Italy lose their minds over a salad green unusually called *rughetta, rochetta, rugola*. It has a peppery taste somewhere between nasturtium and watercress, and gives great zest to summer mixed salads. In central Italy it is served as a special salad by itself, dressed with crushed anchovies and garlic, salt and pepper, lemon and oil. Many a traveler tucks a packet of seeds in his pocket to try back home in the States.

But this delightful plant has been in kitchen gardens in our country since the 1600s and has long since gone wild through most of the South. American seed catalogs have listed it since at least the mid-1800s under the name land cress, garden cress, sometimes (erroneously) upland cress, rarely as pepper cress. Thomas Jefferson, in written instructions to his gardener at Monticello, while he was on an ambassadorial mission in France, lists it as essential for the kitchen garden. To compound confusion, he also instructs that sweet rocket or dame's rocket be planted as well.

This is quite another plant, *Hesperis matronalis* ("vesper flower"), so-called for the fact that its lovely purple or mauve or white flowers give off a highly pleasant perfume in the evening but have no hint of scent during the day. However, the young leaves are gathered for salad, and have a taste as bitey and stimulating as the cresses or rockets.

The confusion of nomenclature is no less in France. In a market in Perigueux, for instance, you can find a heap of fresh greens on one stall labelled *cresson alenois* (it's rocket), on another *cresson du jardin* (it's rocket), and again on a third *roquette* (it's rocket), but you might find another label *roquette* on leaves of the *hesperis* with the same leaves labelled *cresson des dames* on still another counter. All very confusing, especially since REAL watercress is botanically called *Nasturtium officinalis,* and our familiar garden flower with a familiar flavor is popularly nasturtium, but botanically is *Tropaeolum majus.* To make it all more complicated there are several alpine wild plants in Europe with similar flavor in the leaves and they are employed in remote localities under various variations of the *cresson* or roquette names.

Well, let's just take a deep breath and simply point out that a certain peppery-mustardy taste in salad greens pleases almost everybody everywhere. If you check your seed catalogs carefully you will probably find land cress, or any of the Italian or French names. If your vendor is serious, he'll have the Latin name so you can determine exactly the plant *(Eruca sativa)* you seek.

And it flourishes in the South, and on the Gulf Coast goes straight through the winter. Mine survived the first freeze, and only the long protracted deep freeze laid it low. Now a few straggling plants are putting up tasty green leaves again. One tiny patch which was covered with pine needles spilled from around a newly planted azalea survived even the worst. It will obligingly grow in a box in a sunny window, giving you a few leaves to sex up a tasteless salad of, for instance, the elderly iceberg lettuce which leave their retirement homes in the great freezers of California to come here with their insipidity. But even a square foot scattered thickly with rocket seed (use the ones you thin out, let the remaining develop) will give an endless supply.

If you want a good strong Roman salad and have no pressing business in cramped quarters for 24 hours, then pound three or four garlic cloves, and three or four anchovies which have been soaked in a couple of changes of milk, in your mortar, and add salt, freshly ground black pepper, lemon juice and best pure olive oil and toss this well-mixed into a plate of rocket leaves. Unbeatable! Crusty bread and mozzarella on the side.

But this is a first dish for summer luncheon which never fails to please:

Nest Eggs

Cut up some celery heart leaves and some fresh sage leaves and mix them with a little salt and onion juice (NO, not onion salt!) in a big packet of Philadelphia cream cheese. Form small egg-shaped blops and put cheese into refrigerator to firm up. Meanwhile wash your rocket leaves and either swing them in your wire basket or bounce them in the colander until every drop of water is gone.

Make a dressing of lemon juice, pure olive oil, salt, pepper, a few celery or cumin seeds AND a few drops of fresh orange juice and toss your salad. Then arrange nicely on plate or in bowl as a "nest" and place your little eggs in the middle, sprinkling all with finely chopped parsley.

A salad of rocket and mild radishes is very fine, too. So are avocado slices marinated in lemon and onion and mixed with rocket. Plant rocket in your kitchen garden; you'll be pleased.

"I get drunk on it every day..."
Mme. de Sévigné

ROSEMARY

ROSEMARY
Compass-weed, Old Man, Polar Plant, Incensier, Rosmarino, Romero, etc.
(Rosmarinus officinalis)

Rosemary is an universal flavoring in the Mediterranean world, and once was far more widely employed in the United States than now, although much rosemary is grown commercially here to make oil of rosemary, which goes into many dentifrices, lotions, liniments and colognes. Rosemary, in fact, is a principal ingredient in the true and first *Eau de Cologne,* Cologne water.

The Latin name, *rosmarinus,* means "sea spray" or "sea dew," according to some classical scholars, although others prefer a derivation from *rhus,* "shrub," so that significance would then be "seaside shrub." Both make sense, for the rosemary blankets the coasts of Italy, Spain, Portugal, Greece, and thrives on rocky soils and sea mists.

At night, following a hot summer day, one can smell the piquant and bracing perfume of rosemary from miles out at sea. It smacks of pine with a little lavender, or ginger with a little camphor, some think it resembles thyme with a hint of freshly ground pepper. Since remotest antiquity rosemary has been used as a remedy for headaches and as an antiseptic. It has always been considered useful for any and all maladies affecting the head, such as a loss of memory or hearing or sight. I can vouch that oil of rosemary is an almost miraculous cure for headaches: once, after a long night of reading proofs, I had a dull throbbing headache and watery eyes, both unheard-of for me. I rubbed oil of rosemary on my temples and in a quarter hour, the headache was gone, and eyes clear as an infant's!

Rosemary has always been associated with fidelity and with memory, so has always figured in both weddings and funerals. We are told that Anne of Cleves wore a wreath of rosemary at her wedding. The plant had been introduced into England in the fourteenth century when Queen Phillipa's mother, the Countess of Hainault, sent her plants as a powerful protection against the plague.

The plant is mentioned over and over again in every literature. Herrick, in a charming poem, "The Rosemary Branch," writes . . . "Grow for two ends, it matters not at all, / Be't for my bridal or my burial." Madame de Sevigné says, "I get drunk on it every day, I always have some in my pocket, I find it excellent against sadness." And every country has a body of lore and accounts of miraculous cures attributed to this herb. The Sicilians believe that young fairies take the form of snakes and hide in its bushes. The Spanish consider that the bush sheltered the Virgin Mary on the flight to Egypt, and that the bush bore white flowers until she hung her blue mantle to dry on a rosemary bush, whereupon the flowers turned blue.

My favorite story concerns the invention of Hungary water, still employed for stiffness and paralysis. Queen Elizabeth of Hungary, a 73-year-old monarch, paralyzed and failing, had a dream in which an angel instructed her to steep rosemary for five days in spirits of wine then apply infusion to her limbs. She did, recovered completely and was so lovely and sprightly that a young king of Poland wanted to marry her. I can't vouch for any of that, but I do know that a rinse made of rosemary sprigs steeped in warm water is fantastic for the hair and scalp. Cures dandruff, imparts a sparkle to hair whether blond, dark or red.

Rosemary has always been thought to flourish where the lady of the house has dominance; many European husbands have trampled down the rosemary in their kitchen gardens. It is a strong herb, and must be used with caution. The Italians overdo it, especially in their country cooking, but once you've eaten lamb or roast beef which have a few rosemary leaves tucked into incisions in the flesh, you'll never want those meats in any other fashion. For any dish of game rosemary does wonders. If you're cooking over embers, strew rosemary branches on the fire to flavor the meat. Any of the stronger or oilier fish gain from being cooked on a bed of rosemary. If you want a real gastronomic experience, roast a chicken over live coals and baste it constantly with a branch of rosemary dipped in pure olive oil.

Another way to bake potatoes is to rub them well with rosemary, then with bacon drippings, pierce them on all sides and bake. Beans gain greater interest if a few rosemary leaves are slipped into the pot. One of the best Italian spaghetti sauces contains ripe tomatoes, garlic, onion, black pepper and rosemary. You can lay the sprigs among your linens just as with lavender, and if you want to cure a bad hangover just wear a tight wreath of rosemary. You'll be surprised.

RUE
Herb of Grace
(Ruta graveolens)

Most people know rue only from the reference in *Hamlet* from the verb form taken from the plant's name: "to rue the day," meaning to regret. How this expression arose is difficult to say. The plant is quite pretty, a small-leaved silvery blue-green compact shrub with yellow flowers. It has an odd scent which is repellent to many people, but it has been a medicine since the dawn of history. It is not really what you'd call a kitchen herb, although one or two new leaves, chopped fine, add a delightfully different accent to a bland green salad, and the Italians consume vast quantities of digestive *eau de vie* called *grappa con ruta: grappa* is clear distillation of wine leas, the drink is bottled in a pale blue-green bottle with a spring of rue in it.

Rue is always used in small quantities, too much makes one ill, inducing violent vomiting. In antiquity it was considered the best antidote for poisons, from the time Dioscorides noted that weasels, before going to hunt snakes for food, always ate rue. Rue was part of every infusion taken to induce abortion. A weak tea of rue was taken internally and also used to bathe the eyes; both Leonardo and Michelangelo employed the herb for the sight and swore by it.

Like all ancient lore and superstition clustered in the herb garden, the efficacy of rue has lately been found to have a very real basis: a yellow crystallized body called *rutin,* contained in the herb, was discovered during World War II to be of enormous value in treating weakened blood vessels. This trait explains precisely why it is traditionally an eye-strengthener, by increasing capillary action and blood supply to the center of vision. Those who profess the Doctrine of Signatures always use rue as best proof of their arguments, and strangely enough the odd root formations of rue bear a striking resemblance to the arrangement of blood vessels in the eye.

Mrs. Grieve, the greatest modern herbalist, a no-nonsense lady whose *Modern Herbal* (1931) reaffirmed many ancient remedies in the light of modern laboratory science, says bluntly about rue: "If a leaf or two be chewed, a refreshing aromatic flavor will pervade the mouth and any nervous headache, giddiness, hysterical spasm, or palpitation will be quickly relieved." Italian peasants working in the fields chew a few leaves against the heat.

For us, aside from the pleasant occasional addition of rue to a salad, or sipping it in *grappa,* the greatest value of this herb is as a natural and potent insecticide. The leaves are gathered in early morning, dried in the shade, powdered and then sprinkled over any infested plant. There is no creeper or flyer or crawler that doesn't leave town instantly. Besides, rue is very lovely with its blue-green foliage, and as a border for roses makes a charming sight, besides keeping the aphids at bay. Rue is one of the approximately twenty "musts" for any herb garden.

SAFFRON
Zafferano, Azafrán
(Crocus Sativus)

Saffron was already considered an ancient flavoring in the time of Solomon. Thought to have originated in Greece and Asia Minor, this form of crocus was cultivated way back beyond historical record, especially by the Persians. Most scholars feel that the Phoenicians introduced it into Spain and France. The famous gumbo-like fish soup, *bouillabaisse* (the word means "slow boil") is redolent with saffron; one of the most delightful summer dishes on earth is cold boiled seafood and vegetables served with a bowl (perhaps the original "dip") of

Saffron

e.

rouille (rust), which is garlic mayonnaise (*aioli*) liberally spiked with saffron.

In the modern world, saffron is cultivated in many Mediterranean countries and Asian countries. It is a blue or purple-flowering bulb with three orange-yellow stigmas in each flower. They must be gathered by hand; something between 75,000 to a million flowers are required to produce one pound of saffron: this explains why in shops it is an investment, not a purchase. But it only takes a little to flavor a dish, and once you have had a real saffron dish prepared with dried saffron stigmas rather than the yellow dust often sold, you will probably find the mildly bitter iodine-like flavor irresistible.

Many of the rice dishes calling for saffron are often flavored with yellow powdered turmeric, also called curcuma (from the rhizomes of a plant of the ginger family) which is milder and nothing like saffron. Saffron

goes especially well with garlic and seafood, and seems to heighten the sea taste of these dishes such as the Spanish *paella* with its chicken and shrimp. I saw, in a famous Marseille restaurant, a chef preparing a *bouillabaisse* which he flavored with powdered turmeric and *a drop of tincture of iodine* instead of saffron. I couldn't tell the difference. None of the diners complained. If you use the real thing, crush the thread-like stigmas, steep in a little hot liquid, according to recipe, then add to dish. This classic rice dish is good with chicken, veal, or fish:

Saffron Rice

2 ounces unsalted butter
1 chopped medium onion
1 chopped garlic toe
1/2 small green pepper, chopped fine
1/2 pound rice
1 pint of chicken broth (use cubes if you must)
1/4 teaspoon saffron

Infuse saffron in the hot chicken broth. Melt butter in ovenproof casseroles, add onion, garlic, pepper, then the rice, turning until grains are shiny and transparent. Add the saffron broth. Bring to boil, put lid on, place in 350 degree oven for 30 minutes. If you want to be Persian, add finely chopped dried tangerine peel and a handful of white currants. If you feel Spanish, toss in a few flakes of dried red pepper. A little chopped celery is good if you're serving this with fish. I have also thrown in blanched slivered almonds.

Saffron Dumplings

A good beef stew with whole baby onions, 1 or 2 cloves, thyme, celery, whole baby carrots, cooked with 1/2 cup tomato paste and plenty of red wine becomes a wonder when topped with this dumpling mixture.

4 ounces self-rising flour
pinch salt
2 ounces unsalted butter
2 teaspoons finely chopped parsley
¼ cup milk
good pinch of saffron

Sift flour and salt into bowl, cream in butter thoroughly, add parsley. Heat milk and saffron together, add to flour, mix a firm dough. Pat out on a floured surface, roll lightly. Make deep incisions to form little squares, then slide the dough in one piece onto the cooked, bubbling casserole and replace lid or foil. Cook at 350 degrees for about 20 minutes. Serve at once.

The Greek and Latin poets are full of references to saffron. One pretty myth tells of a virgin nymph, Smilax, who was so vehement in her vows of love for Crocus that he was changed into the saffron. Homer mentions that Zeus slept on a mattress stuffed with saffron, lotus, and hyacinth. Over and over, good humor was attributed to this flavoring, and Culpeper said it was what made the English sprightly. Persians, Arabs, and Greeks used it as remedy for many urinary disorders.

Of course it is a dye, too. The brilliant clothes of the children of Israel were colored with yellow from saffron, rose madder (plant of the mallow family), and purple from the *murex,* a sea snail. Because of the price, Rabelais invented the word *safranier* ("saffroner") to mean financially ruined. It is not to be confused with the meadow saffron, or autumn crocus, which is deadly poisonous and of a paler blue, "color of bruises," according to the French poet Apollinaire.

SAGE
Longevity Tea, Livelong
(Salvia officinalis)

The Aryans, those remote ancestors of the Persians and Hindus, knew and used sage. The Egyptians considered it a powerful medicine against a long list of complaints. For the Greeks and Latins, it was the Holy Herb. In the Middle Ages it was often called *Salvia salvatrix,* "sage the savior," for its many uses and its proven health-giving properties. An ancient French proverb says, "Why should a man die whilst sage grows in his garden?" Country people all over Europe and the British Isles make a point of eating sage leaves spread on buttered bread (or bread soaked with olive oil) as a form of preventive medicine and a guarantee of longevity.

In every country sage is associated with long life, and there are so many proverbs and rhymes to this effect that one could fill a sizable anthology. Paullini, in the seventeenth century, dedicated a work of 400 pages to extolling the herb. An old English song says: "He that would live for aye/Must eat Sage in May."

Perhaps the highest recommendation for the familiar herb comes from China. The Chinese who live to a ripe old age all drink sage tea daily, and the records of both British and Dutch import-export houses reveal that in earlier days the Chinese were content to exchange four cases of their China tea for each case of dried sage. Winston Churchill liked sage tea, and once wrote, "We are happier in many ways when we are old, than when we were young. The young sow wild oats, the old grow sage."

Sage is one of the very few ancient pot herbs which has not fallen into disuse. Sage likes poor soil, full sun, hates to have water stand on its feet. Pinch off the pretty purple flowers or plant will go pawky. It goes into countless kinds of sausage, and is essential in our traditional poultry stuffings. But its strong pleasant taste (the herb is considered to be under the protection of Jupiter) makes it delightful for many famous dishes. The Italian dish of veal rolled up with a piece of ham and chopped sage leaves inside is classic.

Many country people in Europe, especially in the Mediterranean world, know no other toothbrush than a sage leaf. Try it yourself: pick a sage leaf and rub your teeth and gums with it. Delightful. Hardens the gums, too. Many modern dentifrices contain oil of sage, as a matter of fact. A brew of sage leaves, lemon peel and honey is a very effective gargle for sore throats. A rinse of infused sage will darken faded hair. A sage leaf placed on an insect bite will relieve the pain and prevent swelling. After a heavy meal of, say, pork, or roast beef, a final touch of sage cheese is very good for the digestion. Simply chop up fresh sage leaves into some cream cheese and soften it with a little milk or cream and add salt and pepper and let it sit for an hour or so. Serve with toast or crackers. On a chilly day or when you're recovering from a cold or just because it's good, try this:

Sage and Garlic Soup
(from Provence)

6 or 8 garlic cloves peeled and cut into quarters
a scant handful of sage
less thyme
1/2 bay leaf
1 egg yolk
a few tablespoons pure olive oil
slices of French bread

Begin with a quart of simmering water; toss in the garlic, sage, thyme, bay leaf, season with salt and freshly ground black pepper. Remove the herbs after you've cooked this broth about 20 minutes. In a heated soup tureen, beat the egg yolk. Pour in your soup a very little at a time, beating constantly. Put slices of French bread into each soup bowl and anoint them with olive oil. Pour the soup over this.

This dish is highly satisfying:

Leek and Sage Tart
Pastry for 8-inch tart

1 cup flour
1/4 teaspoon salt
3 ounces butter
1/4 cup cold water with a squirt lemon juice

Sift dry ingredients. Rub butter into them with fingertips or a pastry knife. With knife, mix water in gradually. Roll lightly and arrange in pan.

FILLING
1 dozen leeks
1 tablespoon chopped parsley
1½ tablespoons minced sage
1 egg, beaten
½ cup cream or whole milk
½ cup grated cheese (Swiss or cheddar)
salt to taste
freshly ground black pepper
4 strips bacon

Clean leeks well; cut into thin rounds. Simmer in a little water until soft. Drain, add herbs, egg, cream and cheese, salt and pepper. Pour this mixture into your pie shell. Lay out your bacon on top and bake in 400-degree oven for 20 to 25 minutes.

Add one or two chopped sage leaves to any salad made with the more banal greens. Try scattering a few chopped sage leaves over your spareribs. Or your pork chops. Good with roast lamb and mutton, too.

SALT

Jogging, the national panic over cholesterol (now somewhat abated), and the shrill cries about salt and the ailments of civilization are all part of one set of circumstances: most people don't walk, climb stairs, carry weights anymore.

Most British doctors smile patiently when they hear the word "cholesterol" and observe, "You must have been in the States lately." They like then to point out that the body needs a certain intake of cholesterol in order to make its own cholesterol. At the end, they argue for common sense and a balanced diet covering a wide range of foods, and a great many doctors, nutrition-ists, researchers in chemistry and medicine, take the present flurry of excitement over sodium with . . . well, a grain of salt.

Salt is the only mineral condiment we use in our food. Sodium chloride was the first salt to be discovered by man. There are two kinds: sea salt, which is distilled from sea water, and rock salt, which is found in crystalline forms in the earth.

The higher the vegetable content of our diet, the greater the need for salt; this is true of the herbivores as well. Carnivores have little need for it. Greedy for salt, all those deer, cattle, gazelles beat the path to those prehistoric salt licks. Man followed: trails became paths, paths became roads. The ancient world used salt as coinage. In primitive pockets of the planet, this is still true today. Roman legionnaires were paid in salt; from whence our word "salary." The ancient *Via Salaria* is the road from the salt flats at the port of Ostia to the Capital, Rome. "Salt of the earth" means worthy, good. The ancient term "Attic salt" means wit. "Worth his salt" is still current; it was the Roman or Greek slave owner's appreciation of a slave bought with, just so, his weight in salt. "Salacious" and "salty" are current to mean frank speech, especially sexually explicit talk or writing.

"Put salt on his tail" means an imaginary way of catching birds or taming rambunctious children. In fact, a rainy afternoon with the *Oxford Dictionary* opened to "S" will amaze and amuse you.

And in all this new roo-ra about "salt the killer," one or two aspects have been shoved aside. One is that people who do hard labor in hot countries and sweat a lot need and crave salt. The other is that the brain is an amazing salt-cell battery, and would suffer in a totally salt-free diet. And we must never forget our origins in the salt sea; the salt content of our own inland sea (blood) is the same as that of the ocean.

It is the kidneys which monitor the body's need for salt. When the body needs salt, the kidneys, which have retained it, pump it back into the blood. When there is an excess the kidneys excrete it. What has alarmed doctors in the last decade or so is that this functional give and take in the kidneys seems not to operate properly in a significant percentage of Americans, a much higher rate than anywhere else save Japan. And when the kidneys retain too much salt, the retained water raises the volume of blood, causing the blood vessels to become more sensitive to nerve stimulation, upon which they contract, whereupon more blood has to pass through narrower channels: blood pressure increases, the heart rate increases and the resultant stress sets up a vicious cycle in which an adrenal gland hormone is released which makes the poor old kidneys retain even *more* sodium and water.

The truth is that we eat an incredible amount of salt without knowing it. It is this we must seriously contemplate. Meanwhile, eat unsalted butter always, and instead of pouring salt into your salad, try lemon juice, grated horseradish and dill for a change.

Salt, we need it, we crave it. For most of us salt means sodium chloride, common table salt, but we get salt in almost everything. Nowadays, when people don't have a chance to eat fresh garden produce and rely more and more on canned or frozen products, the average salt intake has gone far beyond what is needed and up to a level which is positively dangerous. We don't realize how much salt is used in *processing* canned and frozen food, smoked, cured or salted products.

Most frozen vegetables are washed in salted water. Salt as a preservative goes into *all* canned or bottled products. The difference between fresh food and canned or frozen is amazing for the quantity of salt. Or dried foods versus canned foods. For instance, one cup of canned Boston-style beans contains 606 milligrams of salt. One cup of canned beans with pork contains 928 milligrams. But one cup of cooked dried navy beans contains only 3 milligrams of salt. Another curious and interesting thing is the difference in salt content between brand names, based on different methods of preparation. For instance, one raw tomato contains about 14 milligrams of salt, a six-ounce can of Del Monte tomato paste contains 112 milligrams, while a six-ounce can of Hunt's tomato paste has 610!

I quote a bulletin from the Department of Agriculture:

"Sodium is a mineral element necessary for proper body functions. It is involved in maintaining blood volume and cellular osmotic pressure and in transmitting nerve impulses.

"Body needs for sodium are not great. Intakes of 1,000 to 3,300 milligrams of sodium per day are considered safe and adequate for the healthy adult by the Food and Nutrition Board of the National Academy of Sciences — National Research Council. . . One teaspoon of salt contains approximately 2,000 milligrams of sodium. Current estimates of daily sodium intake by individuals are between 2,300 to 6,900 milligrams. . . Many Americans consume more sodium than they need. . ."

And don't they just!

When one totes up the salt count in canned, prepared, processed foods, PLUS the astronomical salt count in potato chips and junk food, it is surprising that we don't see hundreds of people jumping out of their skins every day with blood pressure or hypertension. Surprising we don't see big fat salt crystals popping out of the pores of half the people we know. *Quel image!*

"Taste for salt." A standard conclusion to many old recipes. Nowadays, we are often instructed to add "¹/2 teaspoon" or even "1 teaspoon" by the cookbook writers. "Pinch" is a good measure, and the more miserly the pinch, the healthier. Let's consider some salt shockers: one cup of evaporated milk contains 266 milligrams of salt, while 4 ounces of regular and/or lowfat cottage cheese contains 457. Gruyère has 95 milligrams an ounce, while Roquefort contains 513. Three ounces of fresh herring contain roughly 75 milligrams, the same amount of smoked herring flies to the moon with 5,234 milligrams of salt. Look at the difference in three kinds of oysters, all based on the measure of three ounces: raw have 113 milligrams, fried 174, frozen 323. Three ounces of raw shrimp total 137 milligrams of salt, the same of fried, 159, the same of canned, 1,955.

Three ounces of cooked lean pork contain 59 milligrams, three ounces of cured ham contain 1,114. Cooked brains, livers, gizzards, hearts, tongue, kidney, tripes and sweetbread contain negligible amounts of salt, but if you feel like going to Hell (or intensive care) just add a good glop of soy sauce (1 tablespoon) at 1,029 milligrams!

Garlic salt, that detestable ersatz substitute for the healthful fresh garlic, contains 1,850 milligrams of salt a teaspoon, while one real toe of garlic checks in at something like six milligrams. Baked or boiled potatoes are serenely out of the battle with 5 milligrams of salt per medium tuber,

while one cup of potatoes *au gratin* check out at 1,095 milligrams. One cup of cooked *fresh* summer squash contains 5 milligrams of salt, while one cup of the same, *canned,* has 785 milligrams.

The message is plain. Cut down on salt like mad. Eat more fresh foods! And don't go dumping salt heavy-handedly into dishes you're cooking; use herbs and spices which enhance flavor and make salt almost unnecessary, taste for salt at the end and if you don't really need it, forget it. People who slowly keep lightening the salt load in their food are all unanimous, in fact, glowing, in their accounts of the discovery of the "real" flavor of many foods. A baked potato flavored with unsalted butter, freshly ground black pepper, and a few mashed cumin seeds, *no salt,* is like meeting a baked potato for the first time.

"Hidden salt" creeps into everything canned, processed, pickled, packed, precooked. Even drinking water. The harder the water, the more salt needed to soften it. Aspirin, bicarbonate of soda, Alka-Seltzer: all loaded with salt. Eight ounces of tap water contains some 12 milligrams of salt, but add a heaping teaspoon of bicarbonate to that glass and you reach 564 milligrams of salt. Cereals, baked goods, frozen dishes with sauces are the chief villains.

There's been a great move toward cutting salt in cookery. One of the chief proponents in this field is the amiable master chef and culinary author, Craig Claiborne, from Sunflower, Mississippi, but long a fixture of the New York scene.

When his doctor discovered highly dangerous blood pressure, Claiborne, formerly a salt fiend, did a complete reversal and joyfully proclaimed that his taste buds had been dulled by too much salt for years, and that his new low-sodium diet has led him to discover the "real" flavors of countless items, even the three that most people think would be intolerable without salt: eggs, potatoes, bread.

Well, every European peasant, and every great European chef knows that quite often a mixture of dried herbs is much more delectable to flavor a dish than all the salt on earth. And that's been the sudden discovery of every soul who, of late, has been prescribed a low-sodium diet.

Begin with unsalted butter. It has a sweet, fresh taste of its own. After using it a week, you'll find the slightly rancid taste of salted butter nothing if not positively *yucky*. A baked potato slathered with unsalted butter, and a mixture of ground dill, cumin seed and freshly ground black pepper is wonderful beyond belief. The delightful, nutty, earthy flavor of the skin comes through in a way it never will when salted.

If you pound or grind a few bay leaves, cumin seeds, a dash of marjoram, a few pepper corns and 2 or 3 grains of sugar, you have a flavoring for soups, stews and omelets which will delight and surprise. Why tell your guests you're on a low-sodium diet? Say you're doing Old High Coromandel cookery or early Marengo County.

Flavor an omelet with finely chopped fresh scallions or chives, the inner leaves of celery, a bit of tarragon and a bit of mustard.

Rub your steak with garlic (rub well!) before cooking. Rub with freshly ground black pepper, too. When meat is cooked to your taste, take from skillet and put some dry white vermouth into the unsalted butter and meat drippings in pan. When it boils up and is slightly reduced, add a *very* small pinch of curry, ditto rosemary, ditto

oregano. Mix your gravy well and pour over steaks. Nobody will notice or question the absence of salt.

Here's a traditional north Italian potato salad which contains not one grain of salt:

Abruzzi Potato Salad

2 pounds potatoes
6 hard-boiled eggs, chopped
1 cup chopped fresh chives or baby green onions
½ cup mayonnaise thinned with a little lemon juice
1½ teaspoons curry powder
½ teaspoon cumin seed
½ teaspoon celery seed
1 good splash dry white wine
butter

Boil your potatoes and peel while hot, saving peelings. While potatoes are still warm, splash the white wine over them, then stir in the flavorings and mayonnaise. Fry chopped potato peels in butter until brown and crisp. Put potato salad on dish in a nice rounded mound, surround with little heaps of fried peels alternating with sliced tomatoes, all sprinkled with chopped parsley or chopped celery leaves.

The major flavorings which can make you forget salt include celery (root, stalk and seed) cumin (warm, spicy, salty aroma) curry (choose a mild one, use with pepper and thyme, for instance) dill (this is very versatile and tastes different according to where you use it; it has a salty presence), garlic (rub meats, fish, potatoes, fowl with garlic, then with lemon; this brings out flavor and *tastes* as if you had slightly salted the dish), mustard (both salty and peppery, in powder form; the seeds are great in soups, vegetables, etc.), marjoram (nice mild pungency, good mixed with sage and red pepper), paprika, oregano (the Italian all-purpose flavoring, an indestructible little herb which will grow anywhere, mixed with thyme, rosemary and bay, the four flavors make up what might be called the Italian National Flavoring), savory, winter or summer variety, (great with beans, meat, eggs, stuffings, to sprinkle, along with cumin, or cornbread.)

But then there's lemon, vermouth, horse-radish, capers, all the onion tribe. Try your hand at flavoring. Taste, taste, taste! If your diners protest, you can always produce a salt-cellar with raised eyebrows and a look of lofty patience. But make them taste first! We all eat too much salt!

SASSAFRAS
Salop Tree, Tea Tree, Sassafrax
(Sassafras officinale)

The Spaniards, landing in Florida in 1512, noticed that the Indians chewed an aromatic root for various minor ailments, and took specimens back to Europe, hailing the plant as only another example of what a richness of medicines and foodstuffs could be derived from the New World. For almost a century it was used in Europe in cures for syphilis, rheumatism, for menstrual and afterbirth pains. There is mention of its being cultivated in England in 1633. Up until World War I, in London, on street corners in the early morning, one could buy hot "saloop," sassafras tea mixed with sugar and milk. This tea is still enjoyed in many parts of the rural South, where the tender young leaves are still used in spring salads.

It is native to the eastern United States, from Canada to Florida, and along the Gulf Coast and west as far as Mexico. It is a handsome tree, reaching twenty to forty feet, with both simple lanceolate and maple-type leaves occurring together. Sassafras has inconspicuous greenish yellow flowers followed by blue berries on little red stems. The roots are large, woody, with a reddish brown spongy bark. All parts of the tree are aromatic. Bark, leaves and buds were used in nineteenth-century America as a tea substitute. Many opiates for children are flavored with sassafras to make them palatable.

Ever since its first discovery, sassafras has been praised as a dental antiseptic. The oil obtained from the roots and bark is the heaviest of the volatile oils known, and is used to flavor chewing gum, cough and cold medicines, in a soothing remedy for inflamed eyes, and to make a soothing drink for catarrhal problems. Tom Stobart, in his book on herbs and spices, mentions a Sassafras Cordial made in the United States in the last century and quotes the ingredients to indicate what a wealth of flavorings were used by old-fashioned cooks: sarsaparilla, gum arabic, white wine, juniper berries, pistachio nuts, lemon syrup, rosemary leaves, sweet marjoram, candied lemon and citron, sugar candy, muscatel raisins, sherry, and distilled grape spirits!

The tree is, even as I write, an important commercial crop: a handsome yellow dye comes from the wood and bark, a fragrant oil distilled from the root-bark is employed in the manufacture of cheap toilet soap and perfume. Sassafrid, a kind of tannic acid, is widely used in curing leather, especially in Spain and Greece.

Perhaps you think you have known sassafras only in a childhood tea or perhaps in mouthwash or chewing gum. You have, if you live on the Gulf Coast, consumed gallons of powdered dried sassafras leaves, for

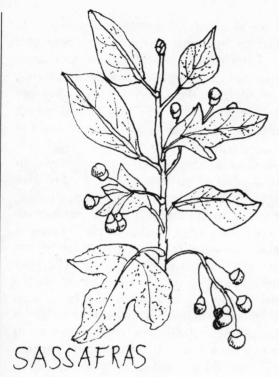

SASSAFRAS

it is the bulk of the thickening agent called *gumbo filé*. Now, attention! Almost ALL gumbo filés (they vary in color and consistency, according to where and how fabricated) are almost entirely sassafras leaves, with some additional flavoring, usually powdered dried thyme leaves, sometimes powdered bay leaves, sometimes—in older versions—a little savory or basil. The best pure unflavored gumbo filé, of fresh young leaves, has always been that made by Dossy Moon in Bayou la Batre. HOWEVER, there are some gumbo filés made entirely of powdered dried okra pods, seeds and all. The okra powder is universal in most of the northern sections of Africa as a thickening for sauces and stews. Although gumbo filé, with us, is usually employed only for gumbos, it makes a delightful addition to many soups and stews, as well as to thicken and perk up sauces and gravies. Sassafras sass!

SAVORY
Sariette, Nun's Pepper
Summer Savory (*Satureia hortensis*)
Winter Savory (*Satureia montana*)

There are some fourteen species of herbs or woody small shrubs of the genus *Satureia* (the name is found in Pliny), most of Mediterranean origin. Winter and summer savory are the most-used, although in Spain a wild member of the family called *Sabroso* is widely employed. The savories are among the most documented of traditional herbs, both for medicinal value and use in the kitchen.

In late medieval France, medical writers were already quarrelling in good testy French fashion over whether the name *Satureia* was derived from the satyrs, "who used it to accomplish their amourous exploits" as Aemilius Macer tells us in his *De Herbarium Virtutibus,* or from a more lowly origin, the *satura,* a humble vegetable stew in which savory was used to give zest. The Greeks and Latins used the savories in many modes: infusions for earache, a concentration for toothache, always for persistent diarrheas or enteritis. The midwives swore by it as an antiseptic during childbirth, and so it goes.

Its widespread use is reflected in the hundreds of popular names throughout Europe: savory, sadre, ass's pepper, nun's pepper, St. Julian's herb, and an amusing galaxy of appellations referring to the herb's use as a remedy against flatulence. And, although the savories are completely delicious in cookery, belonging to a family of musky, mildly peppery flavors somewhere between thyme and marjoram, it is with beans that

"God designated Savory for bean cookery."
GOETHE

e.

ranks as a natural agent against diarrhea, enteritis, intestinal parasites, flatulence, etc. Russian chemists, in recent years, have demonstrated the powers of a powerful essence derived from the savories, rather like thymol, and composed of carvacrol and cymol, and not yet given a final name for the *pharmaceutica*.

For us the savories are a completely delicious addition to the herb garden, to give highly pleasant savor to stuffings, on fish, mixed with unsalted butter, for instance, to serve with a T-bone steak, to use in omelets, salads, in cornbread laced with herbs and seeds (try savory, dill, celery seeds in your next batch of flat-pan cornbread) and . . . and . . . and . . . in any bean dish whatsoever. Brillat-Savarin says that one of the greatest dishes on earth is steamed broadbeans flavored with butter, pepper, and savory. I've tried it. He's not far off.

Summer savory is an annual, easy to grow, likes full sun, is untidy, straggling, and rather unprepossessing with its narrow leaves and small mauvish flowers. Winter savory is woodier, a perennial, with darker purplish flowers; summer savory grows from seeds, winter savory usually from cuttings. A French writer of the seventeenth century says, "These modest little plants look as if they were intended to bloom in the cloistered gardens of the good nuns." Although the exact recipe for Chartreuse is unknown, spies have always reported that vast quantities of melissa and savory go into the liqueur.

Try growing summer savory. Use some young leaves to make a savory bread just as you would make a garlic bread. Or try a simple omelet or boiled navy beans flavored with savory: you'll never be without it again.

they are most mentioned, in fact nominated "bean-herb" in most Germanic kitchens. The whole range of bean stews, soups, loaves in Flemish cookery ALL require one of the savories. And all the recipes for "tonics" for aging gentlemen who'd like to reacquire sexual prowess when "pestered by young and ardent wives" are variants of an infusion of savory with a little angelica and a few peppercorns, said to help such a person "reacquire such virility as to allow him to rival the satyrs of ancient Greece."

Well, as in nine out of ten cases of old wives' tales about herbal remedies and tonics, there's a lot in them. In 1934, Dr. Schulzik published the results of a life's work on *sarriette* (savory's French name, as common on the Gulf Coast as the English one), which placed savory back in the front

SESAME, BENNE
Gingilly, Teel, Till, Vanglo, Ajonoli.
(Sesamum indicum)

An ancient, but ancient, Assyrian myth which turned up incised on a stone tablet, has a grand tale of how the gods drank sesame seed wine when they sat around the table at a committee meeting which was creating the earth. Don't mistake me. I am not laughing. All the myths in every society contain crystallized truths we often are not able to comprehend today, what with our taste for plastics, statistics, and safe mediocrity.

You wonder why *Open, Sesame!* made the cave of riches open in the Arabian Nights tale of *Ali Baba and the Forty Thieves* when the names of barley, wheat, etc. were conjured in vain? Well, oil of sesame is mildly laxative, and it is possible we have there some ancient joke of the type enjoyed by medical students. Benne or sesame has been cultivated for thousands of years, and India and China still produce the most, but it is widely grown in all the tropical and subtropical lands, including the Southern states of the United States.

Benne is a pretty, annual plant about five feet high, with pink or white flowers. The oblong seed capsules contain ivory-white seeds, although they are sometimes red, brown or black, according to which of the twelve species is being considered. These seeds are rich in oil, sometimes 60 percent. This oil is the basis of margarine, but serves as an almost colorless, almost flavorless cooking or salad oil for a huge part of the world of the East, also in Mexico.

The sesame is a native of India and is probably the source of the first vegetable oil used by humankind. Seeds and oil have some element in them which prevents their ever going rancid. A curious thing about sesame: although it will grow like a weed as far north as Massachusetts and the Great Lakes, nobody grows it, save, rarely, in the South. The United States imports some 45,000 metric tons every year. In most of the Eastern Mediterranean and Hindu worlds, a paste made of sesame seeds is considered highly aphrodisiac; it is also delicious. The plant has lovely pink or white trumpet flowers; it resists drought, nematodes, and most insects.

The seeds, slightly roasted, have an exquisite nutty flavor and are used in hundreds of dishes. They are often sprinkled on bread, rolls, cakes or cookies. Ground fine, the seeds provide *tahina*, which is like a more liquid peanut butter and is part of many salad dressings, used to flavor a very good purée of chick peas, *hummus*. But in

Sesame

all the Middle East, the most widespread use of this benne paste is for a universal appetizer dip. The paste is flavored with garlic and lemon juice and served with good crusty bread. In the South Atlantic states, the seeds are used to thicken broths, puddings. Pounded with mustard seeds and honey, they formed a common glaze for ham in the eighteenth century. *Trout amandine* (trout garnished with toasted almond slivers) is nothing beside *trout bennine* (trout garnished with toasted benne seeds and a little dill). Here's an old north Georgia coast recipe:

Chicken with Benne Seeds

Disjoint a couple of young fryers. Wash and dry them. Rub with lemon, then with garlic. Dip them in melted unsalted butter, then in benne seeds. Sprinkle a little salt over them, and a touch of cayenne pepper. Cut up a head of celery, leaves and all, and toss into boiling water for seven minutes. Drain and arrange in buttered flat oven dish. Sprinkle with salt and lemon juice, dot with butter. Place chicken on this bed of celery and cook about an hour at 350 degrees, turning once and adding butter and a little dry sherry to baste. Test with fork; when thickest piece shows yellow juice instead of pink, chicken is ready. Serve in oven pan, with good bread.

Charleston Cookies

Beat an egg, add ½ cup sugar, 2 tablespoons flour, 2 tablespoons melted unsalted butter, 1 teaspoon vanilla extract and enough slightly toasted benne seed to make a good stiff mixture. Grease a cookie sheet and puff a little flour over it. Drop tablespoons of mixture and bake at 350 degrees until done. Let cool a little in pan; they become brittle if handled too soon, and crumble. Store in tight-lidded tin.

Apart from the widespread predilection among Arab males for *tahina* or *tahini* piled on pita bread as an aphrodisiac, all desert dwellers make a kind of "journeycake" or "journey pick-me-up," which is bread crumbs pounded with sesame oil, dates, pistachios, almonds (rarely with candied orange peel, dried currants, raisins, and occasionally dried peach flesh). This is shaped into balls about the same as our jawbreakers and is refreshment and energizer on long journeys.

SORREL
French Sorrel (*Rumex scutatus*)
Garden, or English Sorrel (*Rumex acetosa*)

The cultivated sorrels have been developed from a huge family of plants with pleasantly acid leaves which go by such names as cuckoo bread (from the ancient supposition that the bird ate these leaves to clear its throat before singing), stickwort, fairy bells, hallelujah (since the young leaves were best for cooking during the Easter season when sounds of Hallelujah filled the churches), stubworth, seamsog, sour sabs, green sauce, sour sauce, sour dock.

Many lovers of the table know the herb only in its form of French sorrel and only under the name of *oseille* and particularly as an ingredient of such famous French soups as *potage germiny* or in green sauces for the oilier fishes. To complicate matters, there is a little woodland plant called wood sorrel which has much the same flavor but is of quite another family: *Oxalis acetosella*. Usually, but not always, seed catalogues will

French Sorrel

specify French sorrel or garden (English) sorrel.

They are both delicious, but the French has the better flavor. It has leaves of a kind of elongated heart shape, or buckler shape; it loves moist soil and full sun, and is an unflappable perennial. A little set of four plants will suffice the ordinary family. If you have the French form *(Rumex scutatus)* you will find you dote on the young leaves in a banal lettuce salad, which it perks up in noteworthy fashion. Apart from its use in soups, there is no better accompaniment for veal, pork, eggs, fish, than a purée made from blanched chopped sorrel leaves softened in butter a few minutes. No better summer dish than blanched, chopped sorrel leaves mixed with cubes of cooked cucumber and made into a lemon-flavored aspic (Mrs. Knox and citrus fruit, please, no coal-tar derivative "lemon-flavored") with a few

chopped capers, fresh or dried dill, and a bit of finely chopped parsley. With a cold fish or crustacean dish this is pure delight. Never cook your sorrel in iron pots—a nasty metallic taste will occur.

The Scandinavians use sorrel as an ingredient in the wonderful stuffings they employ for sole, salmon, right up to eels and strong-flavored fish. Sorrel is great in a green sauce to serve with goose, too, just as you would applesauce. This herb is sometimes called "sour-leaf spinach" which indicates something of its flavor and uses. Cut off the flower stems when they appear, so as to have a constant supply of young leaves coming up. There is a round-leaved sorrel which has been developed, which grows rather like spinach, but it is hard to find seeds of this form.

Sorrel Soup

1 pound fresh sorrel leaves
1 finely chopped white onion
1 cup cream
1/3 cup butter
3 cups chicken broth
2 beaten egg yolks
pinch mace
salt to taste
freshly ground black pepper

Pick over sorrel, wash well. Dry leaves, chop them rather coarsely into thumbnail-size bits. Cook onion in butter until soft, add sorrel and simmer 5 minutes, stirring constantly. Now beat your cream and egg yolks together until thoroughly mixed. Bring chicken broth to a simmer, add cream-egg mixture gradually, beating all the while with a whisk. Don't let it boil. Now stir in the chopped, wilted sorrel, salt, mace, pepper. Heat well, serve at once.

Star Anise

STAR ANISE
(Illicium verum Hook)

Everybody knows anise seed. People usually love or loathe the flavor. No middle ground. A slightly stronger flavor comes from star anise. The usual anise is of the *Umbelliferae;* related to caraway and dill, it looks not unlike them. Star anise is something else: seeds from a pretty member of the magnolia family. True anise and star anise have the same liquorice-like taste; they both contain essential oils of the same chemical composition. (Jokey old Mother Nature! Think of cloves and clove-scented pinks and carnations!)

Star anise is a small evergreen tree native to southwestern China, with yellow star-like flowers which, from a distance, look rather like jonquils. The tree begins to bear in its sixth year and lives past 100 years. Traditional Japanese temple incense contains star anise bark, while all over the Orient the seeds are chewed to aid digestion and sweeten the breath after anything containing onion or garlic. Only in 1971 did the United States government lift the ban on importing spices from mainland China, so slowly but surely the star anise has re-entered our spice cupboards. But our dogs and cats have become more accustomed to it than we, for it is a popular flavoring in pet food. The Florida anise tree *(Illicium floridanum Ellis)* is said to flourish all along the Gulf Coast. An evergreen six to ten feet in height with purplish flowers, it occurs as an ornamental in many famous European gardens. I don't know this shrub. I'd love to hear from anybody who knows it or grows it locally.

Old Mobile cooks before the turn of the century knew and used star anise in much the same way as did their Chinese counterparts: to flavor duck and pork dishes. Sometimes garlicky sauces for fish list "1 anise seed, crushed" as ingredient. This refers to star anise, not the true anise. A delicious chowder made of mackerel and oysters was flavored with bay leaf, red pepper, orange peel, garlic, onion, sherry and star anise. There is a spice little-known in the Occident which is called anise-pepper, of the rue family, and is the red hot spicy berries of a little feathery, spiny tree. Again, it goes into fish and pork dishes. Here is a delicious old accompaniment to meat, especially game:

Fig Conserves

1 pound dried figs
1 teaspoon crushed star anise seeds
2 cups water
1 cup sugar
4 teaspoons fresh lemon juice
3/4 cup chopped pecans or walnuts
dash bitters

Soak figs and star anise seeds in water for 4 hours. Bring to a boil, add sugar, cook slowly, uncovered. After about 25 minutes, when syrup has thickened, and figs are tender, remove and let cool. Stir in other ingredients.

And here is an Italian classic:

Anise Cookies

1 teaspoon star anise seeds
¹/₂ cup unsalted butter
³/₄ cup sugar
2 large eggs
¹/₄ teaspoon salt
2 cups sifted flour
1¹/₂ teaspoons baking powder

Crush seeds and mix with butter. Blend in sugar. Beat in eggs. Sift flour with baking powder and salt, then gradually stir in first mixture. Mix well until smooth. Shape into 1-inch balls. Place on greased cookie sheet 2 inches apart. Bake in preheated 350-degree oven 10 minutes or until light brown. Cool and put into airtight jars or tins. Better after sitting a day or so.

SUNFLOWER
(Helianthus annuus)

Sunflowers, of which there are about fifty species, are native to the new world, some found in North America; the giant sunflower which we discuss here originating in Peru and Mexico, was introduced to the northern continent in the 1600s. (The Jerusalem artichoke, *Helianthus tuberosus* or *novascotiensis*, is another valuable member of the tribe.)

The sunflower is easy to grow, not fussy about conditions, thrives in everything from rocky uplands to damp lowlands. The Spanish explorers found the sun priestesses of

the Incas wearing crowns of sunflowers, found sunflowers wrought in pure gold in their temples: they considered the flowers an earthy manifestation of the Sun God. Introduced into Spain, the plant quickly spread through Europe, Africa and the Slavic countries. All are today a big commercial crop, for every part of the sunflower is useful. The leaves are good cattle fodder, an oil pressed from the seed is the closest to olive or almond oil there is; much sought for in salads and frying. A second oil pressed from the seed mass is widely used in soap and candlemaking, and in artists' supplies. As chicken feed, the seeds make for highly productive egg-laying. The stems contain a fiber important in papermaking.

The pith of the sunflower stalk is the lightest of natural substances; its specific gravity one-eighth that of cork, hence its value for manufacturing life-savers and various floats. After the seeds have under-

Sunflower e.

gone a first cold pressing and a second warm pressing, the resulting seedcake which is left is of highest importance in feeding sheep, pigs, rabbits, pigeons, as well as poultry, and all of them relish it.

Roasted like coffee, the seeds produce a delicious drink. Universally, the toasted seed serves as a snack, while coarsely ground seed is used in Portugal and Russia to make a palatable crunchy flatbread. The unopened flower buds of the sunflower are cooked and eaten like artichokes. The black-seeded variety yields one of the best lamp oils known, burning longer than any other vegetable oil.

The dried leaves, flower heads, and stems provide a very good litter and/or nesting material for chickens and ducks. The dried remains, burnt, leave an ash rich in potash, and highly useful to dig into beds where next year you'll plant potatoes or root crops. But right away. If you leave the potash sitting about in the rain, it washes and loses its value. Dried leaves are used as part of herbal tobaccos.

The seeds, browned in the oven, and made into an infusion, make a widely used remedy for whooping cough. The Chinese grow acres and use stem fibers to strengthen their silks. It is a perfect bee crop, supplying large quantities of wax and nectar. But that is not all! Listen to Mrs. Grieve, in her *Herbal:* "The growing sunflower is extremely useful for drying damp soils, because of its remarkable ability to absorb quantities of water. Swampy districts in Holland have been made habitable by an extensive culture of the sunflower, the malarial miasma being absorbed and nullified, whilst abundant oxygen is emitted."

Oh, and one thing I forgot: the petals, steeped, produce a nice bright yellow dye, easily fixed by alum.

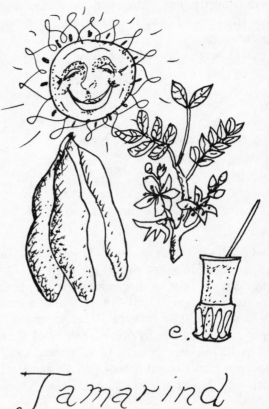

Tamarind

TAMARIND, INDIAN DATE
(*Tamarindus indica*)

Most people, if they know the tamarind at all, know it as the basis for a milky white and highly refreshing bottled beverage sold in hot latitudes around the world and back again. It has the same refreshing sweet sourness or bitey sweetness of lemonade. But the little-known and highly important function of the tamarind pod is as a souring agent for hundreds of curry dishes. It is its high content of tartaric acid which distinguishes this seasoning.

The tamarind tree is very beautiful. It is a member of the legume family, and probably originated in tropical East Africa, but has been grown in India and Ceylon since pre-history. It reaches heights of eighty or even more feet, but is usually seen in examples of fifty or sixty feet high. The seed pods are dark brown when ripe, about six to eight inches long.

The sticky, messy mass of fiber and seeds sold in food shops is rather unpleasant-looking, but the flavor of the prepared pulp adds immeasurably to hundreds of dishes. It is, in fact, the "secret ingredient" of much of Indian and African cookery.

One pours boiling water on a mess of pods, lets them cool, then one rubs and squashes the mess with the fingers until there is a brownish purée. That is the classic method, but the process is different for this famous sauce:

Tamarind Sauce

Soak one pound of tamarind in vinegar until it is soft. Squash it to a purée with the fingers. Pass through a sieve. (Put the fiber and seeds in your compost heap.) Now scrape the peel off 4 ounces of fresh ginger and cut it into small pieces. Clean and peel the same weight of garlic and red hot hellfire peppers. Whizz, blend, or beat this into a pulp. Add 4 ounces salt and 1/2 pound sugar. Boil all this. Taste to see if you want more sugar or more vinegar (everybody's taste for sweet-sour is different). Usually a scant pint of vinegar is enough. This sauce is delicious with chicken roasted after being rubbed inside and out with lemon and garlic. Watercress makes the perfect garnish. For your information, tamarind is slightly laxative.

TANSY
Stinking Willie, Barbotine Tanaceto, Bachelor's Buttons, Bitter Buttons, Etc.
(Tanacetum vulgare)

This bitter herb is native to Europe but has become common in the eastern half of North America. It has very pretty fern-like leaves, and yellow button flowers. The odor is odd, not altogether disagreeable; it has something of camphor or a hint of burning rubber and brickdust.

It has always been one of the herbs used in embalming, and in pre-refrigeration days was a great help in preserving fresh or cooked meats. Tansy, mixed with elder leaves, has always been used to repel flies. In England it is always used to make puddings, breads, teas served in Lent and at Easter. The Danes use it in small amounts to flavor

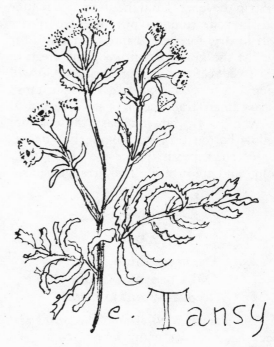

e. Tansy

cookies, and the Finns create from it the rich, dark-green dye found in Finnish woolens. Minute quantities of chopped dried tansy leaves have long been a substitute for pepper in salads, omelets, stews, etc., in the Scandinavian countries, and it is still rubbed on fresh meat to keep away flies; farm workers in Italy, Spain, and France rub the plant on their skin to keep away all insects.

It is a beautiful plant indeed, easy to grow, but has a tendency to take over. Ideally, it is planted in a buried bottomless keg or some such, to keep the runners from spreading. But it is a must for a garden, for it is one of the most mineral-rich of all herbs. The serious gardener can only love it, for its value in the compost heap is enormous. Popping with potassium, resins, oils and acids, its leaves provide rare and sought-for elements. A thriving plant, you can cut it back twice in a season.

Strip the leaves from the stems and scatter half in your compost pile, keep the other half to dry, for rubbed into your dog's fur against the grain, it will keep the creature flea-free. Scattered on pantry shelves, it will keep ants away. If you drag a twig of tansy across an ant trail, they'll bust a little gut to move off. Last, but not least, the cheerful yellow button flowers, looking like daisies minus their petals, dry easily, keep their color, and are nice in dried arrangements.

TARO
Dasheen, Eddo, Ape,
Old Cocoyam, Calliu
(*Colocasia antiquorum*)

This plant is used around the world and back again under many names. Many old

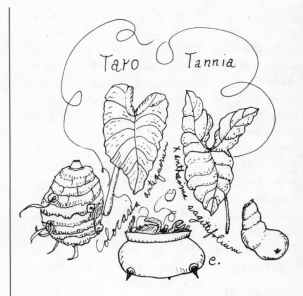

gardens in the South included them. They look just like our elephant's ears. The root is the source of a fine-grained starch, easily digestible, which is used as thickener for stews and dozens of gumbo-like mixtures, from soups to meat and vegetable dishes. The underground corms are the part usually eaten, but the stems and even leaves are used, too. *Taro* is the name in the Pacific islands, in the West Indies it is *eddo* or *dasheen*, in West Africa, *old cocoyam*. An unrelated root is also called *taro* in certain Pacific islands. In Tahiti it is called *ape*. In the Pacific, a paste used in sauces and gravies is called *poi*; this is from the corms of the taro. Our local elephant's ear, botanically *Tannia (Xanthosoma sagittifulium)*, which grows to great heights, even taller than a man in frostless years, is known in East Africa as *new cocoyam* or *yautia* and is used the same as taro.

Here is an excerpt from a letter by Warren Norville, master of the trawler *Nunaliza*, while laying in port at Port of Spain on passage from Monrovia, Liberia, to Bayou la Batre, Alabama, in October of 1974. Norville had seen great blue land crabs in the market and was told they were used in a dish called *calliu*. The ship's cook said he could make it and arrived early one morning with all the provisions, including stems and leaves of taro. Here are Norville's words:

"*Calliu* is very similar to our gumbo, but uses several native vegetables. The *calliu* plant is also known here as *dasheen* — an East Indian name. It is like a small elephant ear in appearance. About the size of your caladiums." To make:

――――

Calliu

1 large bunch of *calliu*. Use stems and leaves. Peel. 16 large okras, sliced not too thinly, 1 large onion, chopped coarsely, 1 coconut, grated, and the coconut milk, 6 to 8 large crabs, the blue land crabs, if you can get them. They are plentiful in Southern Florida. Our blue crabs, from Mobile Bay, should be great, too, as well as shrimp, BUT if you do not have the blue land crabs and wish to be strictly Trinidadian, use salt beef.

Dump all this in a pot, add a minimum of water to cover, salt and pepper to taste, and boil not too hard for several hours. From time to time swirl vigorously with a swirler stirrer. Serve over mounds of boiled rice.

For a side dish serve boiled ripe yellow plantains. Cut the plantains into several large sections and boil them in their skins. When tender remove from pot. Drain, peel, slice longways. Also boil slices of white yams until tender, in the same pot with plantains. They taste much like Irish potatoes. This makes a very good, but different meal.

――――

TARRAGON, ESTRAGON
Little Dragon, Mugwort
(Artemisia dracunculus)

"Tarragon" always means "French tarragon." It is a plant which very rarely produces viable seed; it is multiplied by cuttings or by root division. There is a Russian variety which has coarser growth and stronger flavor; all seeds marked "tarragon" are from the Russian form. But the French culinary herb has a distinctive flavor, slightly sweetish, with a slightly bitter aftertaste, which for many people sums up the delicacy and appeal of French cooking.

Tarragon goes into *sauce bearnaise*, and to flavor the famous chicken with tarragon dish. The ghastly mess passed off in restaurants as tartar sauce bears absolutely no resemblance to the exquisite French *sauce tartare* flavored with tarragon and capers and so delicious with any fish or crustaceans. Tarragon is one of the *fines herbes* of classic culinary fame, along with chervil, chives, parsley. Another classic French sauce is simplicity itself:

――――

Ravigote Sauce

After roasting your chicken, remove the fat from the pan but leave all the juices. Add 1 cup of brown stock, 1 tablespoon each of chopped tarragon, chervil, and chives, and 1 crushed garlic clove. Stir it all well and bring just to a boil. Serve with the herbs in it, over your chicken, or over rice or even spaghetti.

Tarragon is easy to grow. It likes full sun, deeply dug soil. It hates water standing on its feet. Some people grow it in big terra cotta pots which they can bring onto the back porch during our protracted summer rainy periods, for tarragon simply cannot tolerate poor drainage. The plant has delicate fleshy roots—too much water and they simply rot. All herbalists and botanists point out that tarragon, unlike such stalwarts as rue, basil, thyme, and lavender, has no lore or legend attached to it. Throughout its long history it has been noted only as a culinary herb, that and no more. But once one has discovered the tantalizing flavor in any one of the hundreds of dishes it pervades, once one has used real homemade tarragon vinegar, or eaten chicken with tarragon, one cannot live without it.

Tartar Sauce

1 egg yolk
¹/₈ teaspoon salt, mustard, and freshly ground pepper
¹/₂ cup olive oil
1 tablespoon tarragon vinegar
few drops lemon juice
2 teaspoons chopped green olives
2 teaspoons chopped tarragon
1 teaspoon chopped capers

Stir the egg yolk with the mustard, salt and pepper. Add the oil drop by drop, beating constantly until mixture is smooth and thick. Beat in vinegar and lemon carefully. (A minute or two in the blender will do it.) Add the olives, tarragon and capers. Good with boiled shrimp, crab, any fish dish.

Baby Lamb Chops with Tarragon

For four people you'll need 8 to 12 baby lamb chops, 3 tablespoons butter, ¹/₂ cup dry white vermouth, 1 teaspoon tarragon, 2 tablespoons chopped parsley. Sauté chops in butter to preferred stage of doneness. Pour off some of the fat. Place chops on hot platter. Add vermouth, tarragon, parsley to pan

juices. Boil briskly, stirring constantly, until mixture is reduced by one half. Pour over chops and serve at once.

Chicken with Tarragon

3-3¹/₂ pound chicken, cut into serving pieces
5 tablespoons unsalted butter
2 tablespoons finely chopped tarragon
3 tablespoons finely chopped shallots
¹/₂ cup dry white wine
1¹/₂ cups heavy cream
3 tablespoons flour
1 tablespoon Calvados or applejack
Salt and freshly ground black pepper

Sprinkle chicken pieces with salt and pepper. Melt 3 tablespoons butter over high heat and put in chicken, skin-side down. Cook until golden brown, then turn. Sprinkle with all the shallots and half the tarragon. Cover, cook on low heat for 15 minutes. Remove cover, sprinkle chicken with wine, re-cover, cook 15 minutes longer. Remove chicken to hot dish and keep covered while preparing sauce. Add 1 cup of cream to skillet, stir well. Blend the flour with remaining butter and add it, a little at a time, to simmering sauce. Add just enough to make the desired consistency. Cook five minutes, then stir in the calvados or apple-jack and add remaining cream. Put chicken back into sauce, spooning sauce over. Sprinkle with remaining tarragon, serve at once on hot platter.

TEQUILA
Magellan's Revenge

Now and again one reads a heady account of how Cortez and his bullies found the Aztecs drinking tequila. Not bloody likely! They had no knowledge of distillation; tequila is a kind of brandy. The Spaniards noted that the Aztecs consumed a vast quantity of *pulque*, which is a wine made from the heart of the agave or century plant. (More misinformation in the name "century"—the century plant blooms from eight to twenty years, one giant variety in forty.) But the conquistadores soon taught the Aztecs how to distill their wine into brandy, and *tequila* was the result.

The agave, called *maguey* in Spanish, is a family of fleshy-leaved, dry-area plants. Some 400 varieties, including mescalines, have been catalogued and studied; it is estimated that there are probably 800 to 900 varieties. Only five or six, in all the family, produce good wine. The heart of the plant, near the base, referred to as the "pineapple," weighs roughly 75 to 150 pounds. When the plant blooms, the sap, known as *aguamiel* ("honey-water") drains down into this central portion which is cut and shipped to the distillery. The distilled wine we know takes its name from the town of Tequila in the Jalisco state of Mexico, where the principal distilleries have long been located.

No two living creatures agree as to the taste and aroma of tequila. Brandy-like, certainly, more like Greek brandy than French. Something slightly fruity, perhaps suggesting calvados. An aftertaste which reminds many of bourbon. A sharp white spirit, not timid. About 100 to 106 proof (vodka is 190, bourbon 125-150, etc.)

Since 1972 the consumption of tequila has increased noticeably, and most attribute this to the fact that rock singer Mick Jagger and the Rolling Stones, guiding lights for so many young people, drank tequila drinks rather than gin, vodka, or whisky. He was paid to indicate this choice—we are informed by historians of Madison Avenue—by the Heublein Company, which had already mounted a highly successful publicity campaign to convert the United States to vodka.

Habitual barflies love to argue long into the night over the tequila ritual: does one take a nip of salt, then of lemon or lime before each sip or does the fruit come before the salt? (I think lime is much better than lemon here.)

What is less known in the United States are the delights of tequila in cookery. Try pouring a few tablespoons of heated tequila over boiled shrimp or boiled lobster flesh, then setting it on fire. Turn for a moment or so until liquid is burned, then add some heavy cream, a little dry sherry, freshly ground black pepper and a few cups of chopped watercress. Serve on buttered toast. Very fine indeed.

Or if, as I, you are bored stiff with the usual shrimp cocktail, try making such with quite another sauce:

Shrimp Cocktail Jalisco

¹/₃ cup mayonnaise
²/₃ cup sour cream
1 RIPE avocado, peeled and stoned
2 tablespoons lime juice
¹/₄ cup minced fresh dill or ¹/₈ cup dried dill
1 tablespoon finely minced onion
a little garlic juice
2 tablespoons tequila
freshly ground black pepper
salt to taste

Blend mashed avocado, mayonnaise, sour cream and lime juice. Mix in the other ingredients and purée in blender or food processor a few seconds. Mix in your cleaned boiled shrimp. But this is delicious with plain boiled or broiled fish, or crabmeat, too.

In Mexico, Central America and parts of the Caribbean, tequila is employed in dozens of tasty dishes. Look at these:

Hamburgers with Tequila

¹/₂ cup tequila
2 tablespoons olive oil
¹/₂ cup minced celery
¹/₂ cup minced onion
4 tablespoons tarragon vinegar
2 crushed bay leaves
pinch thyme
freshly ground black pepper
pinch salt

Mix all, heat over low flame; don't simmer. Chill in ice box. Brush this marinade frequently over hamburgers while cooking them. (Tough beef can be marinated in this overnight for stew; steaks are delicious broiled with this marinade.)

Avocado Cream

¹/₃ cup mayonnaise
²/₃ cup sour cream
1 ripe avocado, pared and pitted
2 tablespoons lime juice
¹/₄ cup minced or dried dill
1 tablespoon finely minced onion
2 tablespoons tequila
salt and freshly ground black pepper to taste

Purée all and serve with grilled or broiled fish or alongside a green salad. Very good with boiled new potatoes or as a dip for fresh boiled pearl onions or as a party dip.

NOTE: There are many variations of this; the important ingredients are the ripe avocado, tequila, mayonnaise and cream. Some use grated lemon peel instead of lime juice, chopped capers are often included. In New Orleans I ate a nifty version which had Mama's bread-and-butter pickles chopped into it. Pickles more sweet than sour.

Chile Dolores

1 pound lean pork strips
1 pound lean beef chuck strips
1 cup sliced celery
1 big or 2 small onions, sliced thin
2 minced garlic toes
1/2 teaspoon oregano
1 teaspoon cilantro (coriander)
1 1/2 cups sliced mild green chilies
1 big can whole tomatoes, chopped
1 cup tequila
few drops beef bouillon
1 tablespoon or 2 splashes green pepper sauce
(more of New Orleans type, less of
Mexican type: judge for yourself)
salt to taste

Brown meats in oil. Stir in everything else. Simmer with lid some 1 1/2 hours, or till meat is just right. Garnish with sour cream if you like. Serves 4 to 6.

Tequila possibilities: try grated Swiss cheese with a little sweet paprika, mayonnaise and tequila to make a toasted cheese sandwich after the opera or the ballet. Splash your shrimp bisque with a little tequila. Add tequila to a curry sauce. Try a mayonnaise made with tequila and some almond flavoring, served with a platter of chilled, boiled, new vegetables as a summer supper. Picks up even the most exhausted, bored, or indifferent.

Try dressing any fresh fruit salad with tequila and almond extract: you'll be pleasantly surprised. Using honey instead of sugar, of course, and not too much.

THYME
(*Thymus vulgaris* and other varieties)

There are many delightful varieties of thyme, but the one we usually associate with cookery is the *Thymus vulgaris*, which is native (along with many other kinds) to the Mediterranean world. The Romans brought it from Greece, where it provided beehives with its rich pollen; the plant is considered the best for honey-making, with lavender and other plants coming close behind. All the thymes are native to sun-soaked rocky places; they are easy to grow if they have heat and good drainage. The oil thymol is present in highly concentrated amounts. The pure oil is an antiseptic twelve times as powerful as carbolic acid. A tea made by pouring boiling water over a handful of fresh thyme leaves is highly effective at the first symptoms of cold or sore throat. And the oil, rubbed into the temples, cures headaches more quickly than drugs or sedatives. Good for cuts or grazes.

The botanists have as many headaches with thyme as with the mints. They crossbreed dizzily. But some of the best-known and most-used varieties are, apart from our garden thyme, a lovely lemon thyme (*Thymus citriodorus*) wonderful with meats and seafood, and the caraway thyme (*Thymus herba barona*). This last comes from Corsica. Old cookbooks used to mention *Erba barona* to the mystification of the unenlightened: it only meant that thyme was so good with a "baron of beef," a big roast. There is a nutmeg thyme, the tiny-leaved, creeping mother-of-thyme, beautiful golden and variegated varieties. Nothing more pleasant in a garden than a strawberry jar with a collection of thymes trailing from the various apertures.

If carrots, celery, onion, garlic are the Big Four in their realm of basis for soups, stews, marinades and so forth, the Big Four of the herb world for the same dishes would be determined as thyme, bay, sage and parsley.

Thyme goes into so many recipes for mixed meat and fish dishes that a book of thyme recipes would run to several volumes. It goes into the vinegar or brine to flavor olives as they cure; it is one of the ingredients of the famous *Benedictine* liqueur, in most of the vermouths, and many other *apéritifs* and *digestifs*. It has a deep aromatic presence which heightens the other flavors. It is often mixed with marjoram which belongs to the same family of flavors, often flung onto the embers for open-fire roasting or barbecues. Here's an old New Orleans soup which perfectly shows off the flavor of thyme:

Seafood and Tomato Soup

2 pints mussels (or clams), or 1 pound shrimp
4 large tomatoes, skinned and seeded
2 cups minced onion
2 garlic cloves, crushed
²/₃ cup olive oil
1 teaspoon thyme (lemon thyme is best, if findable)
1 bay leaf, torn
2 heaping teaspoons minced fresh parsley
salt and freshly ground pepper
a little grated lemon peel

Scrub mussels or clams with bristle brush; steam them open over 2 cups boiling water, let juice drip into water. (If this is your stock strain through cloth to remove sand.) If you use shrimp, cook with skins on for 5 minutes in well-seasoned bouillon and let them cool in liquid. Peel the shrimp, save liquid. If you like a few crayfish, a few shrimp, whatever shellfish can be combined. Cook onions, garlic, tomatoes in olive oil until just tender, add fish liquid plus enough water to make about 6 cups. Add bay leaf and thyme, and lemon peel and simmer 15 minutes. Strain through coarse sieve: add seafood, parsley. Before serving, a splash of dry sherry, if you like.

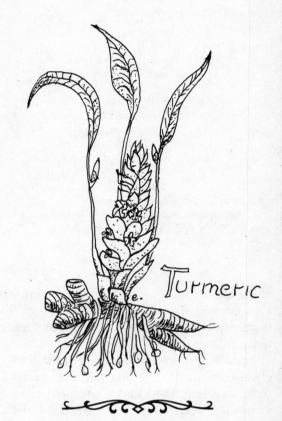

Turmeric

TURMERIC, CURCUMA
(Curcuma longa)

This is an aromatic we all know without realizing we know it. It is very mildly flavored powder which gives the yellow color to piccalilli, chow-chow, and various kinds of mustard pickles and relishes. But it is also a basic ingredient of all curries. There are hundreds of combinations of spices and flavorings, ranging from the delicately perfumed to the blazing hot, which go to produce the enormous range of curried dishes. Four spices are part of ALL of them: cumin, coriander, cayenne and turmeric.

Since long before Christ, this powder has been used as an inexpensive substitute for saffron, and Dioscorides mentions it as a stimulant to appetite and a mild remedy for overeating and indigestion. But it has always been widely used as a dye, imparting to silks, woolens and cottons a range of golden yellow to palest canary tones. The robes of Far Eastern holy men are colored with turmeric, the rice thrown at Hindu weddings tinted with it. In many parts of India, women rub their faces with the powder, preferring a "golden" look to our pinkish or "rosy-cheeked" look. A tincture of turmeric is rubbed on the abdomen of women in labor as well as the umbilicus of the newly-born, both as an antiseptic and an encouragement for "golden" good fortune.

Turmeric is a flourishing perennial of the ginger family, with similar (but rounded rather than flattened) tubers. These tubers, or rhizomes, undergo a long process of washing, drying in the sun, peeling, grinding. Being of an easy culture, it is never adulterated, but, ironically, is often used to adulterate the more expensive mustard preparations.

A delightful soup to soothe symptoms of the common cold is a chicken broth with fresh root vegetables (baby turnips, parsnips, carrots) colored and flavored with turmeric and a dash of cayenne pepper. Both pretty and soothing. But a delightful respite from the usual white boiled rice is done like this: put a knob of butter in a pan and stir finely chopped onions until soft and golden. Put in rice, measuring quantity carefully. Turn until grains are well coated and shiny. Add exactly twice the amount of warm water as you put of rice. Salt, add a little grated lemon peel and juice of ½ lemon, then stir in a tablespoon of turmeric. Mix well. Simmer over moderate heat until rice has absorbed water, stirring well just once. When first grains stick to bottom, turn off heat and cover pan with towel. Let this "hatch" about 15 minutes; then serve. Very good with shrimp, curried or not, or with chicken croquettes, or with a baked fish flavored with capers and dill and a benediction of dry white wine. And this is very good indeed:

Cauliflower in Madras Style

Take two small cauliflowers and cut into flowerets. Peel stems and slice. Sauté 1 thinly sliced onion and ½ teaspoon powdered ginger in 2 tablespoons safflower or peanut oil. Add cauliflower, 1 tablespoon turmeric, 2 teaspoons powdered cumin (or seeds, whole) ½ teaspoon freshly ground black pepper, 1 teaspoon mustard seed, ½ cup water. Cover and cook over moderate flame about 12 to 15 minutes, or until cauliflower is just tender. Stir and add a little more water if need be. Serve with a chutney or green tomato pickled alongside.

VALERIANELLA, MACHE
Corn Salad, Lamb's Lettuce, Rapunzel, Fetticus, Vetticost, Salade Prêtre, Field Salad, Doucette, etc.

(Valeriana locusta)

This plant is an annual, widely grown in Europe and the British Isles for winter salads. A classic French salad mixes valerianella with Roquefort cheese and other winter greens. You can sow the seeds in the open ground in late autumn, and two weeks later you have a carpet of young plants which you can begin thinning out and plopping into your salad bowl. You want the plants remaining to have four or five inches space around them. In spring the plants will flower and cast seed which will sprout the following fall. Once you get valerianella started, there's no problem with replanting it. It goes on forever. It goes well with the more bitter chicory and endive, having a mild pleasant taste and a nice texture. I usually plant valerianella and shallots together and cut them together for the bowl.

Two seed houses have many varieties of endive, chicory and valerianella. They are Le Jardin du Gourmet, Box 451, Danville, VT 05873; and J.A. Demonchaux Co., 827 North Kansas Ave., P.O. Box 8330, Topeka, KS 56608.

VANILLA
(Vanilla planifolia)

Vanilla, the household familiar, yet the unknown friend. Chocolate would be a bore without that bit of vanilla and a touch of cinnamon. Vanilla goes into untold numbers of pound cakes, rice puddings, sweet souf-flés, ice creams, charlottes, a long list, yet any gastronome or cook would be hard put to tell you its origins. Most know it as an extract in a bottle (often synthetic or made from inferior or lesser forms of the vanilla bean) while the serious gourmet will have the real beans buried in a jar of sugar. "Bean" is already a misnomer; the dark pods are the seeds of a rather pretty member of the orchid family.

It is a climbing plant of kudzu-like exuberance, often reaching more than 300 feet. It has bright green leaves, a pale greenish yellow flower, serial roots of the same kind which serves the common ivy to climb where it will. It is rampant in the forests of Mexico, especially in the Vera Cruz region, but also in Honduras, Guatemala, Venezuela, Guyana.

A Franciscan monk, Bernardino de Sahagun, a missionary to Mexico, first brought vanilla to the attention of the rest of the world in his book *General History of the Things of New Spain* (1560), reporting how the Aztecs used vanilla to flavor the chocolate they drank after meals. Morgan, Queen Elizabeth I's apothecary, managed to get hold of some beans, but had an unsubtle hand with them, reported a terrible headache as a result of trying them. Many efforts were wasted for centuries in trying to transplant the vanilla orchid to other climes, but nothing came of it, since no one was aware that the vanilla flower is pollinated ONLY by the tiniest of birds, the *melipona*, which exists only in Mexico. Only in 1841 did Edmond Albius, an aristocratic Creole of the *Ile de las Reunion*, succeed in artificial pollination, based on what he'd learned from Mexican Indians. Afterwards the plant was taken to the Philippines, the Mauritian Isles, the Seychelles, Madagascar, most of Central and Caribbean America.

The vanilla flower has no perfume whatsoever, nor do the leaves, nor do the green seed pods. Only after "sweating" in a closed heated container, when crystals form on the drying pods, does the distinctive and delicious perfume become manifest, and this is what is wanted. The best pods are expensive, but if they are kept in a jar of sugar, and returned to it after use (just wash and dry off) they are no more costly than the far less subtle synthetic vanillas made of the substance *eugenol*, which is found in clove oil, or the various extracts made from other

VANILLA

relatives of the same plant family, such as *Vanilla pompona* from the West Indies. Once one has known what used to be called *French ice cream* or a real *charlotte russe* or *apple charlotte* or a REAL pound cake flavored with REAL vanilla, one is hooked, devoted, and will refuse the secondary forms forever.

The pod is cut into two-inch sections and split. They are steeped in the milk used for the various sweets, then washed, dried and returned to the jar of sugar, which in turn takes the flavor for other sweets.

French Ice Cream

¹/₂ pint milk
¹/₂ pint heavy cream
2 inches of vanilla pod
6 egg yolks
3 ounces sugar

Split the pod, put into sauce pan with milk, heat on low flame, then set aside for about 10 minutes to steep. Whisk egg yolks and sugar, add to strained milk, stir over low heat (WOODEN spoon!) until thick. Still stirring, remove from heat. Whip cream lightly, fold in. Pour into chilled container and place in freezing compartment. Stir once or twice, well, during freezing process.

What the Angels Eat on Sunday

Make your French Ice Cream as above. Have ready 2 ounces diced, candied apricots which have been soaked overnight in one-fourth cup best cognac. Fold into the ice cream before freezing. When serving, pour a little of the very best apricot brandy over each portion. (Marie Brizard or de Kuyper, for instance.)

Try a little pudding recipe with a little more vanilla, with white raisins and diced, candied ginger soaked in white port added before freezing. Try your favorite egg custard or *crème caramel* recipe with an extra splash of vanilla or with bits of pod steeped in the heating milk. Put a small piece of vanilla bean into your coffee pot next time you're making a brew. People will sit up and take notice!

VERJUICE

You may have come across the word in Chaucer or Shakespeare or in some old mustard recipes, but most people have forgotten what it stands for, and have thereby lost an entire world of delicate flavors and combinations. It comes straight from the French *vert*

VERT (green) JUS (juice)

(green) and *jus* (juice). In times past it was the souring agent in hundreds of dishes and preparations, where today we would use vinegar. In England the juice of tart green apples (preferably crabapples) was allowed to ferment by standing a day or so, then scum was removed, the juice was boiled with a little salt, and bottled. It kept well. The juice of almost-ripe plums was employed in this fashion, too.

The verjuice went into salad dressings, to give a bite to many meat or fish dishes. In France, unripe or almost-ripe green grapes were used to make the verjuice, and it went into the preparation of many of the most famous mustards, the Dijon types, for instance. (Once, in the spirit of pure experiment, I mixed juice of seedless grapes and a little bit of lemon juice to Dijon mustard to baste spareribs: the result was delicious.) In some French cookbooks verjuice means simply the juice of ripe white grapes, as in the famous wine-growing region of *Perdreaus au verjus* (partridges with verjuice), and various kinds of verjuice turn up in remoter parts of France in many a game dish.

The principle of the acid or tart fruit taste as first principle in a sauce occurs in a dish served in every famous French restaurant: *sole véronique*, which is fillet of sole prepared with seeded halved white grapes, a tasty combination. In Normandy and Brittany, very fresh cider which has not yet "turned" is used in dishes with veal and cream, or fish and cream, to achieve this delightful aroma and flavor. In parts of the Lowlands and Northern France, since the 1930s, when the Sicilian grapefruit began to be readily available, they have begun to squeeze the grapefruit juice into game, fish, veal dishes, completely in the spirit of the ancient verjuice. In Holland, a sprinkle of grapefruit juice adds a great deal to their carrot puddings and soufflés, and one of the oilier or fattier fish, dressed with baby celery and grapefruit juice (with perhaps one dash of dry white wine), is incomparable. All of which shows it behooves us to reconsider many a forgotten usage which by pure accident has fallen by the way.

In eighteenth-century America, for instance, in both North and South, the blue flowers of the borage, with their cool, cucumbery flavor, went into drinks, salads, fruit compotes, but somehow this widespread practice simply vanished in the early nineteenth century. Think what a great dish would be partridges cooked with lean bacon, crabapples and a local verjuice. Made of muscadines? Of satsumas? Or just plain old seedless grapes!

VERMOUTH

The international appellation "vermouth" comes from the French *vermouth*, which, in turn, is the translation of the German word for wormwood. There are literally hundreds of these apéritif wines made around the world, although the best and better-known all come from southern France and northern Italy. They all have the bitter herb wormwood in them (*Artemisia absinthium*), which was also the basis of the habit-forming and eventually destructive apéritif absinthe, now illegal, although in rural France the country people like even now to steep leaves of wormwood in the imitation absinthes made from fennel and anise which are common today.

The vermouths have a modicum of wormwood, and each vermouth is made from its own secret formula. We know that angelica, calamus (cat-tail) root, cinnamon, cloves, wild thyme, coriander, orange peel, lemon peel, elderberries, quassia, chamomile, gentian root, quinine, nutmeg are among the possibilities. Vermouths are usually fortified with flavored wines, and run in color from pure white to dark mahogany, by way of pale yellows, beige, brown, red, even greenish. One of the most famous manufacturers is the Martini family of Italy, and our familiar martini cocktail, containing much gin and a little white vermouth, is another case of a family name turning into a common noun.

The vermouths are used by many great chefs for some of their most honored creations, but most ordinary cooks have forgotten their many uses. Try broiling a flounder with a little lemon juice and lots of butter and basting it with white vermouth or a dry red vermouth, adding chopped capers at the end. Henrietta Waring, one of the National Treasures of Savannah, invented a wonderful soup: V-8 juice with lemon juice added, some minced onion, a bay leaf, then cook chopped okra in it slowly and long, flavor with vermouth at the end. Mmmmmmmm!

VERVAIN
Herb of Grace
(Verbena officinalis)

The old books call it Herb of Grace, as does Shakespeare. *Herbe sacrée* and Herba Veneris are its other names. The plant has no perfume, but a bitter and astringent medicinal tea has been made from the leaves since the beginning of time as remedy for bladder afflictions, especially calculus. The old Romans gave the name *verbena* to all altar plants, which included hyssop, melissa, forms of clover. But the ancients attributed aphrodisiac qualities to the plant and it figures in many love potions and spells. The Druids included it in their lustral water and the plant has long been associated with magicians and sorcerers. It is part of rites

VERVAIN

and incantations, carried by ambassadors on difficult missions, worn as a charm against snakebite, for general good luck, in warding off the evil eye, as an aid to the eyesight.

Since it grows on the Mount of Calvary and is considered one of the herbs which cleansed the wounds of Jesus, it has always been crossed and blessed with a commemorative verse when gathered. In many Mediterranean countries today, the tea is taken for ailing liver or kidneys; the bitter flavor is much appreciated in many homemade liqueurs and bitters.

VINEGAR
Vinaigre, Aceto, etc.

Since the beginning of time human beings have craved something sour now and again. In the wintertime, especially, dill and other pickles and relishes and "shrubs" or other fruit drinks flavored with vinegar have always been desired. At the same time, workers in the hot summer fields, in many cultures through many centuries, have relished something vinegary to quench thirst and ward off the effects of heat.

Physicians in ancient Persia recommended daily quaffs of lime juice, verjuice and vinegar to neutralize fats and prevent them from accumulating in the body. In the apple-growing shires of England and thereby in much of New England, the eaters of apples and even more, the daily partakers of apple cider vinegar in water prove and have proven over and over that they survive much longer than non-partakers. In recent decades, the members of the medical profession who have scorned naturalist medicine and folk remedies have come more and more to study seriously the healthful properties of apple cider, cider vinegar, and apples themselves.

Before World War I every household had many kinds of vinegar, some homemade, which served for widely diverse purposes. A paste made of salt and cider vinegar is still the best agent to clean brass, bronze and copper. Boiling vinegar will unclog a drain far more quickly than many a highly advertised commercial product. For washing windows, nothing better than vinegar. Or for scouring and deodorizing a fishy skillet or baking dish. In the great country houses of England, the mahogany furniture is always cleaned with 1/6 cup of vinegar mixed with 1 quart of water. Wet a sponge in this, wring it out, polish the ole mahog. A diluted vinegar rinse prevents linens which are to be stored from yellowing.

Vinegar is good for polishing silver when slightly heated and mixed with baking soda. The same paste will clean bathroom fixtures and is sovereign against mildew. Copper and brass doorknobs, drawer pulls, lamp finials, andirons, chrome, stainless steel—even enamel surfaces—can be cleaned thus. A blop of vinegar in the dishwater is very helpful in cutting grease. Does a good job in cleaning the TV screen, mirrors: just add 1 tablespoon of vinegar to 1 quart of warm water. If you have good paintbrushes stiffened and caked with pigment, just simmer them 5 or 10 minutes in full strength vinegar. Vinegar and water will clean aluminum pans, just boil up the mixture.

For minor burns or sunburn, pat on cold cider vinegar and leave uncovered. Some modern Bible commentators, unversed in antique usages, have suggested that the individual who brought vinegar for the crucified Christ to drink was adding another torment for the Saviour. At the ninth hour, "One ran and filled a sponge full of vinegar and put it on a reed, and gave Him to drink." (Mark 15:36) This was a great kindness, since in all the hot dry countries, vinegar is preferred before water as a great thirst-quencher, especially in extremity.

And what about all the cosmetic vinegars that crowd the household manuscript recipe books in all countries and all times? We would say "lotion" or "toilet water" now. "Cosmetic or toilet vinegars were one of the indispensable cosmetic necessities of beauties of previous centuries," writes the head chemist at the old New York apothecary shop of *Caswell-Massy*. "They probably didn't know why toilet vinegar worked so well to keep their skins soft and fresh, but we do now. The pure aged natural vinegar made their basin water slightly acid, so helped preserve the necessary acid mantle on the face."

One of the great antiseptics of the recent past deserves description here. It is known as *Thieves' Vinegar*. The legend says that during an epidemic of the plague in Marseille, four young robbers made their way to the bedrooms of the dead and dying to remove all of value, surviving because they were drenched in this preparation. It was used in sickrooms in the south of France until at least a decade ago, and is still sold in old-fashioned village chemists' shops. Let's consider the formula:

Thieves' Vinegar

Put into a jar a handful each of rosemary, lavender, rue, sage, wormwood and mint, and pour onto it a gallon of strong clear vinegar, cover close and leave for four days near the fire, then strain and add to the liquid an ounce of powdered camphor gum; bottle and keep it tightly corked. Powerful against contagion.

And here is the old formula for a delightful toilet vinegar, still available in country apothecaries in the north of Scotland:

Essence of Summer

Add 2 ounces dried rose petals and 40 drops of attar of roses to 5 ounces rectified spirits of wine and 1 pint of diluted acetic acid. Stand in a closed vessel for 14 days, shaking and stirring occasionally. Strain and bottle, cork tightly.

This sour something has been relished for at least 5,000 years, and probably longer. It is a natural product. The air around us swarms with yeasts and molds. Any liquid containing sugar, such as watered honey, malt liquor, fruit juices, will ferment naturally and form alcohol. Now, unless this liquid is tightly sealed or corked, the liquid

Flavored Vinegars

will be invaded by natural bacteria and turn into acetic acid. Pure spirits or fortified vinegar will not sour, but vinegar left open will lose its strength. That is why, in pickling or preserving in vinegar, it is important to have a good strong vinegar, lest the waters in the matter being preserved dilute the vinegar and harm its preserving faculties.

The strongest natural vinegar comes from wines, with 6½ percent of acetic acid, malt and cider vinegars follow with about 4 or 5 percent. Distilled or fortified vinegars, always labeled thus, are best for pickling and preserving, with up to some 12 percent acetic acid.

When wine is left uncorked and turns sour, eventually a slimy mass forms at the bottom; this is the "mother-of-vinegar," and can be put into a new bottle of wine to turn it into vinegar. In European kitchens, once a really good "mother" has been found, which produces a smoothly sour rather than bitey sour taste in vinegar, it is carefully preserved for generations: I knew a lady in Rome in whose family a favorite "mother" for red wine vinegar had been preserved for 200 years. Wine vinegar is as good as the wine it's made from. Cheap wine makes battery acid, not a vinegar one would use in a delicate salad dressing. The famous French brand-name vinegars go through a long and complicated process of dripping in oak casks at a sustained temperature, with a little drawn from spigots in the bottom of the cask once a week and new wine then added in the top.

Malt vinegar is usually colored and of different flavor from wine vinegar; this is what is wanted for almost all the old English pickling recipes. On the Gulf Coast, this is suitable for many pickles, but chutneys, conserves, piccalillis, and most mixed pickles are better with wine vinegar.

Cider vinegar is very popular in America, but originated in the apple-growing countries of England as a natural medicinal tonic. An ancient and much respected daily tonic consists of 2 teaspoons of cider vinegar and 1 of honey diluted in a glass of water and drunk before breakfast. Cider vinegar goes well with onion or cucumber salads.

There are many flavored vinegars you can make at home yourself, to give interest to many salads and cooked vegetables. A good glop of cider vinegar tossed into water where you boil artichokes improves both color and flavor. Boiled onions should have 3 grains of salt, a pinch of sugar, and 1 tablespoon of wine or cider vinegar in the water. Cabbage and any of its cousins (kale, collards, mustard, etc.) should all have a glop of vinegar added to the water. It makes a great difference.

Avoid like the plague synthetic cheap vinegars. Some are made from factory wastes such as wood pulp, or wastes from canning factories and with synthetic acetic acid and chemical colorings: many have traces of harmful chemicals. Avaunt!

If you would like to capture the essence of your summer garden and conjure it in the coldest and dreariest part of winter, no better way than to make up batches of herb vinegars and line them up in your kitchen. And no pleasanter gifts to bestow at Christmas.

The process is simplicity itself. Gather sprigs and leaves of your herbs in the early morning of a clear sunny day and let them dry in semi-shade for an hour or so. If your garden has no chemicals, all you need do is shake them and blow on them to clean them. If there is dust or grit, go ahead and wash them, but immediately dry them by shaking in a colander then patting lightly with paper towels. Use glass jars and bottles, with plastic tops or corks, please. Metal lids or caps sometimes, according to which herb and which vinegar, can have a chemical reaction which spoils the works.

You simply stuff your containers, pour in vinegar to cover herbs completely, cork tightly and put in a cool dark place for about a month. Check to see that all foliage is covered with vinegar. Sometimes air is trapped under the leaves. If you wish to hasten the process you can bring your vinegar to JUST UNDER the boiling point and cover herbs. If vinegar is boiled, the acetic acid which is the preservative will be destroyed. If you must heat vinegar always use an enamel or a stainless steel pan, NEVER aluminum.

The herbs tend less to discolor if preserved in the unheated vinegar, and for the favorite of all herb vinegars, tarragon, this is important. Some of the herbs used to make vinegar will be strained off, but not so with tarragon: the leaves pickled in white wine vinegar are fantastic to make a sauce for broiled fish, for instance, and the greatest and most wonderful of turkey salads contains fresh celery and green shallots with the chopped pickled tarragon leaves. Any number of crab dishes gain another dimension from these tarragon leaves.

The *dernier cri* among fancy cooks of the 1980s is really an old Provençal favorite introduced into the United States by way of the younger imported French chefs: opal vinegar. The form of basil known as opal or purple or black basil is steeped at least a month in unheated white wine vinegar, along with a few leaves of sweet green basil to enhance the flavor. It turns a lovely red-purple color, almost like a good Burgundy. One can still find pressed-glass cruets and vinegar bottles in the dime stores and dollar stores, especially in smaller communities, and one of these filled with this jewel-like vinegar is indeed a delightful gift. But so are any of the herbal vinegars.

Burnet gives a nice cucumbery taste to salads without the repeat action (burps) of cucumbers.

Orange mint preserved in cider vinegar makes delightful flavor for fruit cups of fresh fruit salads, has a nice pinkish green color.

Dill vinegar gives a little something extra to tomato juice and to any mixed salad. Use leaves or seed heads.

Garlic vinegar, wonderful for salads any time, requires a slightly different technique. Mash your garlic cloves flat with a heavy kitchen knife, but don't go any further with mayhem. Pour unheated red wine vinegar over them, let steep 24 hours, strain through filter paper, pour vinegar into sterilized bottles and cork tightly. I put in some opal basil to color the brew.

Rosemary and thyme want white wine vinegar, fennel, lovage and sage want red wine vinegar, any of the mints are happiest with cider vinegar. Try your own mixtures: *garlic* and *burnet*, for instance, or a mixture of *basil* and *dill* (this makes a Tartar Sauce which makes strong men swoon).

There is a whole world of old-fashioned flavored wines which qualify as vinegars and are used in the same fashion. Take ½ ounce fresh grated horseradish and steep in a pint of dry sherry for 2 or 3 weeks, strain, bottle, use as required in salad dressings or sauces. Chili pepper wine, shallot wine are made in the same way. Celery seed steeped in white wine gives an essence which adds zest to gumbos quite unlike celery itself. Or to tartar sauce or a cream-based sauce for broiled fish.

Essence of Capsicums is doled out by the DROP: infuse ½ ounce of absolutely pure cayenne in a half pint of best brandy, keeping bottle tightly corked for 2 or 3 weeks. A drop or two of this in a beef stew, a soup, a sauce, brings out all the other flavors in rather the way of Tabasco, but there is a sweetish piquancy which is different.

Ravigotte vinegar is completely delicious and completely forgotten; it adds immensely to salads of tomatoes, cucumbers, celery, blanched endive or any mixture of Greens. Take about a couple of heaping tablespoons each of minced garden cress and tarragon, one of minced chives, a small clove of garlic or a minced shallot and IF YOU WISH, 2 or 3 hot chili peppers. Let these steep in a pint

of the best French white wine vinegar for a week, then strain and bottle up. Cork tightly. You can sing to me after you've eaten a salad made with this.

VIOLET

VIOLET
(Viola odorata)

The human race has loved the violet since prehistory. It runs its sweet gentle course through so much poetry, history, herbology, that we must enthrone it with the rose, the onion, and the garlic in humanity's eternal herbal pantheon. It has always been the flower of love. It is emblematic both of Aphrodite and of her son Priapus, god of all fertility. The Greeks called it *Ione*, alluding to the myth where Zeus, fearing the jealousy of his wife Hera, changed his ladylove Io into a white heifer, and created violets for her to eat. And they *are* edible.

A salad of fresh greens with a few violet flowers and young leaves is very good. Thin tea sandwiches of bread and unsalted butter, filled with violet blooms and/or leaves have a long history in the British Isles. The leaves, unusually rich in vitamins B and C, can be boiled as astringent greens, or mixed with other cooked greens, such as collards.

In Victorian language-of-flowers lore, the violet stood for modesty and humility and also could carry the message "I am dying for love of you, but dare not say so." The Romans liked salads of violet leaves, wore chaplets of the flowers to delay intoxication when drinking deep of wine. But they also made violet wine, violet preserves, violet perfume, and a beauty cream based on violets and goats' milk.

The medicinal use of this plant has never abated, and in country towns and villages of Europe and the British Isles, countless home remedies are prepared to this day: cough syrups, mild laxatives (dried leaves made into tea), poultices for fresh wounds or for obstinate running sores.

The candied flowers, which are completely delectable, are easily made and have been used for centuries to ornament sweet dishes. It is easy to "take" the perfume by infusion, which is why old cookbooks with ice cream and sherbet recipes begin by instructing the cook to gather violet flowers in early morning when the dew is still upon them, and to steep them in a quart of fresh cream or fresh milk. (Many older cookbooks define ice cream as made of cream, sherbets made of milk; today we think of ice cream being either milk or cream or a mixture, while sherbets have almost everywhere come to mean water ices.)

Candied violets and violet-flavored lozenges of various sorts are still common; every liquor store carries the violet-flavored-and-colored very sweet cordial called *Parfait Amour*. You can use this to flavor a wonderful milk sherbet, or to pour over ice cream or chilled cooked pears or apples. The violet is the symbol of the Bourbon clan. Napoleon, claiming from exile on St. Helena that he would "return with the spring" (like our subject flower), took the name of "Corporal Violet" and was so toasted by his officers and sympathizers. Vast acres of violets are grown in the south of France for perfumery, and the latest "secret ingredient" used in French perfumes is an agreeable, not-quite-so-sweet scent distilled from young leaves of the plant taken just before blooming.

A delightful vinegar can be made at home by simply gathering young leaves and flowers, stuffing in a jar, pouring heated white wine vinegar over them, then let them sit six days, strain, bottle, cork and use as required. (On a fruit salad, for instance, or with tender spring greens.) A famous spring salad in Sicily and South Italy is made of violets, endive, celery, parsley, dressed with salt, pepper, Marsala wine, a splash of white wine vinegar, and finest first-pressing olive oil. A very good between-meals tidbit in the heel of the Italian peninsula is thin toasted bread spread with a mild white cheese (we'd use cream cheese), piled with chopped violets and a few capers. A highly interesting and appetizing sweet-and-sour snack.

Drying violets is child's play. Gather the flowers in the early morn, rinse them carefully in a colander and dry well, all this without bruising or squashing. They *must* be dry. Use a hair-dryer if you must. Beat up one or two egg whites with a drop or two of water. Take a soft brush and paint the flowers with the whites. (I don't have the patience. I use a slotted spoon and dip them in egg white, delicately bouncing them until they're coated and the rest runs back into the bowl.) Next sprinkle them with granulated sugar, small batches at a time, so that they are evenly coated. Put them on wax paper in a sunny windowsill or into an oven heated and then turn off to dry slowly and evenly. If you wish to be evocative (who doesn't?) you can add a few drops of the liqueur *Parfait Amour* to the sugar, mixing it in well. These keep up to two weeks in the fridge. They're pretty and tasty to garnish sweets.

WILD RICE
Rice, Indian Rice
(Zizania aquatica)

The grain known as wild rice is neither wild nor rice. *Zizania aquatica* is, finally, very very distantly related to white rice, in that both are cereals of the grass family, but the only thing they have in common is they like to grow in shallow water or mud flats. Wild rice is the only grain besides corn that is cross-pollinated. The panicles of blooms show female blossoms on top, male pollen-bearing flowers on bottom. Since they bloom in succession down the stem, it takes weeks for all to be pollinated.

The plant is native to North America (there are two varieties) and once covered all our shores and inlets. Fish and water fowl are greedy about this grain, and the Indians have employed it as a staple of diet since prehistory. Attempts to introduce wild rice into England and Europe, as an ornamental or as food for waterfowl, have failed.

There is a cousin of the American plant which grows in east Asia and is known as Manchurian rice. Long cultivated as a vegetable, it is smaller and less productive than the American forms. It has been grown successfully in England, but never flowers there.

The delightful nut-like flavor of wild rice and its chewy, bitey consistency make it extremely attractive to all, but with prices ranging from eight to fifteen dollars a pound, not all can afford it. The fact that the grains ripen unevenly, plus the difficulty of harvesting them tells the tale. Indians in flat-bottomed boats move through the swamps, whacking carefully at the bent-over stalks, gathering the grains on a stretch of gunny sack. Well, that is the romantic image still evoked. The Chippewa Indians have a legend of the earth itself being created out of a grain of sand—in some versions, grain of rice—which a muskrat brought up to the God Gitche Manitou from the bottom of the Great Sea Water. And on certain Indian reservations in Minnesota, the traditional manner of harvesting continues. But, after World War II, when wild rice caught on with gourmet cooks and lovers of good food everywhere, the American business world cast a cold eye on the whole situation and figured that since white rice had been geared to highly mechanized production, no reason the wild grass couldn't be treated similarly. Modern methods of raising white rice yield four to six thousand pounds an acre, the Indians get about one hundred pounds of wild rice an acre, if they're lucky.

American know-how rolled up its collective sleeves. First, the geneticists went to work: by 1967 they'd developed a shatterproof form of the wild grain which brought the yield of wild rice up to seven hundred pounds an acre. Experimental wild rice paddies were set up. Much greater yield, BUT the inevitable results of monoculture: bugabear insects and plant diseases. Ingenious harvesting machines have replaced the Indians in flat-bottomed canoes, while sorting and packaging machines have taken over from the squaws. Happily, the delightful flavor of the grain remains unaltered, and there is no more delightful luxury than a first dish of it as prelude to a grand dinner, or when served as accompaniment to duck, turkey, squab or the more delicately flavored Southern pork sausage. But I'll tell you one of my dream meals. The menu consists of a kind of gumbo *maigre* which is boiled down turkey broth to which you add quite a lot of chopped celery which should cook only a little, and a tiny bit of minced onion and lemon peel. That's the first dish. Next, perfectly fried lean pork chops with slices of fried apples and a dish of wild rice with mushrooms. Afterwards a salad of fresh sorrel and spinach dressed with lemon and oil. To finish, fresh pineapple with candied violets and crystallized ginger. Then, you go sit in the Dainty Burp parlor and sip peppermint schnapps and talk about old Bette Davis movies. Aaaaah!

Wild Rice with Mushrooms

The mushrooms: Clean well, slice, sauté in unsalted butter with a tiny bit of minced garlic or onion, 2 teaspoons minced lean bacon, few grains salt, freshly ground black pepper, dash of Worcestershire sauce, bit of grated lemon peel. When just right, not overcooked (low heat, stir often, keep covered) uncover, add a splash of pale dry sherry, stir well in a minute, then cover and put aside.

The wild rice: Rinse the rice several times in cold water, pick over for chaff, bugs, bric-à-brac. You need precisely 3 times as much water as rice. Boil water with a little salt and a few drops of lemon juice, add rice slowly, simmer 45 or 50 minutes, until grain is tender and has absorbed the water. Stir in lots of unsalted butter, toss with fork and serve. Bring rice and mushrooms to table in separate dishes; let each diner suit himself or herself as to whether the fungi go on the rice or the rice over the mushrooms.

Willow

WILLOW
(Salix)

What, asks the alert reader, is willow doing in a series on herbs, spices and flavors?

Well, I never tire of pointing out that if you're serious about the table and all its reverberations, you must, logically, be concerned with gardening, poetry, and logic. Read on!

A knowledge of the flavor of *salacin*, derived from willow bark, is almost universal, for it is the analgesic property in aspirin. The willow family is comprised of roughly some 200 varieties, many of them hybrids, for they mingle easily. The final monograph study of this plant family is yet to be written. Many are native to the Orient, but a surprising number are native to the North American continent.

They're useful, quick-growing trees, all of them, powerful in sweetening and draining unhealthy marshes. *Salacin*, antiseptic and analgesic, has been used in the past for the treatment of gonorrhea, for many ovarian disorders, in many types of painkiller. In the Far East, *salacin* is still both a folk medicine and an ingredient in the most sophisticated medications.

But the clamorous recent discovery, proven by repeated experiments, of the powerful root-inducing qualities of willow water, seems bound to revolutionize, not only practices of commercial nurseries, but those of all home gardening.

Everybody knows how easy it is to root willow cuttings. If you've ever had a bouquet of pussy willow in the spring or used a few weeping willow sprays in a big floral arrangement, you know how they put out rootlings almost overnight. Now Dr. Makota Kawase, professor of horticulture at the agricultural research center in Wooster, Ohio, has proven that water in which willow twigs have soaked is a far more efficacious rooting agent than any of the powders or liquids sold for this purpose, mostly synthetic plant hormones.

Simplicity itself: to make a willow rooting substance at home, just cut some current growth willow shoots, take off the leaves, cut the shoots in short pieces, an inch or less. Pack as many as you can into a bowl or mason jar. Cover with water, put on a lid or plastic bag to prevent evaporation and let sit some 24 hours. Then drain off the liquid and use it. For hardwood cuttings, let them stand in the liquid about 48 hours, then plant in soil and water for about a week with willow water. For soft wood or herbaceous plants, place cuttings in receptacle with willow water in the bottom. Let the cuttings absorb the liquid for about 24 hours, then plant them directly in soil. They mustn't dry out; put a plastic tent over them if need be.

What this simple discovery means is that hard-to-root trees like beech, cherry, pine, oak, birch, not to mention countless hardwood trees, woody ornamental bushes, flower, and even vegetable cuttings can be produced routinely and far more quickly than by any system presently in use.

Scientists have long felt that a natural *rhizocaline* (literally "root stimulator") must exist; this may be it. This simple willow water seems to have root-inducing properties which out-distance by light years the plant hormones and other commercial preparations available today.

WOODRUFF
Sweet Woodruff, Waldmeister, Stellina, Glycérie, Galium
(*Asperula odorata*)

A native of the deep woods in Europe and Asia, this delightful, now almost forgotten sweet herb was brought early to America and has naturalized itself all through the eastern and southern part of this country. It likes deepest shade, and is most attractive with its trailing habit, spokelike whorls of

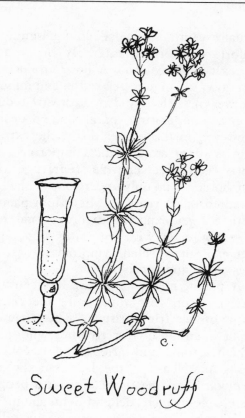

Sweet Woodruff

leaves and tiny sweet white flowers with a perfume of new-mown hay and a hint of vanilla.

In thirteenth-century manuscripts the name appears as *Wuderove* and *Woodderowffe*, the *"rove"* from old French *rovelle* ("wheel") from precisely the look of the leaves. The dried leaves were used to stuff mattresses, to strew in pantries and dining halls to discourage insects, and until quite recently used like lavender to place among stored linens to repel insects and mildew. A tea brewed from the leaves and flowers has always been used both to relax and to uplift, rather like chamomile or certain mints. A crystalline chemical principle called *Coumarin* is found in this herb, much used in perfumery for its own sake, and as a fixative for other odors. This is the same element found in melilot, tonka beans, and certain members of the orchid family. Thus woodruff has always found its way into the great blends of snuff, and is much used in pharmacy to disguise bitter or disagreeable odors and flavors in many preparations. Since earliest times it has been used in countless remedies for troubles of the liver and spleen, for upset stomachs. And most old formulas for *potpourri* require woodruff. In modern times, this delightful plant is still widely used in "May wine," and in countless "cups" and punches, and is the secret in famous cordials and digestives. It is used to flavor many Rhine wines. If you would like a springtime treat (woodruff is part of many ancient spring festivals, and was used on the altar of many churches on May Day), fill a punchbowl with a good Rhine wine, put in a tightly sealed plastic bag of ice cubes (you don't wish to dilute the wine) and plenty of crushed sweet woodruff twigs. Wonderful! It is usually gathered from the woods but in an acid soil can be easily raised from seed, if kept in the shade. Some herb specialists in the United States will supply plants.

YELLOW JESSAMINE
Carolina Jasmine
(Gelsemium nitidium)

This needs no introduction. It is one of the loveliest of the native North American plants, growing in any rich, well-watered soil from Virginia down through Florida, all along the Gulf Coast and into Mexico. The perfume is delicious, and for many is the very smell of spring in the South. It is a

Yellow Jessamine

e.

climber, or really, a sprawler, with a root which runs underground for amazing distances, from a kind of rhizome, both parts being exported in bales from this country for medical uses.

And, yes, pretty yellow jessamine supplies one of the deadliest poisons, which was used by the Cherokee and other Indians for ritual executions. The alkaloid gelsimine is colorless, odorless, intensely bitter and forms crystalline salts. A dose produces a sensation of languor, relaxation and muscular weakness, followed by a drastic reduction in temperature, paralysis and death. However, in the proper doses, the extraction is of greatest medical importance as antispasmodic, sedative, febrifuge and diaphoretic. And only understood in the last hundred or so years. A Mississippi planter with a fever expected to prove fatal was dosed by error with jessamine roots, and, although unexpected symptoms arose, he was cured and survived.

A patent medicine of the last century, derived from jessamine, bore the catchy name of "electric febrifuge." The jessamine drug is still used for treating whooping cough, asthma, and various kinds of convulsions. As well as for "the sleeplessness of the drunkard" and headache. For most people, it is a completely delightful inhabitant of the garden, and no garden can be called Southern without it.

SUBJECT INDEX

RECIPE INDEX